All human beings are on a journey of discovery,
hoping to find a world that surrounds them
with beauty, peace and spiritual love.
Welcome Home!

Published by Corporate Health Dynamics

Produced by Artworks Type & Image
7514 Clairemont Mesa Blvd.
San Diego, California 92111

Design & Art Direction by Nektarios Tradas
Art Consultation by Peggy Robinson-Tradas
Proofreading & Editing by Phyllis R. Bech

ISBN 0-9658665-0-5
First Printing: 1998
Printed in the United States of America

10 9 8 7 6 5 4 3 2 1

Library of Congress Catalog Card Number: 98-96213

To order additional copies of this publication, please contact:

Corporate Health Dynamics
San Diego, California

Telephone: (619) 491-0559 • Facsimile: (619) 293-3166
E-mail: bcoolu@aol.com

Overcoming Addiction

Without A Twelve Step Conviction

Oliver Rhodes, C.T.R.S.

CONTENTS

Introduction

Your Beginning To A New Day, A New Life And A New Way

Spread your wings so that you may fly and prepare yourself for a natural high. You are a beautiful source and it should be known; you were born with greatness to fly on your own.

Oliver Rhodes

It has often been said that today is the first day of the rest of our lives. It is a time to say goodbye to the past, meet today head on and say hello to the future! For today is our past, present and future. The power to make positive changes in our lives begins with today. Everything we need for a successful transition is contained within our beautiful and magnificent minds. Hello, my name is Oliver Rhodes and I have a passion for what I do. That is to get people excited about taking better care of their health, live their lives to the fullest and become more productive in their personal, social and work relationships.

Throughout my life I have always had the passion to make a difference in the lives of people seeking to enhance their health and overall well-being. It is my understanding that we are all striving for self-enrichment, true love and increased prosperity. My passion comes from helping individuals develop an awareness of their inner beauty, spirituality and pure potentiality. My purpose for sharing my life and interests with others results from a connectiveness that I have with people and the universe. My mission is to inspire people from all walks of life to reach their true happiness and develop a meaningful purpose while they are here on this earth. That is to enlighten, brighten and empower you far beyond your wildest dreams. So, I wrote this book for you! It is an autobiography of my life, and a testimony from others. They have all encouraged me to share their experiences, so that you may benefit from years of painful trials and tribulations of overcoming negative addictions. It is our hope that you take these lessons and learn from them, discover your true self and your ability to live and enjoy a fruitful life of peace, happiness and joy.

"Overcoming Addiction Without a Twelve Step Conviction" is an inspirational testimony that addictions are common to all of us and not limited to just drugs and alcohol; inasmuch, a Twelve Step conviction is not always required. Furthermore, understanding how our addictions, habits, pleasures, or hobbies maintain a strong hold on us can empower us to find healthier and more fulfilling ways to live our lives; thus overcoming the devastating effects of negative addictions. Granted, we all have pleasures that we seek to enjoy most of the time, if not all of the time. We human beings are hedonistic in nature and thrive on experiencing pleasure through the five senses. Whether it is food, shopping, gambling, television watching, smoking cigarettes, running, exercise or procrastination, many of us are controlled by these experiences, instead of us having them under our control. These activities eventually become the driving force for our behavior. They are our past patterns of societal conditioning, affinities, habits or passions. What's your pleasure? Whatever we choose to call them, they are the route to whether our behavior leads us to a life of prosperity, mediocrity or dependency.

The readings in this book will help you identify those addictions that keep you from reaching your personal and professional best. You will be motivated towards achieving worthy goals, spiritual fulfillment and a loving relationship with self as well as with nature as it was intended to be. Therefore, the main focus of this book is to point out that it is our negative addictions that are the bases for many of our personal, social and spiritual problems, thus inhibiting our continued progress. The ultimate goal of life is to be happy. We are our happiest when we are doing the things that give us pleasure. Sometimes our choices of pleasure result in painful consequences. As you read, you will discover your true nature and amazing new secrets on how you can become unstuck. One of the skills you will learn to help you break free is to replace negative addictions with activities that provide an equal or greater experience of positive pleasures. Instead of painful consequences, you will be inspired towards reaching your highest human potential. You will discover how these life challenges are necessary for personal growth, development and prosperity.

Since addictions are common to all of us, we are also all in recovery. Contrary to what many may believe, we are all recovering from one thing or another; some more than others. It can be a traffic ticket, divorce, automobile accident, heart attack, personal rejection, illness, being laid off from work or failing our first driver's test. Understanding that we all have addictions and are recovering at the same time makes us all part of the whole. We human beings are special, spiritually connected, and not created to be separate little entities with given "labels of shame." It is my belief that labels such as alcoholic, drug addict, disabled, manic depressive, bipolar or schizophrenic may be appropriate for medically diagnosing patients, but are inappropriate for spiritual beings to refer to themselves as such. These tactics imprison us in servitude to the profitable cause of organized institutions instead of the cause of our own personal interests.

Traditional recovery methods have been based on abstinence—depriving those of their perceived pleasure or happiness. This approach has caused many people grief and anger due to the prospect of loss, and has not been very successful towards creating positive behavior change. In essence, it is much easier to get people to move in the positive than to have them stop doing something negative.

"Overcoming Addiction Without a Twelve Step Conviction" is the discovery for helping you gain personal power, prosperity and true happiness. It is based on ten years of successful hands-on experience, education, love and research. It was written from the hearts and souls of friends, relatives, associates and professionals as told from their perspective. It is also an account of my personal battle with negative addictions and the success I acquired over mind-mood altering substances. Therefore, the methods provided in this book are not based on theory, fiction or personal biases, but

on facts and the universal laws of cause and effect. As a result, *"Overcoming Addictions Without a Twelve Step Conviction"* has been endorsed by many individuals who were at one time stuck, but are now free from the devastating chains of negative addictions.

The road to optimum recovery, spiritual healing and power performance in any endeavor is to break away from old tradition and latch on to a new *Discovery.* That discovery is within us all and does not rest with a specific program. Granted, programs do help many people control their addictions, but one size does not fit all. The ultimate process in recovery is to overcome our negative addictions, not control them. We want to move on to a more prosperous life, not linger in one that perpetuates more of the same rhetoric. Programs are not for everyone. This book offers powerful options that can bring you out of the dungeons of confusion and help you *"discover"* your internal light of happiness.

If the program that you are currently involved in is working for you, please stay with it and the best to you. But if you are looking for ways to reach a higher level of consciousness and greater success in living, please read on. You will learn that the secret to optimum wellness is not always through a system that focuses on fighting disease. It is best accomplished through our spiritual ability to promote health and reestablish ourselves with the biological laws of nature. As a result of this Common Sense Intelligence (CSI), you too can achieve that inner peace, spiritual love and true happiness you so desperately deserve. We are all pure potentiality.

My main reason for writing this book, and my deepest desire, is to make a difference in the lives of those seeking to improve their health, happiness and overall well-being. Therefore, it is with great pleasure that I share with you "My Story, My Glory."

Acknowledgements

I dedicate this book to my mother, Nettie Bell Rhodes, who passed in May, 1984 and my father, Richard T. Rhodes, who passed in December, 1995. It was my father who inspired me to live a healthy lifestyle. My dear brother, Tommie Earl Rhodes, was also an inspiration and guiding light to me throughout most of my life before he passed in March of 1994 due to cancer. I also dedicate this book to my sister who died from alcohol addiction in September 1995; my first cousin, Elijeha Dawkins who passed in May, 1978 of heart failure at the young age of 33 due to drug and alcohol abuse; his sister Christine who was brutally murdered one year later due to her use of drugs and affiliation with drug dealers. I also give thanks to the many recovering individuals for their support, encouragement and for sharing their remarkable stories concerning their plight with the devastating disease of negative addictions.

Many of the individuals who have contributed their personal and professional stories are too numerous to mention. Therefore, I can only say to those who were a part of this work that your contributions are greatly appreciated and will significantly inspire and encourage those who continue to seek freedom from the painful experiences of negative addictions. I could not have completed this book without the willingness and cooperation of those special individuals who shared their personal and sometimes very painful experiences that surrounded their recovering lives.

Last but not least, I sincerely want to thank Nektarios "Nick" Tradas and his wife Peggy Robinson-Tradas, owners of Artworks Type & Image, for their support, time, creativity and hard work in the design, layout and production of this fabulous publication. Thank you Nick and Peggy for being a part of my world and for helping make my dream come true.

Poems to Remember

Throughout this book I have included special literary works titled *"Poems to Remember"* in selected chapters and sections. They are a recollection of excerpts from the preceding chapters that will summarize and capitalize on thoughtful ideas and information to provide enlightenment, excitement and joy to your reading pleasure. These poems are all creations of my personal and interpersonal experiences with people who have found peace, health and happiness while discovering a world that goes far "beyond recovery."

What's Beyond Recovery? Discovery!

We human beings are forever
evolving. We live in search of
self and continuously strive to
reach our full potential in
accordance with nature and
our own individual spirituality.

Oliver Rhodes

THE DISCOVERIES

Discovery 1

My Story, My Glory – Telling It Like It Is!

Everyone has a story to tell. It is their own reality, truth and experience. We may not agree with the truth of others, but it is through their eyes that they hold their experiences to be true. If we keep an open mind, the lessons that they have learned may be as spiritually rewarding for us!

Oliver Rhodes

Television was in its infant stage back in 1954 and so was I. Even at the tender age of seven, I remember how I used to sit and watch those early black and white children's programs for hours, particularly the cartoons. Humor was the theme for me then just as it is today. I marveled at how that mysterious picture box could bring life to still pictures and words. Situation comedies and variety shows were also among my favorites to watch. What made television appear so real and alive was how good the actors were in playing out their parts. Even the cartoon characters had me convinced that they existed. During the early stages of my life, I honestly believed that what I was seeing were real life situations, not actors playing out their roles in front of a television camera. The actors that I found to be the most amusing, were the ones that portrayed their characters with their eyes at half-moon, staggering as they walked and slurring their speech due to intoxication. Jackie Gleason, Red Skelton, Dean Martin and some well-known cartoon characters were a few of the many that demonstrated this drunken behavior on early television shows.

Their portrayal of a drunk was so funny and amusing, that I was always trying to live out that experience by mimicking their behavior. Unaware that this powerful influence would someday peak my curiosity toward using alcohol and drugs in my later years. What went wrong? How could I have allowed myself to fall victim to the devastating effects of negative addiction and substance abuse? It has been said that the environment has an incalculable effect on the human mind and the choices we make. And I guess that's how many of us, if not all of us, get hooked.

You see, I am a survivor of drug and alcohol abuse. You may have noticed that I didn't use the old familiar expression, "Alcoholic-addict" commonly used by individuals suffering from both drug and alcohol addiction. This is a type of labeling that many people in recovery have conformed to calling themselves. I don't believe in labels. Labels are for pickle jars. Especially the ones with negative connotations such as the ones just mentioned. I strongly feel that people who have acquired a serious health problem, be it cancer, AIDS, anorexia or chemical dependency should not be labeled with negative terms that may hinder their quest for optimum recovery.

So, what's my story? I didn't start out to become negatively addicted to drugs or alcohol. No one does. My negative addiction was a consequence that resulted from my need to experience those pleasures of the worst kind. Like many of us, I personally got caught up in all the excitement, curiosity and fun of chemicals and wasn't totally aware of the monumental dangers involved in excessive use of harmful substances. I wanted to experience the mystical magic that was labeled taboo. Although I had been warned, the drugs and alcohol seemed oh so tempting. Everyone I observed appeared to be having a festival of fun, and I wanted to get on the band wagon. I didn't want to be left out. So I indulged in the forbidden fruit and did not take heed to what my parents, relatives, friends, educators and, of course, my body was trying to tell me about the plight of drug and alcohol abuse.

After the initial hypnosis of societal conditioning towards the use of harmful substances, I began my pursuit of the forbidden fruit. I started out smoking cigarettes at age fourteen, then moved on to alcoholic beverages such as wine and beer. The hard stuff came later. What was my motivation? What would drive a vibrant young boy to indulge in such crude and lewd acts of destruction? Could I not see the writings on the wall that this behavior harbored dangerous consequences? Oh the writing was there all right, but it was covered up and disguised by the popularity given it by my surroundings. That was the trap. "Everyone was doing it." And today, that cliché still seems to hook many young people into these precarious behaviors. You see, all my friends were smoking and joking, and I just wanted to be "one of the boys."

During my pre-teen years, I was in no way interested in using any harmful substances. I was always encouraged by my family, friends, and school officials that smoking and drinking alcohol was destructive behavior and could possibly lead to a negative addiction and worse. My concerns were more with where I was going to get my next candy bar or piggyback ride than my next drug fix. I had a passion for art, drawing, roller skating and comic books. Why were those activities a popular pastime with me? They were popular with me because they were popular with most kids my age back then. Throughout my life I have found that most of what we do in life is not instinctive; it is learned. I discovered that we tend to take our cues from those around us. We say that we like a particular food or style of clothing, but how does that like come about? I learned my desires and behaviors from others just like everyone else. It became obvious to me that what we see we become, what we hear we become and what we touch we become. We are the metabolic end products of our sensory experiences and our interpretations of those experiences. For example, the way I followed my peers around resembled a platoon of processionary caterpillars. That's how I became sick. I followed in the foot path of those before me without question as to whether they were qualified to lead me. But I didn't start out following negatively addictive people.

During those early years, I was fortunate to be immersed in a very caring environment. The people that made up my world were church going and God fearing souls, particularly Mrs. Rudibaker. She was a very special neighbor, friend of the family and "my hero," whose gregarious nature made her liked by all. She took a strong interest in me as she did with all the other kids in the neighborhood. Her jubilant voice and attitude would always make our insides feel warm and tingle with joy every time she greeted us. Whenever she passed by our house, she'd look up at my mother sitting on the porch, smile and say, "How ya doing today, Mrs. Rhodes? Where's my boyfriend Oliver?" I was lucky and grateful to have such a loving woman spend time teaching me all about the joys of healthy living. She was a beautiful lady both physically and most importantly spiritually. She taught me healthy eating habits and the importance of having a good education. Mrs. Rudibaker always spoke with humor and passion. Her teachings included fun ways to exercise, how to make good friends and to be one with the Lord.

Mrs. Rudibaker was very firm with me about the dangers of smoking and drinking alcohol. "Don't you ever let me catch you with a cigarette in your mouth," she boasted forcefully. This woman inspired me by showing that she cared. She was one of my biggest role models. The teachings that she embedded in my mind were important to me. She, and everything she stood for, was very important to me. Since we tend to do the things that are the most important to us, there was no way I was ever going to put a cigarette in my mouth. She made a promise that if she ever caught me with a cigarette in my mouth, she'd make me eat it. Now, I really didn't believe she'd resort to those measures. It was just her way of getting my attention.

Although I was exposed to many people who drank, sniffed glue and smoked reefer (that's what marijuana was called back in the fifties) I didn't see using harmful substances as being fun or exciting. Also, I never believed that I would ever develop a desire to use any substance that was not designed for human consumption — not even in a million years. I could not have imagined that drugs and alcohol would one day play a major factor in causing some of the most painful experiences in my life. I was too busy being a child. What went wrong? Everyone I had associated with during my childhood and early adolescent years were very supportive and nurturing. How does one go from an amusing lifestyle to an abusing lifestyle? Much of my change in attitude came with a change in my environment.

Smoking and drinking alcohol were adult behaviors that I found repulsive. But it wasn't difficult for me to fantasize and romanticize about their mysterious hold on human beings. This wasn't hard to do when the glamour that surrounded television and billboard advertisements touted the values of smoking and drinking. They associated these behaviors with fun, success, fortune and wealth. Anyone who was anybody came up to the "fresh clean taste" of Kool Filter Kings cigarettes. Johnny Walker Red Label (Scotch) was the man's drink that gleamed with success. How could anyone not be a Johnny Walker Man?

Television stations discontinued cigarette and whiskey ads, as more and more people became aware of the devastating affects they were having on the lives of millions. As a result of the cutback on these promotions, many of these deadly advertisements on television are scarce nowadays. But nevertheless, they are still strategically imbedded in our programming, both on the screens, at home, and at the box office. The allure or more appropriately named, "the trap" that gets most of us, is not so much the product itself, it is the association that's attached to it. Once you are inside the jaws of the allurement, the notion that "every one is doing it" causes the relentless doors of pain to come slamming down on any prey who gets snarled in a life of negative addiction.

Mrs. Rudibaker had taught me values that were important. As a result, I maintained my stature not to participate in destructive behaviors. Well, for a while anyway. It wasn't until I entered high school that I began to change my attitude and my value system. Through experience and the school of hard knocks, I soon realized that our values change based on the compensation we receive from our environment. This payoff comes to us from our sensory experiences by way of the five senses. If the environment provides a bigger payoff than our current values, there is a great probability that we will drop those values for other ones. For example, I used to love chili con carne with loads of beef in it, until I learned that large consumption of meat contributed to heart dis-ease. The payoff here was a healthier heart and lifestyle. Therefore, I developed a taste for foods that were less fattening and more nourishing. As a result, I cut meat out because it was not *important* to me anymore.

For years I believed there was nothing that could encourage me to ever want to smoke cigarettes. But as I got older, my priorities changed and so did my interests. I had graduated from elementary school and was now on my way to bigger and better things—high school! For the first time in my life I was exposed to girls who had large bumps and curves on their bodies. They were very impressive as I noticed that these bumps and curves were causing bumps and lumps of my own. The lump in my throat, the thump in my heart and the goose bumps that formed every time the girls smiled, swarmed and charmed. The bulge that protruded from my chest cavity (my heart) seemed almost obvious when one of their smiles came my way.

These changes that were occurring in my life had a dramatic affect on my behavior as well as my attitude. I was now beginning to understand my reasoning for going from an attitude of not wanting to smoke cigarettes to an all out passion to give them a try. As I think about it, the allure had nothing to do with the cigarettes per se. It had everything to do with fashion, style, flair and communality.

My first few weeks in high school were a blast of fast action cars, pretty girls, parties and football. I got to rub elbows with people who were practically adults. This was the first time in my life I attended the same school that my older brothers and sisters attended. Coming from a large family of nine, I was next to the youngest who was still in junior high.

Even though my older brothers and sisters ignored me most of the time at school, I could still point them out to my friends and say, "Hey, check it out, there's one of my big brothers." Most of the time my older siblings didn't pay that much attention to me so, many of my friends didn't believe there was any relation. You know how it is in high school. The older guys didn't want their younger brothers getting in the way. When I asked my older siblings why they didn't respond to my greetings they said it "cramped their style."

As a freshmen, I was exposed to many wonderful experiences. The girls were fabulous, and I got caught up in the art of girl watching. They came in all shapes, shades, heights and sizes. But of all the girls I checked out, none were sweeter than Alexis Jones in my fifth period art class. She had a set of legs that wouldn't quit, a figure that made your liver quiver and a smile that would cause a melt down in the most sophisticated nuclear plant ever built. I made up my mind that I had to get to know this young lady better at all costs, and costly it was.

During one fall afternoon, I decided to wait for Alexis near the main bus stop many of the students used. This was a common area where most of the teens would meet to talk, show off their supped-up cars and hang-out. Many of the guys would smoke cigarettes (Kool Filter Kings), listen to the music on their transistor radios (vintage music device from the forties and fifties that "boom boxes" today now represent) and illegally drink beer or wine. The favorite drink for these young offenders was Sweet Rosio Gradi wine. The makers of this drink made it very convenient for kids to get their hands on this beverage as the bottle resembled most soft drink brands. Although it was difficult to distinguish the soft drinks from the wine coolers, many students felt it necessary to drink from their bottles wrapped in brown paper bags trying to disguise the obvious. Who were these kids trying to fool. Even someone as green as myself could tell what these guys were sipping on. The brown bag was just a symbol that represented "being cool," manhood and being just one of the boys, or girls. It is what's known today as being a follower.

A follower is a person who blindly follows those before them just so they can be known by the rest of the group. It would have been great if we played follow the leader, but there weren't very many back then, and it seems the same way today. Sure there were a few. But most of us are motivated by numbers and unfortunately, there are more followers than there are leaders in this world. For many young people, they just want to belong. In our society wanting to belong, that communality, is what's important, because the deepest craving for many young people is to be just like their role models and to be liked by their peers. Although most teens want to be seen as making their own decisions, many do not realize that they are taking their lead from the environment they have chosen to fit in with. Our ideas had to come from someone. They just don't pop into our heads. Remember that what we hear, see, feel, touch and eat we become. Our ideas generally come from the company we keep.

I had been standing on that corner waiting about a half hour for the lovely, heart stopping, mouth dropping Alexis Jones. Nervous and scared, I was trying to think of what I was going to say to her when she eventually came by. I knew she would be coming this way. I was on that corner everyday for the last four weeks and had seen her walking home in this direction. She lived only a mile or so from school. Her house was located on Grand Avenue and this was the most direct route to her home.

Of all the times I'd seen her pass by the favorite student bus stop, this was the first time I mustered up enough courage to say something to her. It had been thirty five minutes now and she still hadn't shown up. Did she take a different route today? Did her mom pick her up? Was she staying late for cheerleader or band practice? All kinds of thoughts were going through my head. Darn, the one day I get the courage to talk with her she decides to break her daily routine. What luck! I was just getting ready to leave when all of a sudden, I saw her walking my way. She had a smile on her face and a sparkle in her eye. Did she notice me standing there? I wondered if it was too obvious that I was waiting for her. She started moving much faster now and appeared to be looking my way. Was she thinking, "there's that "cool" guy in my fifth period Art Class." Just as I begin to open my mouth to say hello, it abruptly shut as she called out someone else's name. My smile became a frown turned upside down. Not to look foolish, I pretended to be looking in the direction of someone else myself. As I looked out the corner of my eye, I could see and hear her talking with another male student. I was devastated and broken hearted. I couldn't help but eavesdrop on their conversation and my crushed body couldn't take it. Oh, the disappointment!

The first thing she uttered out of her mouth was, "Hi Harold! Can I have one of your Kools?" She embraced him with a hug and as their bodies touched he put two cigarettes in his mouth. He then pulled out his "Zippo" cigarette lighter, and in one fast action move, popped it open and lit both cigarettes at the same time. It was like magic. I was so impressed! I thought, "how'd he do that? The way he lit up those cigarettes was so cool, I had forgotten all about the fact that he was holding on to my Alexis. I noticed she too was impressed. She was mesmerized by his ability to perform tricks with those sticks.

I didn't think he was all "that." So what! He can light up a couple of cigarettes with one move. Big deal. Well, it must have been a big deal to Alexis because she was holding on to him so tight he could have popped a blood vessel. As they walked away, she asked him if he would like to visit her at her house that evening—not to do homework—but to listen to some "rock n' roll" on her record player. She also asked him it he would teach her how to do that cigarette trick.

As I looked around, there were other guys with their packs of Kool Filter King Cigarettes rolled up in their tee-shirts displaying the Kool emblem. I couldn't help but notice that there were many fabulous looking girls responding to cigarettes the way Alexis did. They too were asking these guys for a smoke. Almost everybody was lighting-up. I felt dejected, alone and left out. My value system wasn't recognizable among these high school kids. Just about everyone was smoking because it was the "Kool" thing to do. Anybody that was somebody was lighting-up. Even my older brothers and sister were sneaking a cigarette just to be part of the in crowd. Not I. I chose to stand by my values. I wasn't about to give in to the peer pressure of the many. "Stick with the morals of the few," I said. I was going to stand my ground. And I did until I was put to the ultimate test.

During one afternoon, I was leaving my art class when Alexis asked me about my artwork. She thought that my work was the best in the class. Now that was something I was good at. I loved art and if anyone could draw and paint it was me. Shucks, I didn't need to smoke cigarettes to impress Alexis. She didn't need to ask me for a cigarette and I wasn't about to perform like old Harold either. She was impressed with my art work. She asked me if I would come over to her house to help her with the art homework assignments we were tasked with. I was ecstatic. Finally, the chance I had been waiting for had arrived and I didn't have to light-up to get it.

At about 7:00 p.m., I arrived at Alexis's house with artwork in hand. We studied, talked and laughed about our instructor's teaching style. Making fun of your teachers was something that all kids did even today. After our assignments were done, Alexis put on some "rock n' roll" and we slow danced to the Shirelles, Impressions and the Supremes. Our bodies were touching for the first time and I was in heaven. I couldn't believe it. There I was, dancing with the beautiful Alexis. Our cheeks touched and the greatest thrill of all happened. Our lips met and I was propelled into an orbit of puppy love. After our initial kiss, we only thought it appropriate to take a short walk outside. I wasn't prepared for anything further than just a kiss, besides, her parents were in the very next room. During our walk, we kissed again, and again and again. I was putty in her hands. We sat on the steps of a neighbor who was not at home. We talked about our assignments and kissed some more. The discussion got very deep as we shared our ideas about the perfect romance. I was hoping and praying that she saw me as the likely candidate for her. Even at fourteen, puppy love seemed like the real thing. At least it appeared to be.

The conversation we shared was sending me into a higher orbit. The flow was all systems go with me at the helm, and Alexis as my co-pilot. All of a sudden my instrumentation began to malfunction as she finally popped the question. I was not prepared for this abrupt change of course that Alexis had just charted. Right out of the blue she hit me with a request that sent me for a loop. My orbit began to descend, drag and spiral earthward. I was losing consciousness as I struggled for the proper response. How could I forget that this young lady was a smoker and that it would only be a matter of time before she lit up in my presence. But it was bound to happen and that was the question she had just popped. She passionately asked, "Oliver, do you have a cigarette? I immediately responded with a quick boldfaced lie — "I'm fresh out." Why did I lie? Now I'd gone and done it. I was so into her, I did not want to disappoint or spoil the evening by telling her I didn't smoke. Then she asked me, "what kind of cigarettes do you smoke?" I immediately told her, "Kool Filter Kings." She was pleased and asked me to meet her after school tomorrow for smoke break.

Alexis and I finished our homework assignments, kissed and said our good nights. I was in love. Moreover, I was also in trouble. The trouble was due to my big mouth and that cock-and-bull story about my smoking cigarettes. I did not smoke and didn't want to learn, but I didn't want to lose Alexis either. What it came down to was I had to make a value call. I had to determine what was important to me, Alexis or my good health.

After only two months into the high school scene, I was tired of being banished from social functions because I wasn't a smoker. People made fun of you and called you square if you didn't follow the trend. In other words, if you wanted to be accepted by your peers, you had to play the game of "monkey see, monkey do." That is, you had to learn how to smoke and drink.

I was beginning to reevaluate my priorities. My inclination toward wanting to smoke was being justified by my need to keep Alexis. I found myself saying, "Oh, smoking never hurt anyone." "Where's the proof?" "I know people who have been smoking for years and they're still kicking." Isn't it amazing? When the wants of our personality override the needs of our souls, it's easy to justify the cause of our ills. There are many people who use those same excuses today. The truth of the matter is that we set our *values* based on what's *important* to us. As a result, the important things become *priorities* in our life and that's what determines our *choices*. This is what I call the "Determination Equation": *(CE+VIP = C)*. "Values are Important Priorities that result in our Choices." The Compensation Expectation *(CE)* is the payoff we expect to receive from our Choices.

Everything we do is based on this equation. There are people right this minute who are dying from lung cancer, but won't give up their cigarettes. They know that smoking is not good for them. They smoke because their smoking is *important* to them. In order to change, our *VIP=C* (Values, Importance, Priorities = Choices) requires that we explore finding an equal or greater payoff from some other stimulant. In my case, I placed Alexis and smoking over my good health. For me, Alexis was a greater payoff *(CE)* for my personality, but not for my soul. I was about to sell my soul to the devil as so many of us do when we decide to abuse and misuse our minds and bodies. And I don't care what people say about their bodies being theirs. They are still violating the biological laws of nature when they neglect the needs of the soul. It doesn't matter which way you look at it, the first time you light-up, shoot-up, drink-up or snort-up, you are starting the dis-ease process. Like nature, the human body degenerates at a snail's pace. Although we may not immediately experience the ill effects from the toxic substances we ingest so carelessly, we are still setting ourselves up for ground zero (disaster). Although subtle, we seldom give these warnings a single thought. As a result, many of us acquire a false sense of security and assume everything is okay and continue our negative addictions thinking that the dis-ease inside does not exist. This is called denial. Why go through all the unnecessary pain when our bodies are very capable of warning us of the up-coming flash, followed by that shock wave of destruction.

I was so excited about Alexis and just couldn't wait to show her off to all my friends. She was my first high school sweetheart. She was beautiful and she was mine, at least for now. I never will forget the night I walked home from our first romantic encounter. I could only think of her. Then the thought occurred to me about the cover up. She will eventually find out that I lied to her about me smoking. Even though I didn't want to smoke, I also didn't want her to think I was a square or liar. I had to make a decision whether to learn to smoke or not to smoke. So, I did a quick on the spot rationalization session. I would give it a try, and if things didn't work out with me and Alexis, I can always quit. No big deal. I had it all figured out.

I still remember the excitement when I arrived home. It was the fall of 1962. I was just fourteen years of age and ready for my first adult experience. I felt like a man, no, twice a man, after that first date with Alexis. It was about 9:00 p.m. when I arrived home. Now that I had made the big decision, who could I get to teach me how to smoke? I know! I'll ask Eloise. She was one of my favorite sisters, older by two years. I could get her to teach me how to smoke. Besides, I was always doing things for her. Now it was time for her to return the favor. Every morning before school I'd always tie her ponytail. On many occasions, I would steam iron her school clothes while she waited her turn to use one of two over-crowded bathrooms in our home. With six of nine kids still living under the same roof, bathroom time was at a premium.

The hardest thing for me to do that night, besides asking her to teach me to how to smoke, was getting her alone from the other family members so I could pop that big question. With so many of us all sharing the same little house, there was seldom a time any one of us were ever alone. Finally, I saw an opportunity to get her away from the others. Without hesitation I said, "Eloise, will you teach me how to smoke?" Although nervous and afraid she would tell Daddy, I honestly believed that I could trust Eloise. Her response floored me. Surprisingly, she said yes! The only question she asked me was why. I told her of the situation with Alexis and how everyone else looked down on you if you're not a smoker. She said, "I'll teach you but, you better promise me one thing." "I'll do anything, I exclaimed!" "If daddy catches you smoking, I didn't teach you, understand?" I agreed.

It was really strange that Eloise didn't seem too surprised that I asked her to teach me how to smoke. Smoking and other negative behaviors were a sign of the times. Again, everyone was doing it, and it seemed as if I were being initiated into the adult world of vices. I now felt like "one of the boys," a new member of an old club. I now owned the badge of acceptance. Check me out! There was a new smoker on the block. And that was my beginning of the end. The end of a strong *values* system.

Everything that Mrs. Rudibaker taught me about the devastating effects of smoking had just gone down the tubes—my wind pipes. The values of healthy living were exchanged for a new set of values. Wanting to belong both to my peers and most importantly to Alexis, I had sold out to smoking. As a result of the new habit I acquired, I avoided Mrs. Rudibaker like the plague. It was very difficult to face her after I had broken my promise not to use tobacco. As for Alexis and me, after two months of a shaky relationship, she dumped me for some guy with a souped-up car and ten years her senior. I had been smoking cigarettes for two months now and was just too depressed to give them up. As a result, I was feeling down on my luck and stuck with the butts!

The moral of this episode in my life strongly suggests that the behaviors we choose stem from what *value* we place on our activities based on the compensation (payoff) we receive from our sensory experiences. Again, it is not so much the behavior or substance that compels us to become hooked, it is the association. Our associates are the hosts that transport the ideas, notions, attitudes and beliefs we embrace. These INABs (Ideas, Notions, Attitudes and Beliefs) generally become our own and are the catalysts that inspire us to act in much the same manner as those around us.

Often, if not always, the mannerisms, attitudes and habits of others influence our behavior. Therefore, our habits can be changed in much the same way as they were acquired. As a result of the many changes I have personally experienced, I have come to the conclusion that, if one soars with eagles (interacts with positive and influential people) that's what they become. But, if one chooses to scratch with turkeys, (interact with negative thinking people) that too is what they will become. Giving up negative addictions for positive ones or vice versa, can be as easy as whom we choose to associate with and what payoff that association provides. It doesn't matter if it's negative or positive, as long as it provides some form of pleasure. Although your payoff may be in the form of negative pleasure, it is important that you understand that your magnificent body will intelligently let you know what it doesn't need. It must do so in order to maintain its equilibrium.

The body will do everything in its power to get you off the negative forms of pleasure, even to the point of making you sick. You'll have no choice but to give in to the needs of your soul. If only people would realize this truth of cause and effect, they could prevent going through a life of excruciating pain, despair, heartbreak and misery. All we have to do is listen to what our minds and bodies are telling us. But many people do not wish to hear what can be heard so easily. Unfortunately, the price we pay for our disobedience can be costly. Even to the extent of premature death. And the only thing that's worse than death is the unnecessary suffering that precedes death. Death is just the final stage.

During the difficult days of my adolescent years, I was beginning to learn how to weigh the pros and cons on what things were important to me based on compensation. In my case, I chose a dysfunctional relationship over my good health because I valued the intimacy of a woman's love. Through the experience of trial and error, I managed to give up smoking for another trade off. That's what we do when we go from one activity to another. We trade one experience for a new and more rewarding experience.

Realizing that smoking wasn't good for the body was not what helped me kick the habit. It was the pleasure principle, not the fear of disease, that helped me give up cigarettes. I found that improvement was not viable motivation toward positive behavior change. It was the excitement of knowing you were going to experience a greater payoff from a new activity than the one you were currently experiencing. We do this all the time. Even with drugs. People will go from one drug to the next because they feel that the new drug will give them a greater high; not because it's a different drug or that it costs more. Again, it is the payoff (compensation). This is how I gave up smoking. I found another activity that provided a bigger and better payoff than what the smoking was providing. The payoff was not better health; it was the opportunity to sing with a band. I had a life-long dream to sing professionally with a well-known local band. And that dream came true on the Island of Guam. That was my first overseas duty station after I joined the navy in 1964.

It wasn't a doctor or counseling professional who suggested that I give up smokes to improve my singing voice. It was one of the musicians in the band. Doctors were no authority on music. They were authorities in medicine. I wasn't interested in medicine. I was interested in singing with this band. So I gave up smoking at the drop of a hat. I quit in *one day* at 19 years of age and never smoked another cigarette in my life. And that was more than thirty years ago.

Everyday doctors are providing people with staggering amounts of medication instead of providing them with the things that are important to them. If you can find out what's important to people and associate that with good and healthy habits, people would change their behavior on the spot. People will become excited about the process and follow through with whatever they need to do in order to change their lives for the better. You see, we human beings tend to do the things that are important to us, and it is that *excitement* that is the key to motivation.

Doctors are not versed in this unique method of change. They are in the metamorphosis of changing one's biochemical makeup through the administration of mind-mood altering chemicals and medications. Many people think that the medical model is the best way to improve our health because of strong societal conditioning. Living our lives in the medicine cabinet is not the best way for acquiring optimum health; it is the most common way. This way of thinking results in millions of people becoming dependent on drugs instead of the unique ability of the human mind and body to heal and take care of itself.

The dynamics of spiritual health and healing is a product of every living thing on this planet. Many people are just not aware of the vast healing potential that's present in all of us. Doctors don't heal. The human body heals itself under our directions. At times, this process can be stimulated with the help of doctors, counselors, therapists and the like, but the final process in healing, rests within the human mind. The mind is where dis-ease originates and that's where it ends. When a person is sick and tired of being sick and tired and believe they can use their mind to heal, the healing process will begin. Please, do not doubt the magnificence of your spiritual mind and body to heal itself. Now there are those who say that only doctors can heal. There is evidence for and against what the mind and body can do. It all depends on who or what you choose to believe. Check out this evidence at any medical library about the many who have been diagnosed with certain types of terminal diseases. Read about how they overcame their diseased conditions against all odds, in spite of their doctors' predictions and medical knowledge. There is no greater source for healing than what God has given to us all. The human mind.

When I gave up smoking for a career in singing, I had no awareness of this unique power of exchange. It was a swap; a trade; a switch from the grave. I gave up the negative addiction of smoking for the positive stimulation of singing. So simple, yet so difficult for me to understand during that time. Even today, many people are under the misconception that they can get rid of a habit without swapping if for another habit. This difficult process of getting people to give up old behaviors go on in treatment centers throughout the world. Taking someone's perceived pleasures away without giving them something pleasurable in return is disheartening. It is much easier to take up something more positive and enjoyable than it is to give up something negative. So, why are drug and alcohol treatment centers still clinging on to this outdated method of having people give up their drugs and alcohol without furnishing them with more than a life-long sentence of a program, the Big Book, meetings, Twelve Steps and a sponsor? Old habits just don't go walking off the job. They must be relieved by another habit that's going to take over the job of providing the hedonistic human being with its daily dose of better pleasure.

It is imperative that we as human beings understand this process of trade. Trade is the key to improvement and developing healthier lifestyle values. It is a must for anyone seeking to master the art of change.

Although I gave up smoking for something more rewarding, I later fell into another *trade off* that *wasn't* so rewarding. Still just in my early twenties, I didn't quite understand the dynamics of change in a positive sense. I found myself getting sucked in to a deadlier game of trade. Hadn't I learned my lesson by now? Wasn't the smoking experience enough to help me see the light. I was beginning to realize that right or wrong did not play a part in most of my poor decisions. It was the association that linked alcohol, pot, speed, methamphetamines and inhalants to the pleasure principle. Believing that if everyone else was using or doing it, it couldn't be all that bad. That was bad. I was part of a crowd that personified success. Most of the people I associated with were not the average thugs on the streets. My associates were respectable people who were upstanding citizens in the community. Their socio-economic and political status ranged from school teacher to professional athlete; circuit judge to police officer; commissioned military officer to hospital surgeon; commercial airline pilot to nuclear plant manager.

Many people aren't aware of the staggering number of professionals who regularly use illicit drugs, harmful substances and alcohol excessively. And as dangerous as it may be, many use while they are on the job. I've been there. Nevertheless, I allowed myself to follow in the footsteps of my associates.

The drive was on again to move from one source of

pleasure to a higher source. Unfortunately, I was making all the wrong choices. There was a new form of pleasure I was excited to give a try. Again, much of this behavior was due to the company I kept. After I got a hold of these new drugs, I thought, boy, what a rush! At first I thought I had died and gone to heaven. I was totally absorbed by the glamour of it all. Oh yes! The girls, parties, trips and camaraderie were too infectious to give up. I had learned a new form of pleasure that I thought I would be able to control for the rest of my life and without any limitations. Besides, there were professional people all over the world indulging. So I didn't feel out of place. I fell right in place, wanting to be just like my friends. Excruciatingly, I later learned that the human body was not designed to process harmful chemicals or control a controlled substance indefinitely. I eventually began to feel the pain of the psychological trap I had allowed myself to fall into. As I thought about how I got caught up in my obsession, it was like the bait, hook, line and sinker story. I felt like the unsuspecting fish that generally gets snagged on the enticing lure of the fishersman's trickery. Substances control and alter the mind, and since the mind controls how we think, it also controls our body. The drugs and alcohol I once perceived as my pleasure eventually became my terror.

My drinking and drugging days went from a perceived joy to a distorted ploy. I went from a social drinker to a problem drinker where these substances interfered with every aspect of my life. They controlled and hampered my physical, mental, emotional, social and spiritual growth and, my overall well-being, which consequently left me bewildered and lost. The helplessness that I felt at times was so overwhelming I became totally out of control. My continued and excessive use of these substances had gone far beyond its intended use. The problems that I created while under the influence extended from a broken marriage to numerous hospitalizations. Often I would drink and drive during peak traffic hours without any concern for the innocent people I was endangering. My ex-wife of four years came under the attack of my behavior while I was using. I was very disrespectful to her. Under the influence, I was verbally abusive and for no apparent reason. I was neglectful, and on many occasions would direct my attention on other women. Infidelity played a big part in my life when I was sauced to the gills on alcohol. On some occasions I would stay out until the early morning hours partying with friends. Calling home to let my wife know that I was all right was the last thing on my mind. As a result of my drinking and irresponsibility, I tormented my ex-wife during the four years we were married. She divorced me after I refused to give up my gallivanting, drug use, alcohol and other women.

Drinking and Driving - No Problem You Say?

My chemical dependency played a major role in a terrible automobile accident that almost took my life and the lives of innocent by-standers. While driving under the influence with a blood alcohol concentration of .35 percent, I allowed an antagonistic stranger to provoke me into a high-speed chase through Balboa Park, San Diego. How could just a one finger hand gesture turn a fairly good day into a day of tragedy? This irresponsible act on my part to chase down this person caused a major turn of events in my life. Had I just shaken it off and kept going, the shattered lives, auto damage, surgery, wreckage, finances, time off work, hospitalization and military reprimand could have all been avoided.

I often reflect back on that day and the events that occurred at that cursed intersection. That was the focus and start of the perilous chase through the park that ended in disaster. Although I was highly sedated on ethanol, I clearly remember how I reacted to such a worthless and senseless hand gesture. This horrible situation unfolded after I had entered an intersection giving me the right of way. In other words, it was a two-way stop sign for cross traffic. As I proceeded to cross this intersection, a speeding car suddenly cut right in front of mine. Like a scared jackrabbit running from hounds, this car came just inches from taking out my front end.

As I sounded my horn in protest, he yelled in defiance and gestured in compliance. To put it in more acceptable terms, he yelled out, "screw off," and gave me the one finger salute. As a result of my lack of better judgment, I gave him the power of control. I changed my course of direction to match his direction and speed. The chase was on. The driver in the other car was determined not to be overtaken or forced to stop. As we sped through Morley Field (one of San Diego's city parks), I eventually managed to pace his car. We were now side by side. I shouted with fervent anger, "Pull it over and let's do it, man." "Come on, let's get it on, I'll take you apart with only one hand," I threatened. Apparently, I got him running scared. He had no intentions of having a confrontation. In his attempt to make a clean get-a-way, he viciously rammed my car causing me to lose control. I became increasingly angry. In all my rage of "getting this guy," I was unaware of the parked truck sitting right in front of me. I somehow swerved off the road where it was waiting for me to crash right smack into its rear. With shock and horror, I slammed on the brakes but don't remember ever slowing down. But I do remember stopping with the help of that parked pick-up truck.

My car became an out-of-control steel projectile. I forcefully crashed into the back of this parked pick-up truck at a speed of 35 miles per hour. Like a thief in the night, the driver of the other car fled the scene with no concern or regard for the tragedy that had just occurred. The impact of the crash was so great that it forced this parked pick-up onto the picnic grounds and rolled several times before it came to a complete stop. Had it rolled one more time, it would have injured several people that were having picnics in its path. My car was totaled and I almost along with it. I was seriously injured but lied to the investigating police officer that I was okay. Witnesses told him that the other car was at fault, and I was cleared of any wrong doing. In the state I was in, I wasn't about to argue with credible witnesses. I could not believe that I walked away from a car that looked like it had been turned into an accordion.

The investigating officer asked if I wanted to be taken to Balboa Naval Hospital noting that I was U. S. Navy, active. I emphatically refused and said that a lift home would suffice. I knew, had he taken me directly to this military installation, I would have been severely reprimanded for conduct unbecoming. I went home and tried to sober up before having my girl friend take me to the hospital. I figured if I couldn't sober up, I could always say that I went home immediately from the accident and out of disgust downed a bottle of Scotch. And that's exactly what I did.

My girl friend eventually took me to Balboa Hospital where I stayed for a week to heal from neck surgery. Due to the condition I was in, I was not tested at the site of the accident for driving under the influence. Had I been, I would have definitely spent time in county jail. Suspicious corpsmen and doctors drilled me about my dangerously high blood alcohol count and repeatedly asked had I been drinking while driving. Well, you know what my story was, and with no way for them to verify whether I was telling the truth or not, I weaseled my way out of a possible court martial.

Drinking on the Job - No Problem You Say?

The devastating effects of my drug and alcohol use eventually reached the work place and caused numerous problems on the job. As a result of my divorce, I became depressed, despondent, and anxious. These emotions interfered with my performance, and I could not function properly without the use of chemicals. I then resorted to drinking on duty. My changed behavior became increasingly noticeable. My disposition and attitude towards many of my navy co-workers was negative and disrespectful. I occasionally missed special military meetings and called in sick quite frequently due to being hung over from the night before.

In May of 1983, my superiors discovered that alcohol was affecting my performance, conduct and military bearing.

They allowed me two options to get it together. One was a chemical dependency treatment center and the other was a pink slip normally called an Undesirable Discharge. They warned me to shape up or ship out. My past nineteen years of continuous military service was about to be wiped out. I was teetering on a very precarious path of destruction.

Good old retirement was in sight, and I did not want to blow my career. I respectfully requested that I be given the chance to shape up on my own. With my naval career on the line, I seriously made a paradigm switch from boozer to a cruiser. I cruised from heavy drinking to positive thinking. I mean, I got my head together for the better and completed a total of twenty-one years, one month and twenty-one days.

Although I gave up alcohol during my last two years in the service, I still had a desire to drink. My sound and most logical decision to stop using was based on that ultimatum given by my superiors. The threat of losing my career was too great to jeopardize. I knew that all I had to do was give it up for two or three more years and I was home free. No one could tell me what to do after my time was up.

During those last two years, I learned to live my life, not with substances, but with a new found passion—recreation. As a result of the "natural high" I was creating, I discovered that boozing and using was an artificial feeling that distorted reality. These false feelings of euphoria gave way to true feelings of bliss and happiness.

Recreation - A New Found Natural High

Upon completion of my naval career and my victory over negative addiction, I vowed to work in the field of recreation therapy, holistic health and motivational speaking. This is where I would spend the rest of my life helping others find healthy alternatives to addictive drugs, alcohol and other abusive behaviors. Since my recovery, I have lost two brothers, one sister, two cousins, a nephew and many friends to the devastating effects of drugs and alcohol. In the process of following their lead, I almost lost my identity, my life and my soul to mind-mood altering chemicals. The pain and anguish I went through trying to produce the ultimate high almost rendered me disabled. Fortunately thereafter, I discovered that the use of our creative minds can produce the ultimate high on its own.

In December of 1985, I retired from the U. S. Navy and immediately enrolled at San Diego State University. After just three years of arduous study, I graduated with honors and received a Bachelors Degree in Recreation Administration with emphasis in Therapy. Up to the publication of this book, I have worked in six recovery homes, three adolescent residential treatment centers and five hospital rehabilitation programs. It wasn't unusual to discover that the hardships and pain that many of these clients experienced were similar to my own experiences. It also became apparent to me that many of their struggles were fruitless; that's why many of them failed to overcome the chains of negative addiction.

One of the main reasons for failure was the labeling and conditioning. "Once an addict always an addict." "You're going to need this program for life." "You can never be cured." It was difficult for me to agree with these premises. As a result, I found this "labeling" to be one of the main reasons why many people avoided traditional recovery programs. Basically, they did not want to be handed down a life sentence of "program" and neither did I. This kind of labeling brands you as a "diseased person" for life. If you're in a traditional recovery program and you think that this labeling is appropriate for your recovery, then by God you should stick with it. But remember, the "program" is just one way, and may not be the best way or appropriate way for others.

I like to think of us human beings as being the parts of the whole and not categorized as separate entities. Everyone has problems and we are *all* recovering from one thing or another. Recovery is recovery. Some people are just recovering more than others; but nevertheless, it's pretty much all the same. Once we establish the notion that we're all in this together, we can start making greater progress towards a state of health and happiness that goes far beyond the mind set of just recovery.

My Passion for Sharing

I wrote this book with one purpose in mind. To help bring people to a new state of balance in their lives that offers an exciting and fun filled journey through the power of their beautiful human minds and bodies. If your dreams are to acquire true happiness, then live your dreams. But it is imperative that you rid your mind of any preconceived notions you have about traditional recovery. You must be willing to let go of past patterns of "program" conditioning. If you're not happy and your current program is not meeting your personal expectations, do not completely discard it. Maintain that part of the program that works for you and allow my story to fill in any gaps that may bring you to a new state of awareness. Who knows, some of the experiences you read about in this book may be the key that opens the door to the peace and happiness you may be trying to find. This consciousness is extremely important and necessary for your speedy and permanent journey beyond recovery.

My ultimate objective towards helping people discover their true potentiality is based on the love and caring that I have for all human beings, particularly the children of our world. A part of being healthy and truly happy is being able to recover successfully from the things that happen to us during our daily interactions with life. It doesn't matter whether we're recovering from our first fall as a child, failed marriage, high school examination or traffic ticket. It is knowing and understanding that we are all going to be challenged in life. We are going to have to muster up all the power and energy that God has given us. The "Serenity Prayer" that's often recited at AA meetings is a prime example of how we should live out our lives. It goes like this:

God, grant me the serenity to accept the things I can not change, the courage to change the things I can, and the wisdom to know the difference.

It's as simple as that. If we lived our lives accordingly, our lives could be transformed almost immediately. Who says you can't get immediate gratification living clean and sober? This unique and truthful statement has been uttered many times in meetings, treatment centers and recovery homes. I've chanted the "Serenity Prayer" on many occasions and make it a habit to reflect on these words daily. God knows I have communicated with him as much as I've communicated through AT&T. I'm just thankful He hasn't sent me the long distance bill.

I have personally witnessed children being born to chemically addicted parents. On many occasions, these innocent and unsuspecting children also suffered the devasting effects of these harmful substances. Fetal alcohol syndrome (FAS) and crack infested babies stand little chance for surviving pregnancy. These pickled fetuses that are being treated in chemical baths will never be able to lead a normal life.

There were many painful situations that I experienced when I used; far too many for me to discuss or want to discuss. You see, I don't want to live in the past. My past is over. I only wish to share that part of my life, and the lives of others that may assist you in your journey. Many professionals suggest you should go through life talking about your past. Personally, I disagree. Today is the most important time we'll ever have.

The past is just a review, not a major study.

I believe we should learn from the past and move on. Unfortunately, there are too many people stuck in the past trying to recapture old lifestyles. Or they are trying to make sense out of something that doesn't exist anymore. Their past may exist, but only in their heads. I believe people should lead their lives as if they were driving a bus. Surely we should occationally look in the rearview mirror but remember what we are seeing is only a reflection of our past. Our eyes should be on the road up ahead: the future. However, you can only reach your destination by focusing your attention on the drive: the present. In doing so, you will achieve true happiness along the journey of life. Unfortunately,there are many people driving their bus seated facing the rear, watching where they have been instead of looking where they are going. This aimless approach to living can cause many serious consequences and painful "pot-holes" in one's life.

Our future lies beyond the sign post straight ahead, around the bend and up the hill. It's that light at the end of the tunnel. It is Discovery!

Be Aware of The Cave

You know, it's sad and sometimes ironic, but many people find solace deep within the confines of their own little dark tunnel. They are afraid of coming out to see the real world and to see all the beauty that exists in real life. The air is much fresher when you're out of that ominous cave. I know. I was one of those moles who was blinded, not by the light, but by the darkness of my own little tunnel. It was truly a hell hole.

How many of you are in a similar situation at this time? After a while, I got sick of that darkness. I also got tired of the same old people who urged me to stay. I wanted out but as the saying goes, "misery loves company," and those who were suffering wanted me to continue to suffer with them. Isn't it amazing that when you want to come out of the darkness into the light, there are always going to be those who want to ride your coattail up or pull you right back down like rats in a pit. I definitely didn't like what I saw in myself while in my own dark cave. After shaking off those old ties that were holding me down, I managed to rise up out of that pit. I sifted through the ashes and fought like hell, to return to a world that made some sense.

In order to recreate my life, I had to change. For years I was trying to change everything and everybody but me. Who was I kidding? Only myself. I soon learned that if it is to happen out there, it must first happen within me. As Zig Ziglar emphatically states, "If it is to be, it is up to me." I changed and my whole life began to change. I know there are a lot of people who feel as I do. I also know that there are practically thousands, maybe hundreds of thousands who are suffering from the devastating effects of harmful chemicals. As a result of their suffering, their friends, families and co-workers are suffering too. Right now as you read this book, there's someone you know that needs help or maybe it is you. As I once did, I know there are many people who are stoned on the job, driving on the roadways, operating passenger trains, performing surgical operations or probably transporting passengers on airline flights. If you are one of those who are consuming harmful chemicals while at work, you are making an unjust decision regarding the innocent lives that you are endangering.

In each of our lives, we will all receive a wake up call to reality that will someday be knocking at our door. Personal responsibility and accountability will have to become the forefront in place of blame. It's just a matter of time. But how many people have to suffer before we are called to make restitution for our ignorance. One day we will all be held accountable for the wrongs we have caused others and the heavy burdens we have imposed on our own minds, bodies and souls. Ultimately, it is the children who will suffer from the poor role models who refuse to set good examples. Although we are different in many ways, we human beings all share one common characteristic—Spirituality.

We are not human beings having a spiritual experience, as some may think. We are all spiritual beings having a human experience. When we are being spiritual we radiate compassion, empathy and love. When we are being human we can easily be influenced by our human selfishness and greed and ignore the important things in life. We begin to think in terms of dog eat dog. We exploit each other and harbor feelings that using people is a means for survival. We strive to steal from those we come in contact with and take advantage of their every being. We take more than just their material possessions—circumstances permitting—we'll take their heart, soul, spirit and their lives. Is it any wonder why the children of our world are failing to learn desirable lifestyle values? With few role models to lead them, and a surplus of unqualified deviants to encourage them, many young people will miss out on the nurturing, companionship and love that's needed in order to develop, grow and prosper. For children to become whole, responsible, loving, prosperous and happy, they must be led by positive and caring role models.

We Are All Role Models

We are all role models whether we want to be or not. I'm reminded of a famous sports personality who appeared in an athletic shoe commercial where he stated emphatically, "I am not a role model." Whether he knows it or not there are many young people who are inspired, motivated and encouraged by his talents on the basketball court. If this is not being a role model, then what is? These impressionable youths will follow his lead in spite of what he considers himself to be. If we fail as responsible and caring human beings, our children will fail as responsible and caring adults. If we as a society do not project and demonstrate ongoing responsibility, love, care and pride, it may be difficult for our young to develop these qualities. You see, it takes more than one or two parents to raise a child, it takes a society. The reason for this is that children are not restricted to two parents. They are exposed to a society as a whole. And it is also that society that will have a strong influence on what many children will learn. If the environment for which that society exists fails as a whole, it is quite possible and very probable that many young people will swing to the left instead of to the right.

We adults must all be accountable, reliable, responsible and encouraging by giving of ourselves to our most valuable resource—our children. See yourself as a positive role model for these impressionable young people. And always remember that a song is not a song if you don't sing it, a bell is not a bell if you don't ring it, and love is not love if you don't give it. Plant that seed of love and watch it grow. It is no doubt that when we are wrapped up in our own little worlds, others in our lives become insignificant, even our closest and dearest loved ones. We are so busy working from the outside in, when we should be focusing on the inside out.

It is my belief that the reason we are here on this earth is to be here for one another and to interact harmoniously together as one. I see the world as a big jigsaw puzzle where each one of us has a specific goal in life. That goal is to create peace and happiness within that larger picture by giving of ourselves. We are all parts of a whole and must coexist as such. If we do not see ourselves as one, we'll never be able to create that harmony or peace on this earth. What better way to create that peace than to share our lives with each other in hopes that someone may benefit from our experiences. It is for that reason that I share with you my story, my glory, and my purpose for being on this earth.

To me, life is a big college and we're all in class. And if we don't see it as such, how do we expect to pass? Whether we like it or not, birth is automatic enrollment in "Life 101." This life-time course can be awfully painful at times. But if we aspire to turn a profitable gain, it's sometimes difficult to avoid the inevitable pain. The lessons that I have personally learned over the years have served me well. But as painful as these experiences seemed to be, they were necessary to bring the best out of me. When life landed its merciless force upon my world for the poor choices I made, I used to mistake these happenings as punishments from God, or felt that life was unfair.

I had to wake up to the fact that life is not unfair, and God – that's if you believe in a higher power – doesn't single out any one person to cast down his wrath upon. In my opinion, God is a loving God and life is never the same for me as it may be for others. My life is a creation of my own imagination. I'm often bothered by the comments people make when things aren't going their way. With anger and frustration a person will protest, "life sucks" unaware that much of their pain and suffering is due to their own lack of effort and personal responsibility to live according to the biological laws of nature.

As a result of the lessons I have learned over the years, I have a much deeper spiritual awareness of who I am and how my life is to be lived. Although those lessons were blessings, they could have resulted in a much deadlier fate. The dangerous and deadly plight I've experienced with harmful substances almost destroyed my career, my health and my existence. I guess you might say that I was lucky, blessed or both. It could have been much worse.

It is for this reason I share my passion with everyone I come in contact with: To raise your awareness to a higher level of consciousness. It is to enlighten, inspire and educate the readers by sharing those truths I hold so dear to my heart. These pages house the pain, suffering, discovery and conquest of many souls that have struggled to find peace and freedom from the chains of negative addictions and dysfunctional lifestyles. I hold these beliefs to be true for I have witnessed many desperate people suffer needlessly. This epidemic of suffering permeates our societies. Why? Because the truth for optimum health, healing and spiritual recovery has been tarnished by ignorance; shaved for profit and suppressed for the benefit of those who seek social and professional status. Much of this status seeking continues to go unchecked throughout the world, all at the expense of the ill-informed. My purpose is not to sell books or to become rich and famous. I'm already rich. That is, rich in spiritual health. My health is my wealth and I'm a happy man. And it is my deepest desire to share this wealth of knowledge with those who aspire to be just as healthy, wealthy and wise.

The wealth of health I now enjoy today wasn't always that way with me. For a long time, I forfeited my health and my soul for the harsh life of chemical dependency. It wasn't all bad, but as time pressed on it became really sad. The drugs and alcohol became solutions to my dilution and confusion, and I paid the price. I know what it's like to suffer and it was a costly sacrifice. Living on the dark side of alcoholism and drug addiction was not what I wanted to see in myself or anyone else. I sifted through the ashes of depression and degradation, and now live a life based on success and revelation.

My life was such that I was always trying to get things that I considered I needed to feel whole. I never dreamed or realized that what I was trying to acquire, I already possessed. I was already whole. The drugs and alcohol that I used only distorted my perception of real life. I honestly believed that my drug use was responsible for my happiness. But in reality it was an illusion that created that delusion and an obstruction to my creativeness. How many of you out there have lost your creativity because you've allowed yourself to become a slave to outside stimulants? Many people, including myself at one time, thought that it's those things that are outside of us that create happiness such as cars, jewelry, drugs, alcohol, food, people and of course cash. It's no doubt that things can make us happy as long as we can continue to produce them. When they are gone, our happiness goes right along with them. For many people their happiness comes from outside sources. They become object referral. That is, they rely on objects in the environment to bring some kind of order to their world. This is how people get hooked. Just like that fish I talked about earlier. If a person's happiness is tied to objects such as the string that's tied to a baited hook, well you know the story. I often hear people profess that "people who have money are happy." Sure to a certain extent, but it's just the opposite. People have money because they are happy first. Happy people know how to create situations that net large incomes. Their happiness is independent of outside objects.

For the truly happy people, objects only add to their happiness, for happiness is an inside job. In other words, these people would be happy even if they did not have material possessions. In this manner, they would be able to focus their energy on the perfection of the inner self. You see, everything in life flows from the inside out. The sun doesn't shine from the outside in, it radiates from the inside out. And when it shines, we all shine. It even shines on those planets that go far beyond our world. When you drop a pebble into a pond, the ripples it produces move from the center outward. The energy from sound waves function in the same manner, where its transmission goes to infinity. In weather systems, winds circulate clockwise and outward around high pressure centers. That's why the weather associated with these systems produce fair weather and clear skies. And it's not coincidental that these systems are called high pressure patterns. On the other hand, weather systems that have winds circulating counterclockwise and inward are associated with adverse weather patterns.

With nature, everything in life even our human energies, originates from the inside and gradually moves outward. This is why we human beings lose heat — which is energy — in cold environments. We also lose our energy to emotionally needy people. The emotionally needy tend to drain our energies because they have very little of their own. It is important that we share our energies, but make sure that our energies are evenly exchanged in relationships with others.

If one partner in any relationship tends to take more than they are giving, they will feed off the other leaving that person emotionally worn out. This is called a dysfunctional relationship. There must be an equal exchange of spiritual energies in order to have successful and nurturing relationships.

Plants extend up and flourish outward, always gravitating towards the light. Clouds condense to saturation until they produce a burst of rain that comes pouring out of them. We human beings are conceived within an embryo until we are thrust out into the world by the laws of nature's will.

Consequently, it is within self that our greatest achievements are *Created and Re-created.* Therefore, as we evolve we re-create ourselves through our projects. If our creativity involves health promoting activities, we develop the skills necessary to overcome many difficulties while simultaneously promoting happiness and good fortune.

This is why it is important that we recreate ourselves after we have been created. What you are and who you are is a *creation* of your *imagination, socialization and imitation*. It is without a doubt that we become exactly what we imagine (think about) and whom we associate with (socialization). As a result of the continuous association with the people we like, we eventually begin to act, think and live just like they do (imitation). If the end product (who we are today) of our sensory, personal, social and spiritual experiences are not to our liking, we need to find better ways to re-create ourselves. I will thoroughly go over the Power of Re-creation in *Discovery* 6. But let it be known that recreation is not only an activity, it is also the result of actively participating in health promoting activities and projects. Just as one changes the oil in their car, or refuels the engine after driving extensively, we human beings need to refuel in pretty much the same manner. Besides satisfying our nutritional needs, we must also restore and refresh our mind, body and soul through these recreational experiences and do it on a regular basis.

Qualitative Recreation Lifestyle Principles

Qualitative Re-creation Lifestyle Principles (QRLP) are health promoting activities and projects. They lead to spiritual re-newal. When you are following *QRLP,* you are enhancing your center of influence. You become more spiritual and less material. Although material items may add to our happiness, often times we become rigidly attached to those objects of reference. With principles, we begin to give more of ourselves because we feel that there is more of us to give. We develop an understanding that life is not about receiving as much as it is about giving. Therefore, it's not what society can do for us, but what we can do for society. Unfortunately, many people get caught up into believing that society owes them something. To think that society is in your debt will have you waiting aimlessly for something you haven't earned. This process of waiting for unrealistic frills leaves many people disappointed, angry and frustrated with life and all of humanity.

These feelings of dissatisfaction will not be against society as much as it's going to be against us as a whole. There are those who feel that all they need is for society to drop that perfect soul mate into their laps in order to be fulfilled. I've heard people say on many occasions, "if I can just get my feet back on the ground I'd be okay." If they are not walking on the solid ground, where have they been walking? We tend to fall into society's trap if we think that society has all the answers. There are no such things as "pat" answers. This is why people get hooked on trying to find answers to their problems and wind up looking in all the wrong places. The real answers are inside your mind. The trap is getting you hooked and dependent on objects and things that glitter in the environment. Objects take your awareness off the fact that you are a unique and special human being with the power and the means to be happy and successful within yourself.

For years we are conditioned by our society that we aren't valued if we aren't wearing Levy's 501 Jeans, or drinking a particular beverage, or smoking a certain brand of cigarette. In our attempt to be accepted and liked, we run rampant trying to please others and at the same time we neglect ourselves. Our rush to acquire these goods keeps us dependent on outside stimulants. It took me years of painstaking trials to realize that I am unique, special and valued. Whether I have those material things or not. However, if I choose to indulge in those outside luxuries, I have to remember that they only add to my pleasure, but they are not necessary for acquiring true happiness. The universal law of cause and effect states: if you want it, you must first give it. How many of us go through life not understanding

BOX 1

The Dynamics of Optimum Health is in Understanding

Cause and Effect

Understanding that things come to us in the form of Wholesome Rewards or Negative Consequences is the key to optimum health, wealth and happiness!

(As Bobby McFerrin would say, "Don't Worry Be Happy")

Anyone can be happy and free of worry by understanding and knowing that everything that happens to us comes as either a consequence or a reward.

Rewards are the results of our efforts, and consequences are the results of our lack of responsibility.

Knowing that we have that choice empowers us to do something about changing our lives. We also have the power to differentiate one outcome from the other — That is, we should not expect positive outcomes from minimum output, or negative outcomes from maximum performance.

When we understand these dynamics, we can better apply our true potential, but we must be willing to listen, not defend, the cause of our ills. This allows us to act accordingly towards improving our health, wealth and happiness.

The Magic all begins within Self!
This is known as CSI
("Common Sense Intelligence")

We all have it!

that simple but effective law. Whatever the effect of your life may be, it will definitely equal the cause. Good cause good effect. Bad cause bad effect. So simple, so perfect, so true. What goes around comes around.

I have a "thought for the day" that I would like to share with you. This is one of my own creations that I wrote one month after I began living according to the biological laws of nature. Again, I prefer not to say living drug or alcohol free, or living a sober lifestyle. To me that means living without. The reason is that many of the addiction programs are based on abstinence instead of sustenance. Filling my life with nourishing substances replaced the behaviors I lost or the ones I discontinued. It was this thought that I share with you now that helped me establish and maintain a much healthier lifestyle. After twelve plus years, I still read this thought on a daily basis (see Box 1, page 54).

If you are making a contribution in life, you won't have to worry about retributions from life!

Life will always return to you in rewards what you give to it in service. Also, it's important to note that your returns will not always come when you expect them to. So be patient. Your efforts will be rewarded serendipitously! If you are doing your part in giving of yourself, do it unselfishly. You will get your just dessert. Let's hope it's sweet!

Many of us want things, but at times find it difficult to put out the effort to obtain them. We lose interest in the magnificence of the human machine and settle for inanimate objects of pseudo pleasures. For example, state lotteries are waxed rich by the millions who play it, all hoping to win their fortune. Now there's nothing wrong with hoping to get rich quick, but millions of people are left disappointed and depressed because they didn't win the "big one." I've spent years tormenting myself with drugs, alcohol and dysfunctional relationships because I didn't win that pot of gold at the end of the rainbow. I felt that life was being unfair. Disgusted with life because of my failures, I was always pointing my finger in the direction I believed was responsible for my misfortune. But what I "failed" to realize about pointing the finger was that there were three pointing right back at me. It took a while before I realized that if it were to be, it was up to me. My retributions were the effect of not making any contributions. There are many of us that want the effect without the cause. Earl Nightingale says it's like the man sitting in front of the fireplace who says, "Give me some heat and I'll give you some wood." It doesn't work that way. We've got to pile in the wood first.

I once thought that drugs, alcohol and other mind-mood altering chemicals were responsible for enhancing my life with sophistication, glamour, masculinity and confidence. I actually believed that these chemicals would give me virility; making me the man that I always aspired to be. My interpretation of success was in using and boozing, with thoughts of women beating paths to my door. These thoughts were all false feelings of euphoria. Sadly enough, these substances almost made the man that was not going to be—deceased. Fortunately, I am still living and breathing, and I thank God for walking with me through those most difficult times of my life. The *cause and effect* of my experience with drugs and alcohol nearly destroyed my life. Personally, they were a total bust and left searing scars in my mind that I shall never forget.

Rediscovering Passion in Health-Promoting Activities

The dynamics of our behavior stems from our need to experience pleasure, fun and excitement. Why do you think we use and abuse harmful chemicals? Happiness being the ultimate goal in life, we will do almost anything to accomplish this goal even if it means hurting ourselves or others in the process. We possess feelings and emotions that must be satisfied by interacting with others. We possess a burning desire to be needed, loved and to love others ourselves. We are social human beings and simply can't get along without each other. We are the happiest when we are doing the things we love. I have often stated that if you ever find a job that you truly enjoy, you'll never work a day in your life. It is a part of human nature that much of what we humans do is based on some form of compensation that stimulates the five senses. Adam reached for that forbidden apple because he wanted to taste the sweetness of that fruit. Christopher Columbus had an itch to discover a new world. The Wright Brothers wanted to experience the magic of flight. Even Hitler wanted to experience this power by trying to conquer the world. What do all these people have in common? They all wanted to experience some form of pleasure or power. Even if their behavior resulted in destructive consequences, the initial idea was not to wind up in the red. Their hopes were for power, wealth and happiness.

It is not so much the people and their cause that's important as much as it is the dynamics of their behavior.

We human beings are driven by a need to feel, see, touch, taste and smell pleasurable experiences. Our emotions play a much greater part in our need to act on pleasurable sensory experiences such as to be loved, wanted, respected, recognized, honored, revered and challenged. What this is saying is that it is the carrot more than the stick that motivates our behavior. More than anything else, *pleasure leads the field in motivation.* If it is not immediate, we are still inspired by anticipated pleasure. We are either doing something that we love or doing something we dislike with hopes of a happy outcome. The drawback with the latter is that if we are not immediately rewarded, we tend to give up. In other words, there must be a pay off or we may feel that our efforts are in vain. *No compensation, no continuation!*

This happens often in our society with such things as exercise, treatment programs, diets, dead-end jobs, etc. The most desirable way to accomplish our goals successfully is to first seek positive and pleasurable rewards. Only then can we find both success and happiness.

If you seek improvement, first seek enjoyment and you'll find both.

Re-creation is Compensation

Getting off drugs and alcohol was not an easy task because I didn't understand the dynamics of my behavior. All I knew was that I wanted to feel what everyone else was feeling. I wanted to experience excitement by getting high, socialize with people I thought were cool and being a part of the crowd. It was like receiving a badge, a membership card and diploma all wrapped up into one. It was wanting to belong. Unfortunately, I was just following everyone else around in darkness and not sure where those before me were headed. I was one of the blind following the blind. What made it even more difficult to give up a harmful substance was that I had failed as a responsible and upstanding club member—social drinker. As a result of my abusive behavior, I was ousted, banished and suspended from the very club that I was recruited by—the using and abusing population. Most of society got to indulge in boozing and using, but I couldn't play anymore.

Needing to belong to a group is very healthy as long as the group you are involved with practice health promoting activities. Are the people you're involved with living according to the biological laws of nature? Check your inventory and see what's happening in your life.

To be ousted or suspended from a group, club or any organization is similar to getting fired. It is not a good feeling. No one likes to be shut out of a lifestyle they've become accustomed to over the years. This is why so many people feel cross, burned, deprived and deserted when they are forced to give up their chemicals. To be truly healthy, it only makes sense to find an alternate club, and make sure that it's going to provide you with the means to enjoy life on life's terms; a form of living that will take you far beyond recovery. For what's beyond recovery but discovery. And this is where I discovered my true self—exploring new areas of happiness, success and pleasure.

Overcoming the devastating effects of negative addictions can be just as easy as going from one form of addiction to another form. We *practice* this method of change throughout our entire lives. It's called "compensation." Isn't it true that we go from cigarettes to alcohol and from alcohol to pot. Aren't we encouraged by our club members to try new ways to get high when drug lords fashion new poisons for us to abuse? We are forever looking and searching for more powerful drugs to get stoned on due to the fact that the old ones have lost their punch. We go from one chemical to stronger forms of drug use in our attempt to get a more powerful high. Unfortunately, our bodies develop a tolerance to these foreign substances. As a result, we are forced to use more of the same or find a new game.

Exploring New Game

Many people who I meet often ask, "how can you be so full of energy and be so happy without the use of drugs or alcohol?" I turn it around and ask them how can I not? Drugs and alcohol are a total bust. I have found new games to play and a form of re-creation that my old drug use can't compare to. Many in traditional recovery find this hard to believe. They think I should be stuck in the Twelve Step program for the rest of my life. They feel that I will always have an urge to use, but nothing can be further from the truth. These harmful chemicals are no longer an option in my life.

When you find new and exciting ways to live, play, work and socialize that promote health rather than destroy it, drugs become insignificant. The reason so many in the "program" are opposed to this "common sense" approach to recovery is that it's not the Twelve Step tradition set forth by Alcoholics Anonymous (AA). Alcoholics Anonymous is a worldwide fellowship of men and women who meet together to attain and maintain sobriety. It originated in 1935 when Bill W., a New York stockbroker, and Dr. Bob S., a surgeon, met in Akron, Ohio and started to help each other stay sober. Although this program has helped many people attain sobriety, it often becomes a lifetime of propriety. Many people profess to such rigidness, but others find that it's not always the best. In my experience, I have found that this form of rigidness keeps you hemmed in and forces you to follow a strict life-time program that is well overdue for a face lift.

The single most important factor that saved my life was the *realization of compensation*. I knew in order for me to kick the negative habits, I would have to find healthier habits that provided just as much pleasure, if not more, as the chemicals I was using. I also knew that I would have to stop scratching with the turkeys and start soaring with the eagles.

It may be difficult for you to change your habits without changing your environment. And it doesn't matter how adamant you are about keeping your drug using friends. You may be denying and lying about what is real and how you feel.

How did I accomplish this? First of all, I sought out people who were living healthy and happy lifestyles and studied how they went about their lives. I found that almost all of them lived with passion, instead of just living sober. I didn't want to continue a program that required having you look over your shoulder for the rest of your life. Instead of worrying about what things to avoid, I wanted to bring things into my life that were positive and fun. So I got in to *play* and *sound re-creation*. Re-creation in its original Latin form means the "restoration to health." The French expanded it to mean "to create anew, restore, and refresh." English dictionaries now define recreation as a "refreshment of strength and spirit." Spirituality is that common denominator that involves us all, and the key towards developing a "re-creation" lifestyle attitude. Since we are spiritual in nature and material in form, our spiritual well-being must be recreated. This state of well-being can best be achieved by actively participating in projects that nourish the soul. See more on Re-creation in *Discovery 6, "QRLP Defined and Applied."*

Our spirituality is our highest component. We are 99% spirit and 1% form. When our destructive use of foreign chemicals enters the body, it draws on our spiritual strength disrupting our connection with the biological laws of nature and the universe. When our spirit is unable to function in accordance with those laws, the human form is directly and seriously affected. It becomes unable to discern, reason or manage itself within the realms of spiritual, mental, social, physical and emotional well-being. You become lost and unaware of the damage you are causing your inner spirit. When the spirit goes, every part of your existence goes with it.

I have worked with hundreds of sick people who have lost their souls to harsh chemicals, prescription medication, inhalants and alcohol. I have worked in two recovery homes, four hospitals, residential treatment centers and many drug and alcohol rehabilitation facilities. If you are using these substances and having problems managing your life, then you are lost too!

As a licensed recreation specialist and as someone who has also recovered, I have a passion for helping others find their way home—to the soul. I've conducted many workshops, lectures and group presentations all relating to disorders of the mind, body and spirit. I have read countless numbers of patients' charts and have found that the one component that they all lack was that positive recreation lifestyle attitude. Over ninety percent of these individuals had no idea what recreation was. Fun and games was the typical answer to the question, "What is recreation?" Many were not aware of the power of recreation participation and the positive effect it has on the human spirit. Recreation can result from a good volleyball game to a college course in physics. Whether it's a Ping-Pong game or CPR class, recreation gives us the chance to create ourselves anew.

Since our spirits are destroyed by chemicals, it only seems logical that we allow ourselves to become "re-inspired" through pleasurable activities that revitalize our spiritual well-being. There is no better way to heal ourselves from the devastation of disease than by following Qualitative Recreation Lifestyle Principles. *QRLP* are basically Health Promoting Activities (HPAs) that lead to Desirable Lifestyle Values (DLVs).

My First Encounter With the Program and Its People

My decision to get involved with the Twelve Step program was not your typical method of indoctrination. I rather slid in the back door. Due to the success I had with overcoming the devastating effects of drugs and alcohol, I was burning with desire to help others manage their lives more effectively. I was gung-ho and wanted to take the ball and run with it. I was like that kid on the bench yelling, "Send me in coach." I wanted to play. I was so excited and wanted to share my new found approach to optimum recovery with many others the same way I used to share my drugs and alcohol with them. Not only had I been successful with my recovery, I was successful in encouraging others to give up their abusing for something more amusing — re-creation! I'd lost friends, relatives and associates to this devastating disease, and didn't want others to suffer those same consequences. I wanted to make a difference in the lives of those who were still fighting to stay sane as well as alive.

During my quest to do my best, I landed a job as a Youth Counselor and Activities Coordinator at a recovery home in Escondido, CA. My primary function was to provide leisure education and recreation for teenagers and adults who were in drug and alcohol rehabilitation. This was my first encounter with the people of the "program." Before I could begin performing my functions, I was instructed to attend a mandatory staff meeting where I was to be initiated, indoctrinated and appropriated. I personally felt that I was given a set of conditions, or militarily speaking, a set of orders to be carried out without question. Those orders were to follow strictly the teachings of Bill W., founder of Alcoholics Anonymous, that include the Twelve Steps and the Twelve Traditions. I was given copies of the Big Book, AA meeting directory, disease concept literature and program description. Without question, I was expected to read and familiarize myself with the Twelve Step conditions, ideologies and beliefs.

The Administrator drilled me as if he were the Gestapo. Before I could take the ranks in the program, I had to agree to abide by their by-laws. He was very adamant about following the "program" to the letter. Accordingly, I was to learn and understand the disease concept and the fact that negatively addicted people were powerless. I personally didn't have a problem with understanding dis-ease. It was the idea of being "powerless" that didn't sit well with me.

I understood that being powerless meant that there are those who can't use drugs and alcohol anymore. Their lives are now unmanageable, and they have no more control over certain situations, drugs or other mind-mood altering chemicals. Unfortunately, there are too many people who mistake being powerless for *helplessness* and *hopelessness*. For example, I often hear in recovery programs that people refuse to stop smoking, attend school, lose weight, eat healthier, or seek careers based on the idea of being "powerless." In my experience, this "stinking thinking" prevents many in recovery from taking action towards improving their lives.

I also had, and still have, difficulties with addiction being considered a disease. I can honestly say that "negative addictions" create disorders within the body and mind. But what about those people who are positively addicted. Are they diseased as well? Remember, addiction is understood to be a disease that also means that people with a disease are sick, ill, infected and contaminated. Do they have this disease for life or are they ever going to fully recover? I felt perplexed and confused whether to accept the idea that people with an illness can never be healed? Patients who have survived cancer see themselves as being healed. So, why can't people with other diseases be healed?

Of all the people that I've known to contract an illness, be it cancer, AIDS, diabetes, hypertension, diverticulosis, atherosclerosis or worse, they have survived, and now consider themselves to be cured. Many people will argue that you can only control some diseases but you can never cure them. Well, if you believe that tale, maybe you should read the thousands of case studies on people who have survived the most serious of diseases and are now living a healthy and normal life. Isn't it true that when we live our lives in accordance with nature we are promoting health while at the same time *preventing disease?*

If certain diseases are considered to be incurable, how do we account for all the thousands of people who have successfully recovered? What do you call these people? Lucky? When man cannot explain these miraculous recoveries through medical science, he refuses to recognize these alternative measures as viable treatment. For example, there's mounting evidence on the healing power of meditation, nutrition, exercise, play, recreation, laughter and visualization. If the successful treatment of these diseases are not contained, studied, radiated or chemically treated in a medical environment, they are considered quackery by the medical establishment.

I consider myself to be fortunate that I discovered the true dynamics of optimum health before I allowed myself to fall victim to "program" conviction. A program that focuses on what things to avoid instead of looking at what things to enjoy was not my idea of optimum recovery. So, I never considered myself to be diseased or negatively addicted. I wasn't about to stand up in front of a group of people and say that I was an addict. In my opinion, we are all addicted to something and we are all recovering from one thing or another. There are those who are negatively addicted and those who are positively addicted. In my opinion, people who are negatively addicted are dependent on harmful substances that destroy the inner spirit. They find life difficult without the use of drugs and react negatively during withdrawals. On the other hand, people who are positively addicted are involved with lifestyle practices that enrich the mind, body and spirit. People who actively participate in health promoting activities (HPAs) develop skills for acquiring a natural high. They go after these new found activities with a passion. It is called the pursuit of happiness, life, liberty and freedom.

Individuals engaged in the pursuit of negative substances do it because they "have to," whereas, individuals engaged in the pursuit of positive lifestyle practices do it because they "want to." It is a part of a healthy lifestyle. Excessive drug and alcohol use only abuses the user and renders them incapable of functioning in a positive manner.

The negative addict is living dis-eased, while the positive addict is living at-ease. One is destructive and the other is constructive.

My entire attitude towards drugs and alcohol had changed. The using and boozing that once almost shattered my life were things of the past. And the past for me does not exist. My new outlook on life, happiness and peace of mind hinge on new found interests of value promoting activities. I guess you can say that I "re-created" myself through activities that were fun, challenging and exciting.

I went back to school, started to play again (fun first fitness) and also learned how to play the piano. Art became a big part of my life, and I also decided to teach. It was these activities that helped me discover my true self. I refused to allow drugs and alcohol to interfere with the value I now placed on myself. These chemicals were not going to be held over my head for the rest of my life like the "old rugged cross." Discovering myself further, I was amazed by who I became and where my life was going. I was now experiencing a part of my life that I never knew before. As far as I was concerned, I was still addicted and still getting high, but it was a positive addiction. And for the first time in my life, I was getting high on life itself.

Many people in recovery blame drugs and alcohol for their misfortune. I blame myself and I am glad that I woke up to the realization that it was not the drugs and alcohol that were responsible for my distortion and destruction, but I, and I alone. The using was a factor but I was the creator. I created a broken spirit that led to a run-down body. Thus, in finding my true self, I recreated a new day and a new way to enjoy life without the use or abuse of drugs and alcohol.

Living drug and alcohol free was a lifestyle I had never experienced before. Often I thought, "Why couldn't I have discovered my true self years before?" Well, as stated earlier, life has its way of teaching us lessons. The real deal in life here was waking up and learning about myself. That's where my true happiness lies, within my soul. Everything else is icing on the cake. Although these harmful chemicals caused great pain in my life, the experience has significantly heightened my inner awareness. Therefore, I have developed an in-depth inner awareness of myself and a greater love for life!

Wanting to Belong Can Be Costly

Once I was formally indoctrinated and oriented into the Twelve Step program, I began my work with recovering teenagers and adults. My passion in life, after the death of my past, was to help others give up using for a lifestyle more amusing. I was motivated and energized. The positive energy that I exuded spilled out to almost everyone I came in contact with. It was a refreshing feeling knowing that you were making a difference in the lives of those who were fighting to find a healthier way to live their lives. I wanted to teach individuals more than just living a sober lifestyle. I wanted them to experience the excitement and pleasure that God intended for them to experience without the use of harmful substances. I wanted them to know that life can be more rewarding than abstinence alone.

The job of creating challenging and fun projects for recovering teens and adults had begun. The activities that I scheduled were just what the doctor ordered. Within two months I managed to get nearly all the teens and adults involved in recreational activities. The magic was happening, and I was making a difference in the lives of those who had been struggling to get off their drug of choice. In addition, I helped them find more rewarding activities to engage in. More importantly, I assisted in helping them find their true selves.

The recreation program was making a big difference in the lives of the residents. Unfortunately, many of the counselors felt that it was taking away from the traditional Twelve Step program. I personally felt that it was boosting the program with fun, variety and excitement. I had assumed that the change in attitudes of the residents would be a welcome sight for staff as well as for new clients. I was not immediately aware that there were hidden agendas and some staff members felt slighted because much of the credit for residents feeling better was due to their participation in recreation. It was soon apparent to me that dedicated staff members felt their importance losing ground over what was important for the clients.

I begged to differ. My observation was such that it made the counselors that much more important because there had been a new component introduced for their benefit as well as the clients. Many hard-nose Twelve Step counselors didn't see it that way and began challenging the importance of recreation.

Another factor that didn't sit well with the counselors was that many were traditional Twelve Step followers and resented the fact that I did not consider myself to be an addict. My argument to them was that I once had a problem with drugs and alcohol, but that problem has since been resolved. Wrong answer! They didn't want to hear that. They argued that I'd always have that problem according to the big book. It was insisted that I was in denial and was full of "it." "It" being a popular word of profanity spoken by many in recovery who use "it" and another form of "it" to demonstrate anger and frustration.

Over a period of time I was discriminated against simply because I didn't see myself as a negatively addicted person. Even when I was introduced by staff to others in the program, they referred to me as a "normie." I was perplexed and asked what this terminology meant. I was informed that since I didn't consider myself an addict, I was "normal." I was not impressed that people in recovery did not think of themselves as being normal. This negative terminology that permeated the program was enough to keep me from adopting that kind of "stinking thinking."

Many hard-core Twelve Step members warned that if I didn't "fess-up" and admit that I was an addict, I would eventually sabotage my program and fall right back into drug use. I continued to profess that using was no option in my life. That was in the past. Many in the program weren't satisfied with that. They would counter with rude statements such as, "oh, so you're cured?" I would respond with, "aren't you?" In all their harassment, insults and accusations no one ever asked me if I was happy. They were not interested in the fact that I was successful in recreating my life. I had completed college and graduated with distinction from San Diego State University.

I gave up cigarettes, coffee, sweets, junk food and unprotected sex. I incorporated pleasurable physical activity into my life. My attitude on life did a complete about-face—a 180 degrees from a destructive lifestyle to a constructive lifestyle. I wasn't just living sober, I was living my life with purpose, meaning, success, challenge and happiness. I wasn't sitting around doing nothing like so many in recovery do. Many people in recovery programs do nothing but go to their meetings, smoke cigarettes, drink coffee and eat donuts.

In my understanding of the "Big Book" it states: "In order to establish and maintain continuous sobriety, one must abstain from all mind-mood altering chemicals." I know for a fact that the majority of recovering people are not following this protocol. What this says is that you are not sober if you are smoking, using excessive amounts of caffeine or sugar. Many people in recovery aren't doing anything to improve their health. Whatever disorder we may be experiencing, we need to consider enhancing our minds and bodies through diet, exercise, meditation, higher education and spiritual revitalization.

I have gone beyond recovery into a state of well-being that has far exceeded my past experience with harmful chemicals; and I don't ever care to look back. There's just no need to since my life has been enriched with the wisdom and awareness of my true potentiality. I believe that people should mind their own store and stop taking other people's inventory. In doing so, they just might find their true selves.

The motivation and enthusiasm that I shared was about a new state of bliss that others seemed to miss in their pursuit of this happiness. Helping others find the pieces of the puzzle to happiness was a challenge. My sincerity and convictions towards helping others was always being challenged by many of those in the program. I wasn't trying to steal anyone's thunder, but there were those who felt that I was similar to a false prophet. Because I displayed so much joy and happiness, many people thought that the happy feelings I experienced without drugs were a put on. Many felt that I couldn't be that happy living a sober lifestyle. I wasn't living a sober lifestyle. I was living far beyond that. I was living a terrific and exciting life, and I wanted to share it with the world. In my excitement, I felt like the old gold prospector that discovered "gold in them there hills." Now, I was playing out that same scenario with excitement and wonder of the gold-like happiness I had discovered in my new life. Anybody can discover their own gold if they are willing to look within their personal gold "minds." For it has been said that the mind is so valuable, it's like an undiscovered gold mine.

I was so excited about my discoveries I wanted to impress upon others to dig as far and as hard into their own marvelous minds to see what wonders they could find. In working with recovering people, I found that sobriety provided a pittance in the way of true happiness. The Websters Dictionary defines sobriety as "abstinence from mind-mood altering chemicals." That's all! It barely resembles the pseudo joy and excitement people once experienced while they were using and abusing. Abstinence alone hardly creates the excitement that motivates people to change. Is it any wonder why you hear so much ruckus about what causes *relapse*. This could also explain why you find so many people who are reluctant to go into a treatment program. They need more fun and excitement in their lives in order to create the opportunity for positive behavioral change.

Evidence will show that if our new experiences provide equal or greater pleasure than our past or present experiences, the chance that we would give one up for the other is highly probable.

Due to the payoff involved, positive behavioral change would come expediently and with little resistance. We have been practicing this give and take method throughout our lives. It's like giving up our old car for a new and improved one. It is called compensation. Dr. Deepak Chopra of the Center for Mind and Body Medicine has developed a fantastic compensation program. In his own words he states, "Our clients are bathed in *pleasurable experiences* so that they develop a permanent desire toward positive behaviors."

This magical method of transformation from "pain to gain" was my wake-up call in February 1986. That's the date I totally gave up all mind-mood altering chemicals for activities and lifestyle practices much more rewarding. Why aren't there more programs out there offering fun and excitement in conjunction with their treatment objectives? The reason why this "make sense program" isn't being used widespread is because many loyal Twelve Steppers don't believe in it. Besides, they have their own program already in place: The Twelve Step program. They believe in saturating their clients with 90 percent program, program and more program. They feel that the only way today is the Twelve Step way.

Fun and excitement in the "program" is not encouraged enough. Other than the Annual Recovery Games and a few softball tournaments, many in recovery don't get the chance to explore their true potential in re-creation. For this reason, I find some programs to be short on excitement but high on resentment. This was evident by numerous heated confrontations I had with many gung-ho Twelve Steppers who believe that recreation is a waste of time. I find the "program" works like going on a diet. People go on it and after they have struggled with it for a certain period of time they come off it (relapse). Some people seesaw more on a diet of AA than on a diet of food.

Life should be exciting and full of wonder including the "program." But excitement is not promoted in treatment programs. Ninety percent of the time what you see in AA meetings are these sad, bovine-like faces displaying pain and despair. These meetings consist mainly of smoked filled rooms. With "coffee pots" at almost every entrance, recovering neg-addicts are now getting their fix on caffeine and nicotine instead on their Benzedrine, codeine and amphetamines. Many appear as if they have lost the best and only friend they ever had—their old drug of choice. For some, these meetings are no comparison with that old flame.

As a result of the negative politics associated with my first experience with the program, I decided to move on. I resigned my position with that recovery home in Escondido and accepted a position as a recreational therapist at a local hospital in Poway, California. My responsibilities were to develop the entire recreation and leisure program. Although I felt more at home in this new position, I was still working in an environment that minimized the power of recreation. The word that kept coming up in treatment and recovery was program, program and more program. I mean there was so much "program" they hardly had time for anything else.

As a recreation therapist, I created and performed many exciting activities for patients' health and dynamic recovery. To provide for their specific needs, I was tasked with evaluating and assessing their strengths, weaknesses and interests. Most of this raw data was acquired through personal interviews and reading each patient's medical chart. On many occasions I discovered that my past life was just as gruesome, if not worse, than many of the patients I was supposed to be helping. To develop a stronger bond with my clients, I shared my most intimate drug and alcohol experiences. I knew what it was like living in pain because I had been in their shoes and knew exactly what it was like to suffer the consequences of substance abuse. Still, I found my sincerity and commitment to helping people being challenged again. I was being accused of lying and denying being an addict. I was bombarded with statements such as, "If you were just as sick, why aren't you following the program?"

The people in the "program" had such a strong influence on my own beliefs that I began to question if maybe they were right and I was wrong. I wanted so desperately to help others that I was willing to do anything. It's no fun being shackled to a debilitating habit, lifestyle or predicament. After careful and arduous deliberation, I bought into the idea that maybe I was an alcoholic-addict.

In January of 1989, I positioned myself in front of a group of recovering people, stated my name and affirmed that I was an "alcoholic-addict." The response that followed was astonishing! There was a wail of cheers accompanied by big hugs, applause and strong approval. It was like winning an Oscar at the Academy Awards. Although it was no act, it resembled an awards ceremony because of the overwhelming reaction from the "program people." The response was so forceful and dramatic that I thought I had won the nomination for best actor. It seemed more their cause than it was mine. It was a hollow victory for me, but appeared to be a glorious accomplishment for the program and its people.

It has often been said that "misery loves company." All sorts of confusing thoughts ran through my head. Did I make the right decision? Was I being honest with them as well as myself? It didn't matter that much now. I had become "one of the boys."

I had taken the "plunge" and decided to live with it. Deep inside I felt that the "eagle had fallen." I had come down from my soaring altitude with the eagles, allowed the crowd to clip my wings, and I perched myself among a breed that did not soar. This new breed was not into flying. They were into sadness and sorrow. They sulked in misery and wallowed in anger because of their loss of dangerous chemicals. I was now one of them. Even though this was where they currently lay, I honestly believed that I could help them fly again in some future day. I had found a new family of supporters and co-horts.

I wasn't at all comfortable working the program, but it felt great to belong. I had received my badge. Now I could go to meetings and other AA functions and say that I was one of them—a "normie" no more. Again, "normie" was one of the names many in the "program" labeled people who were not in recovery. I carried that label for an entire year and allowed it to get the best of me. As a result, I carried a new label—an AA robot.

It's difficult to exist as normal in the company of those who consider themselves to be abnormal. How did I allow myself to become entrenched in a system that did not promote fun, excitement, holistic health and optimum well being? How did I "fall" victim to a program that limited its principles to only twelve steps when I believe it takes that and more to get to cruising altitude?

I found myself acting and responding contrary to my former beliefs. The eagles I once soared with had since left me on the ground of despair and uncertainty. I gave up my position of living beyond recovery and accepted, in my opinion, an inferior lifestyle attitude. Déjà vu was happening all over again. This was how I was influenced to take up smoking. I wasn't sticking to my values. Many years before, I had forfeited my soul to smoking for a girl who left me stranded. Now I was giving it up to belong! This is not to say that the Twelve Step program doesn't work for people. I just found that it was not the most effective way to help people recover expediently and willingly. This may not be the case for many out there. These are just my feelings and opinions on how I perceived the "program."

As a reformed Twelve Stepper, I seldom found people living a happy and exciting lifestyle. Many professed that they were happy, but their body language spoke otherwise. Many appeared to have no idea what true happiness was. The only happiness that they ever knew was the false feelings of euphoria brought on by the use of their drug of choice (DOC). Without their DOC, they had become miserable and aimless souls hoping that happiness would fall from the heavens and down on their heads. Unfortunately, the only thing that fell on their heads was more boring dread. I witnessed an awfully high rate of relapse in the Twelve Step program. A lack of happiness in conjunction with tremendous amounts of medication, coffee, cigarettes, sugar, and junk foods was a sad experience for most.

You see, people in the "program" are in recovery. Before I came to the "program" I had gone "beyond recovery." I lived, worked and played with people who were moving towards higher levels of enlightenment. By becoming a Twelve Stepper, I allowed myself to come down from my soaring altitude to ground level only to realize that it was a mistake. In my attempt to seek approval and the desire to belong, I lost sight of who I was. This happens to many people who don't hold on to their true feelings. They get mixed up in other people's belief systems and lose sight of their own. I went into the program hoping to bring people to a higher level of consciousness, but only found myself sucked into a lower level of bitterness. I desperately wanted to get back up to cruising altitude again. When you soar with the eagles the view is much brighter as you fly higher. The air is much fresher because you are above all the pollution. There are few crowds when you are among the clouds, and you can see your way through much better. It was then that I created my "Eagle's Creed":

Eagle's Creed

Soar high, climb far.
Your aim the sky, your goal the star.
The view gets much brighter, as you fly
much higher.
Become that star, for which you are.

Wanting to belong to the program was costly and caused much anguish, distress and unhappiness in my life. As a Twelve Stepper, I did witness many people who found sobriety in these programs, but not much more than that. Being sober is not what life is all about. It's about being happy, and I wasn't happy living something I did not truly believe in. I wanted to have more than just a sober lifestyle. I wanted to live again and not have to worry about going to meetings and being hemmed in for the rest of my life. Is it any wonder why so many people relapse in these programs. It doesn't take a rocket scientist to understand if someone isn't happy, they aren't going to hang around for very long. I believe that we should all be given the opportunity to grow past our current developments. A program that does not allow one to go beyond the Twelve Steps is similar to a mother eagle not allowing her offspring to venture beyond the nest. I personally find restrictive programs stifling. They hinder creativity, personal growth and development, and in many instances do not encourage *alternative means* toward acquiring true happiness. A program that promotes limitations, and the idea of being locked in tends to make life seem boring, tasteless and stale. I personally found that the "program" used the stick instead of encouraging the carrot. The stick provides temporary results, but it is the carrot that produces permanent happiness.

I renounced my position as a neg-addict, and re-established my true feeling and beliefs on optimum recovery, holistic healing and spiritual well-being. I needed to move on because the resistance that I was up against with drug counselors, rehabilitation therapists, AA members and treatment centers only impeded my progress towards further growth, happiness and prosperity. I had succumbed to the rigorous pressures of the "program," but resurrected to a higher level of enlightenment due to the blessings and lessons I learned from going astray.

There is more to recovery than meetings (See Discovery 2). The world has more to offer than programs and we are all entitled to find our true selves. We are all destined for higher heights, prosperity and happiness. If our wings are pinned, we'll never live as eagles. Only eagles are free. Non eagles squander their valuable time in misery and despair never knowing or discovering their true selves—true potentiality and spirituality. Going beyond recovery takes you to levels of spiritual growth that allow you to live free of material influences. It is a lifestyle where the magnificence of your marvelous mind provides the personal power towards overcoming the most difficult and painful circumstances. Better yet, you'll discover all the joy and happiness your heart desires knowing that it's not what happens in your life but what you can do about it. You will develop an understanding that people who are successful are not without problems. They have learned that they have the power to bridge the gap between them and what it is they want to accomplish. Going beyond recovery is a *state of mind* and not a *factor of time*.

People who live beyond recovery don't see "time being sober" as a major achievement. Although "program people" may feel good about accumulating time being sober, this becomes a burden to bear since it can all be lost at the tip of a drink. Once time has been lost, they must start all over again. Time is a figment of the imagination. It's not real and only exists in the minds of those who are pressured by constraints, schedules and deadlines. As a result of losing that time sober, many give up trying to acquire sobriety a second, third or fourth time around because of the unrealistic thought of having to accumulate that time all over again. Why not live just for the day, and let go of the debilitating thought of accumulating time, for in reality you only have one day.

It Only Takes One Day

People in recovery have asked me on many occasions, "How long does it take to acquire optimum recovery and a positive lifestyle attitude?" They look at me rather strange, perplexed and skeptical when I tell them that it only takes one (1) day. Many have responded with anger and opposition because of the time game. I call it "time, time, whose got the time." They identify their status in recovery by having the most time sober. That is, people with the most time are to be honored. But many are shocked to find those who have had years of sobriety suddenly fall off the wagon. These people may have been sober for that duration of "time" but many may have never acquired a new "state of mind." Well, let me tell you something about time. Living a successful and healthy lifestyle is not a *factor of time*, it's a *state of mind*.

Time is a myth, an idea, a notion that has no form or other redeeming value. Once the day is over, that time ceases to exist. We refer to time being in the past or future, but there is no such thing. Time only occurs in the present. Time is not something you accumulate, have, possess or earn. It is something that becomes available when your interest and desires motivate your behavior. The rate of your success in anything is directly proportionate to your degree of desire. The higher your degree of interest and desire, the higher your rate of success will be in accomplishing your goals. All this occurs in due time that's right now! The time is now. You don't have any other time periods. It doesn't exist anywhere else. It exist today, right here, right now. When you are aware that your time is now, you will have succeeded in living in the here and now. This is where everything is real and is now happening.

You only have today for today holds your future, and ironic as it may seem, today also holds your past. The dilemma is not the past or the future, it is today. Expending your energy in either the past or the future is a waste of today. So, use today as a tool to build the future and a platform to say goodbye to the past.

People living "Beyond Recovery" recognize time as just an idea, notion, or place in the mind. They are spiritual in nature as opposed to being material in time. Although thoughts of the past may linger in their minds, they know that past events are just stepping stones to a more rewarding future. Everything that occurs or happens begins and ends today. Everyday we live is the first day of the rest of our lives, but we should live it as if it were our last. In most cases this day is our last until this day shall pass. What makes this notion so difficult to believe? We take for granted the present day thinking that tomorrow will always be there. No day is promised to us. Our notion is that tomorrow will bring a brighter day. If you wait for tomorrow to recreate yourself, then all your tomorrows will be just like today— dark and lugubrious. You must make today bright, for if you do not, the day can only bring darkness. Ever wonder why so many people are unhappy? I know if I want to be happy, it must happen today because for me there is no other way.

I've often gone toe to toe with those in Alcoholics Anonymous about how much time it takes to change one's lifestyle habits. Since we are only allowed one day to recreate ourselves, then recreation begins in that one day. It can't happen in the past or the future. Ponder on this thought for a moment. Do the things we work for come to us "in time," or do they come to us as a result of what we do for ourselves today? We set our goals and objectives, create that means to that end, and make sure we follow through by living each day as successful as we can.

What many people don't realize is that the end is the means and the means is the end. It all happens in just one day everyday. Everything that happens to us is either a reward or a consequence of what we do in that present time and space.

People live their lives thinking they will always have tomorrow. This way of thinking sets us up for procrastination. We often catch ourselves saying things such as, "I can always do it tomorrow or next week," maybe or maybe not. Life holds no guarantees. Tony Robbins, a well-known motivational speaker and coach, often says, "The past is like a canceled check and the future is like a promissory note." What he means is that today is like cold hard cash. How you spend your day will influence your personal investments in yourself and your future.

What do people really mean when they say, "it's going to take me some time?" While they are looking ahead, they ponder the long and arduous journey of life wondering if the rewards are worth their efforts. When you're looking for that pot of gold at the end of the rainbow, the lack of immediate gratification can play havoc on your psyche. Some people don't have time to wait to be happy. It all begins now.

Life demonstrates that people who tend to run out of time start doing things they never had time to do before!

It is my experience that people who have been diagnosed with a terminal disease — and don't have much longer to live — begin to appreciate today. And why does it have to take a tragedy to bring us around to the power that's contained in just one day. The first thing these people start to consider is doing things they have always wanted to do but didn't have the time. Now that they don't have time, why are they now taking the time?

Taking the time as opposed to finding the time is the solution to the problem of not having the time!

Looking too far down the road of life may cause people to have second thoughts on plowing new ground. In the same manner, looking too far in the past can impede one's progress and stifle their ability to perform at their best in this present time and space. This is what I call the double edged sword of fear. What keeps many people stifled is fear from the rear and sorrow from tomorrow. For example, I have watched many people who downhill ski come to the top of the slope and stare in horror at the long way down. They take a few moments to build their courage. After such time, they carefully and reluctantly make the precarious trip down. At that moment they reflect on the past dangers that have befallen others before them. This division of energy interferes with one's concentration and may be the direct cause of their inability to function at their highest human potential thus causing mishaps and accidents. This is known as a self-fulfilling prophecy.

There have been many people whom I encouraged to try accepting the fact that they can change their lives in one day. For success comes effortlessly for those who refuse to wait for change to happen. Instead, they made it happen just by accepting that life is now and so is change. Many people who are reluctant to live this way are missing out. Isn't it true that many in the Twelve Step program refer to living, "One day at a time?" Maybe it's not fully understood, but that's exactly what I'm talking about. This change must first occur in the head before it can be said. In other words, you just can't say I'm a changed person unless you truly believe it. Therefore, it becomes a *state of mind*, not a *factor of time*. Time does not exist; your mind, body and soul do. And if change occurs first within your full being, you are there, with time to spare. Now you have all the time to enjoy the true beauty of life and not spend it on programs that focus on what things to avoid. You are free and alive. Whatever occurs first in the mind will cause the body to follow with no more worries about tomorrow. Live for today and make it pay, for you only have just this one day.

A Poem to Remember

You Only Have One Day

It's often been said, "if I had the time," I could
get a lot more done.
I could create a new day, lay in the sun, and
even have time for fun.
For what is time, but an imaginary line, that
originates within our minds.
It has nothing to do, with what's really true, it's
the idea that tends to confine.
When people plea, "I don't have the time," is that
really what keeps them behind?
Blame it on time, what a convenient line, but it's
more a state of mind?
With a new attitude, you can change in a day, if
you live with true gratitude.

For relying on time, as a factor for change, can keep you stuck in strict servitude.
Many are confined to that factor of time, but I guess it's a personal call,
They squander their time, in a fictitious bind, and realize they've dropped the ball.
Blaming it on time, instead of our minds, leaves us dark, with barely a shine.
We sit in the dark, and don't start that spark, of the light that's one of a kind.
Responsibility is the name of the game, not poor time, so let's stake our true claim.
Time is no factor, when we seek pleasure, but when it is pain, poor time takes the blame.
There's only one day, to expend our energy, so let's live like the morning sun,
It's up and down, and makes its rounds, giving warmth, and then it's done.
It shines each day, and doesn't share one ray, with the past or suspecting future,
The sun can't divide, what it provides, for that's not a true act of nature.
Consider for a moment, we lived like the sun, shining one glorious day at a time,
We could live for today, look forward to the future and leave our past and troubles behind.
Past events, are a muck in the dust, but teaches a variety of lessons.
They pave the way, to a brand new day, and give reasons to count our true blessings.
Remember "one day" is all that we have, so let's make it one of success.
Living in the past, and dwelling on grief, can turn "one day" into a hell of a mess.
Appreciate today, for it holds the power, which is contained in every new hour.
For within just one hour, contain the minutes,

that our spirits can bloom and flower.
Seize today with all your might, and let your new energy flow,
Focus on your strengths, not your past, and let your weakness go.
Now if you're thinking, "I can't do that," I'm just not strong enough.
You're more than you think, so believe in yourself, and drop all the negative stuff.
If you can breath, then you have power, and the ability to recreate anew,
You can change in one day, by the way you think, then watch your dreams come true.
If you aspire, to fly much higher, make sure it's a natural call.
For scratching with turkeys, can be very jerky, and you most likely are destined to fall.
I mean, please be aware, that you can't compare "time," with a new state of mind,
Change starts within, before you can win, what it is you are trying to find.
Some will disagree, if they hear you say, that it only takes you one day.
They're not into change, and play that old game, that the "program's" the only way.
But we should have choices, to express our true voices, to move up and out of the gutter.
Let's explore new turfs, find out what really works, and get rid of the old cookie cutter.
Life is a college, and we are all in class, which is more than just a discovery.
You don't get stuck, in one discipline, but go far "beyond recovery."
It only takes one day, I am happy to say, that there is more than just one way,
I've learned from the best, and gained happiness, from living the holistic way.

If you're willing to say, that it's just "my" own
way, I have news for all to hear,
There are millions out there, that live and
compare, then work, to put it in gear.
If you live this day, with a new state of mind,
and rely less on a factor of time,
You are on your way, because now you believe,
that you only have just one day.
I wish you the best, in your new quest, for health
and true happiness,
For when you succeed, be sure that you breed,
the joy which has come from the best.
It is that inspiration, and strong motivation,
that ties the bonds that hold,
Give back what you've gained, to those living in
pain, with all your heart and soul.
Going beyond recovery, is more than drug free,
it's an experience in finding true love,
Take it from me, and you too will see, that true
love is within and above.
To find peace in time, takes only one day, and
I'm sure you'll be wanting to say:
A factor of time, or a new state of mind?
I'm living now, for I only have one day!

I often refer to the mighty eagle as a symbol of strength and agility. During my stint in the U. S. Navy, I was stationed in Alaska for three years out of the twenty-one that I served. There were eagles everywhere. It was a sight to behold to see those great birds spread their wings, lift to the sky and gracefully soar through the air. It takes great strength and ability to propel their huge bodies into the wind. It was a marvelous sight to see them hunt, soar, glide and dive. I like to think of myself as an eagle because they flow with nature, and move with grace and never lose their way or their time in space. That's the mark of the great eagle.

A Poem to Remember

The Mark of The Great Eagle

The mark of the great eagle
Represents the spirit and the soul.
It has been revered by all legends,
so it's been told.
They are self sufficient and proud in every way,
and don't fall victim to an unproductive day.
They're strong and reliant and don't hang
around
For some other creature to bring them down.
It is amazing watching these great birds of prey,
And the dangers that they face each glowing day.
No fear, no foe can ever match their grace,
For it is these great eagles that have set the pace.
Their ways are cunning and forever stunning,
They can nab their food, even when it is running.
If ever they find, an eagle in distress,
They band together to give it a rest.
The mark of the great eagle is strong and bold,
They live off the land, and are more precious
than gold.
They are a valuable sort and can only be found,
Soaring high in the sky, while peering down at
the ground.
It's obvious to see why these birds are so free,
They're on top of the world, where we'd all
like to be.
You can become an eagle, if you're willing to try,
But it takes more than a wish, it requires a
passionate high.
Just return to nature and live accordingly,
And you will discover, how great life can be.

We human beings all possess this greatness, but fail to believe in our magnificence. What causes this lack of truth is that many of us have been conditioned by society to believe that forces outside of ourselves are responsible for our success or failure. For many people, happiness must occur outside before they can be happy inside. In this case, happiness becomes an object instead of a state of mind. Believing that outside forces are your focus of control leaves you vulnerable to every whim, idea, notion and belief about your true potentiality. You lose sight of who you are and what you can become. Since outside forces influence how we think, our self-esteem becomes tied to those forces and could possibly give us the roller coaster ride of our lives. Many become fixated on harmful chemicals because they believe it is the resource for their distorted discourse. This is what causes human beings to participate in destructive behaviors.

When the mighty eagle spreads its wings it bears a need to be free and fulfilled. It has a hunger inside that moves on instinct that lifts his enormous body into the sky. In addition, they carry more than their own weight, packing their food up high from a morning catch. In this sense eagles know that they must put forth more effort or they won't eat. It is the spread of their wings that fulfills their needs, and it also needs strength for which it breeds. Eagles are a symbol of strength that we all should follow, for they put great effort in ways of reaching their destinations. It is that opening of their wings that keeps them on top.

Similarly, we humans must open up the wings of our hearts and minds if we are to accomplish our goals and reach our destinations. It is in this same fashion that the great eagle opens its wings. If our thoughts, dreams, ideas and desires are to be fulfilled as the great eagle, we must be open to new challenges and ideas before we can take to the sky.

Throughout life all progress begins with the opening of its doors. We need only to walk through. The eagle will never get off the ground if it doesn't spread its wings and fly. Confining it to the ground will only cause it to die. If we human beings don't open the wings of our minds, we're going to be left very far behind. You'll find that life can be very jerky, down on the ground with all the turkeys. So spread your wings and take to the sky.

An open mind can create wondrous delights, and bring beauty to life that once seemed a fright. You're not stuck in a muck, or living in pain, you're experiencing pleasure that continues to gain. People who find that life is boring don't allow their minds to do much exploring. Just taking a few minutes a day to broaden your horizons can make all the difference from a destructive way to a more productive day. So, "Spread Your Wings."

A Poem to Remember

Spread Your Wings

Spread your wings, so that you may fly,
And prepare yourself for a natural high.
Your are an eagle, oh yes you are,
You have unlimited power, to fly high and far.
As an eagle, you must spread your wings,
It's a must if you want, what true happiness brings.
Nothing reaches down, out of the sky,
To get you in motion, and cause you to fly.
You are a powerful force, and it should be known,
You were born with greatness, to fly on your own.
It's a beautiful sight, soaring among the clouds,
No mess or stress and very few crowds.
So, spread your wings, and see what life brings.
You may be surprised, what appears before your eyes.
Your dreams will come true, and you will know too,
That you have great potential, oh yes you do.

Now, this is a natural high, so please be aware,
All the drugs that some use, could never compare.
Drugs leave you hanging, not soaring, that's clear,
They devour your soul, leaving you frantic with fear.
Soaring is fun, and that's no doubt,
You can soar too, so please check it out.
It's a trip with nature, so try it if you dare,
You'll never go back to drugs, after breathing fresher air.
You may contest, "It's not easy and life's not fair,
It's hard to keep trying, and too painful to bear."
If you lay wallowing in the midst of your pity,
You may lay drowned like a flood drenched city.
For who in this world, has reached greatness with ease?
Just show me one and I'll show you a sleaze.
Eagles toil diligently in order to get high
But turkeys remain on the ground using drugs to get by.
What makes some people think that they can fly free?
Flying takes effort, wouldn't you agree?
But if drugs are your thing beware of its sting,
It's the lure of the fling that resembles a swing.
It takes you up and down then whirls you around,
Destroying your life as you crash to the ground.
It's a flight of chance with a negative stance,
Where you're moving back but never in advance.
Many think they're flying but unaware that they are dying,
And sad as it seems they are throwing away their dreams.
They think using drugs is the life of daisies,
But wasting it all on a bunch of crazies.
Life can be a dream and as difficult as it may seem,
You can soar too but you must turn on the steam.
To soar like the rest you must give it your best,
For success is that crest that yields true happiness.

So spread your wings and spread them wide,
Soar with the eagles and show your pride.
Ride with the wind and stay with the breeze,
And you'll soon be soaring with the greatest of ease.
Keep abreast of your direction and fly with perfection
For your aim is to experience a new resurrection.
So, follow the stars because they are your path,
That steer you clear of any hazardous aftermath.
You're now approaching home and it's a glorious sight,
For the rewards of your efforts were the results of a great flight.
It was the spread of your wings I guess you can say,
That you've soared much higher than you did yesterday.
As you come down from up above make it a point to share what you love.
Teach others to fly like the eagles up high,
So they may experience the view from the sky.
So, spread your wings great eagle and soar with style,
Share your love from the heart and share it with a smile.

You are the Main Focus

The key to remember throughout this book is not meetings or "program." It's not even about sobriety. It's about you, your attitude, lifestyle and over-all well-being. The reason is that sobriety should not be a goal in your life—although many individuals think it should. Sobriety comes as a result of individuals following *Qualitative Recreation Lifestyle Principles* with a purpose to serve yourself and others in a sincere and meaningful manner. Again, these principles lead to establishing Desirable Lifestyle Values (DLVs). These VALUES are your labors of love and are defined as follows:

Vocation	Gainfully Employed Enrollment in School Success / Leadership Programs Research Studies	
Arts	Dance Music History Theatrical	Art Drawing Literature Performing Arts
Leisure	Hiking Camping Backpacking Surfing Reading Arts Crafts Biking Fishing Boating	Roller-skating Walking Movies Gardening Photography Music Theme Parks Museums Socializing Motorcycles
Ultimate nutrition	Vegetarian Cooking Helath Food Stores Health-Oriented Restaurants Balanced Meals Fruits and Vegetables Healthy Snacks, Whole Grains Baked or Broiled Fish and Chicken Plenty of Water, Fruit and Veggie Juices	
Exercise	Dancing Walking Aerobics Biking Weight Training Running Swimming Basketball	Volleyball Rope Jumping Calisthenics Yoga Stretching Gymnastics Rowing
Service	Volunteer Work Teaching Lecturing to Community Groups Gainful Employment Public Speaking Entrepreneurial Private Business Community Leader Divinity and Religious Work	

Figure 1.1

These activities are to you as cement is to bricks. They are a cohesiveness that brings your life together and keeps it structured. They build a strong foundation for self-esteem and self-worth. Sound eating practices helps rebuild damaged cells that result from the devastating effects of drugs, alcohol and years of abuse. It is a proven fact that individuals who develop this healthy *VALUES systems do not* allow themselves to become involved or re-involved in destructive-compulsive behaviors. (See *Discovery 6* for a further explanation of *Qualitative Recreation Lifestyle Principles*).

Qualitative Recreation Lifestyle vs. Sober Lifestyle

My success in overcoming the devastation of negative addictions was not a very easy task. It took painstaking effort and a desire to live a healthier lifestyle. As a result of my success, I am frequently challenged by many in the Twelve Step program on the healing approach I "choose to use." My response has always been the same. I choose to live a productive lifestyle that involves health promoting activities (HPAs). It's more than just going to meetings. I have tried living a sober lifestyle with little to no success. It didn't work for me and similarly, it just isn't working for a large percentage of people trying to escape the devastating clutches of drugs and alcohol. As a result of working a "program," I had no concept of Qualitative Recreation Lifestyle Principles. For me, the program was a deterrent that caused me to overlook one of the most simple and logical ways to optimum healing and rejuvenating the whole mind, body and soul—the Power of Re-creation.

Recreation produces Desirable Lifestyle Values (DLVs). Drugs and alcohol destroy the spirit. When the spirit goes, the body goes with it. Recreation restores the spirit to health, refreshes the mind and heals the body. Basically, it does more than help people unwind, it enhances their entire physical and mental well-being. It helps to create a whole new person. Recreation also acts as a diversion. Therefore, if you are under a lot of stress, you need to take a mental health day off and go out and play. I know this may sound simple, but shouldn't life be simple. Isn't this what is stated in recovery programs throughout the world, "Keep it simple?" Maybe some people need an arduous program to keep them busy, but I think that millions are missing the target.

The ultimate goal in life is to experience pleasure while at the same time work to avoid pain. How many people do you know who are living their dreams merely by being sober? An exciting life is what gives joy to living. Therefore, one's main focus should be on establishing a Qualitative Re-creation Lifestyle and allow sobriety to manifest on its own.

In my experience, I found treatment programs that did not provide Qualitative Recreation Lifestyle Principles, were like taking a shower and stepping right back into the same old dirty clothes. You are still going to stink. You have to put on fresh clothes and splash on the fu fu juice (cologne) as well. In other words, allow yourself to develop a whole new attitude.

Floyd D., a patient I worked with in January of 1992, is grateful to the "program" and says, "It's not that I don't like the program, I'm concerned about what comes next. Here you are on a diet of meetings, Twelve Steps, sponsors and reading the Big Book. I need a replacement for living a fun-filled life. Drinking at one time was fun to me. What do I do for fun now?"

Living without your old drug of choice requires painstaking effort if you don't have a plan to incorporate other activities into your life. On the other hand, developing *QRLP* is effortless and is in line with following the biological laws of nature. We need recreation in our lives. If you live without these principles, you're setting yourself up for failure of the worst kind. With *QRLP* one lives their life at-ease as opposed to dis-ease. The Qualitative Recreation Lifestyle Principles approach is totally opposite in comparison to just living a sober lifestyle. It is much easier to learn and do something positive than it is to discontinue something negative. *QRLP* produces

BOX 2

Q.R.L.P. ▶ Values

Developing a Values System.
A values system is created by actively participating in health promoting actives (HPAs).
See pages 89-90.

Values are the result of the # of QRLPs you participate in, and can be acquired within the time it takes you to learn new activities (sometimes as soon as a week). "It's not a factor of time, it's a state of mind." Now that's immediate gratification.

Values are significantly more stable than having years of sobriety. The more values you have, the more stability you have.

A strong values system does not allow for relapse. These people are spiritual and don't need alcohol or drugs to get high. They get high on life!

When values are present you take pride in everything that you do, especially yourself.

You cannot have continuous sobriety if you don't have a strong values system.

Values remain with you in times of trouble or a crisis.

SOBER LIFESTYLE ▸ Abstinence

1 Working toward Sobriety.
Drug and alcohol free.

2 Sobriety is valued by # of years a person has been sober (this takes time).

3 The more years you have, the more sobriety you have, but not much substance.

4 People relapse regardless of how many years they have. Many are not spiritually based and still have a need to use. This shows a weak values system.

5 Being sober does not necessarily create self-pride or self-esteem.

6 You can have years of sobriety and lose it without a strong values system.

7 Sobriety, on the other hand, tends to go right out the window, and the person with it, during a crisis.

Desirable Lifestyle Values (DLVs) while sobriety produces *Abstinence* (strict habitual and usually complete self-denial in the gratification of appetites or passion).

Recreation: A Values System That Can't Be Beat!

It is the good intentions of this book not to steer anyone away from whatever *program* they are currently working. The main objective is to get you to continue progressing and not stop at the shower door. Put on some new and refreshing clothes by going beyond recovery. Allow yourself to experience other areas in your life that will provide healthy pleasurable experiences. Consider this an opportunity to rejoice!

Find in yourself that inner child that's been yearning to explore life's real wonders and not the drug blunders. Augment your program and learn to live not only a sober lifestyle, but a bolder lifestyle.

Life is filled with an infinite number of activities that are much more rewarding than the minuscule and pseudo effects of mind-mood altering chemicals. Life is a parade of events! We must learn to discern the real treasures in life, not the pits. I don't fight to stay sober anymore, I promote health and now "Soar with the Eagles." As a result of the difficult, but successful fight I had overcoming drugs and alcohol, I live better than I ever have in my entire life. I wish you all the best in your quest for peace and happiness. You deserve it!

Discovery 2

There Is More To Recovery than Meetings

Happiness is knowing and understanding that variety is the spice that gives life its flavor.

Oliver Rhodes

Have you ever been on a restricted diet which consisted of certain foods that did not include your favorite ones? During that time, did you ever become frustrated or angry because you did not acquire the desired outcome of losing a few pounds? Did you find your efforts ineffective and the need to succeed overbearing that you just up and quit? Well, you're not alone. There are many people, including myself, who have tried this approach and have failed. Taking someone's "perceived" pleasures away without compensation is doomed to failure. Is it any wonder why so many people "keep coming back?" What's so ironic about this process is that it works well for the top echelon of many ineffective programs and less for the clients involved. Programs that keep you coming back tend to have a hidden agenda that benefits the establishment's cause more than yours. It is this recidivism that is predicated on profitability. The more dependent you are on a particular person, place or thing, the more you are going to continue to seek them out.

This is a treatment process typical of that given in many agencies that rely on deprivation as a tool for recovery. These methods of deprivation have been the standard practice in many weight loss programs, hospital-based rehabilitation centers and Twelve Step programs nationwide. Unfortunately, many people who check in to these programs check out with very few recovery skills necessary for permanently staying off harmful substances. Just like restricted diets, sobriety is difficult to maintain without some kind of balance. You yo-yo back and forth, hardly making very much ground. You go in and out of these recovery programs just like a needle going through loose fabric on an out-of-control sewing machine.

As a result of the boredom and frustration that's associated with typical rehabilitation programs, many clients find it much too easy to resort to relapse. Programs that deprive their clients of recreational activities are hollow and lack a balanced curriculum. Clients entering a treatment program must be provided with a variety of challenging activities that offers that needed drive and motivation towards establishing optimum health and ongoing recovery. The balance that I am referring to are those programs that provide activities such as super nutrition, pleasurable physical activity, art therapy, sports, athletics, music, dance, field trips and educational opportunities. Along with group therapy, there should be play therapy where everyone is encouraged to participate in "New Games" that provide physical and mental challenges. It is absolutely essential that these activities provided be emotionally stimulating, creative, fun and exciting!

It is my experience, and the experience of others, that a diet of Twelve Steps, the Big Book, sponsors and meetings is incomplete. Diets are based on deprivation and denial of pleasurable experiences. Since we are hedonistic in nature, we humans can't last very long in a constant state of denial. Eventually we are going to swing the other way to satisfy our pleasure centers the only way we know how, through drug use. Unfortunately, if we have not learned alternative ways to experience positive pleasures, we are going to be left with only one recourse. That recourse is a reunion with some of our old friends: drugs, food, chemicals, gambling and alcohol.

As a result of the extensive research and personal experience in my recovery, I have found that many people see recovery programs as the final straw. They feel, as I once did, that their life has come to an end. "No more fun."

Just all work and no more play. You know what that did to "jack." It made him a dull boy. Many people just don't know how true that statement is when it comes to traditional treatment programs. Granted, we must come to grips with our problems and our chemical dependency. But that doesn't mean that you have to "dry up" and die.

Programs should be fun as well as educational. Unfortunately, many of these "cult-like" programs are very strict, controlling, and don't allow for very much play time. Is it any wonder why most people wait until they hit bottom before entering such a rigid treatment program? With little to no pleasurable experiences to look forward to in recovery — only the "humdrum" emptiness of sobriety— one feels trapped, hemmed in, with no way out. Many are horrified to think that this new way of living leaves little to be desired and may not have been such a good trade-off for their drinking and drugging days. Programs that don't offer their clients variety, do not allow them the opportunity to flourish, grow or develop outside of the program. This growth is necessary for optimal recovery.

Generally, clients are locked-in to a curriculum that's based on concepts leading to brainwashing and one-way thinking. Many of these individuals use these meetings like they once used their drug of choice (just another fix). Now they are addicted to meetings, treatment centers and smoke-filled rooms with coffee pots brewing at every entrance. Many recovering people wouldn't attend these meetings if they couldn't get their new fix of caffeine and nicotine—two of the most widely used mind-mood altering chemicals in the world today. A drug is a drug is a drug! That's saying a lot about their sobriety—claiming to be clean and sober. Condoning cigarette smoking and excessive coffee drinking is no better than providing fat people on fat farms with chocolate donuts and twinkies. It's a poor means to a dead end.

Joan L. was a registered nurse who worked in the Drug and Alcohol Rehabilitation department at a local hospital in San Diego, CA. She was a recovering "alcoholic-addict" who followed a very rigid Twelve Step program like a church congregation followed their pastor. I first met Joan when I worked at Paradise Valley Hospital in July of 1990. She was forever quoting the "Steps" as she fumbled for her cigarettes, drank extra large cups of coffee and ate sweets like "Willie Wonka in the Chocolate Factory." Although she had been sober for nine years, Joan was a nervous wreck and could not function without her two pack a day smoking habit. The cups of coffee that she consumed in a one-hour setting was enough to keep "Juan Val Des" and his mule packing back to the mountain for more coffee beans.

Under pressure, Joan doubled her use of soft addictions such as cigarettes, coffee and sweets. On one of many occasions, she blew up during a staff meeting and stormed right out the door saying, "I've got to go have a cigarette." She would leave right in the middle of important office functions to smoke just like a person with an alcohol problem would go out to sneak a drink. Joan displayed every characteristic of a practicing user of drugs and alcohol, yet she'd quote the "program" like a minister preached the gospel.

The Big Book states: "To establish and maintain continuous sobriety, you must abstain from all mind-mood altering chemicals." Does this mean that people who smoke and use coffee excessively are not clean and sober? According to the Big Book they are still using and have not passed day one! They cannot collect $200.00 and must go straight back to rehab! It appears that these soft addictions have a "monopoly" on those who have not changed their state of mind.

In the case of Joan, she had stopped using alcohol and illicit drugs, but she still demonstrated the behavior of a problem drinker. In recovery programs they call this behavior a dry drunk. Here again, I choose not to use labels, but in this situation it will help you understand what Joan was going through. She was following a pattern that is common among many people in Twelve Step programs.

Joan, like many, was following a program but had not developed a new "state of mind." She had accumulated time sober, but spent much of her time looking over her shoulder. Every time she became stressed out, she would seek out an AA meeting as she once sought out a bar. The only difference in the case of Joan was that her blood alcohol count was zero. Unfortunately, Joan had a new blood problem—high blood pressure. Her use of cigarettes, coffee and sweets, compounded by worry, had created a propensity for hypertension and angina. Although her drug and alcohol use had ceased, Joan was only a "Step" away from relapse. This scenario is in no way unique to Joan. There are many people who live their lives worrying about what things to avoid instead of finding new ways to enjoy their lives. Apparently, they didn't understand that the use of cigarettes, caffeinated soft drinks and excessive consumption of coffee and sweets were no different from excessive amounts of drugs and alcohol. They are still mind-mood altering chemicals. Why is this behavior condoned in these programs? Evidence shows that this is still a negative addictive behavior. The only difference is that these new chemicals are condoned and acceptable.

The main reason cigarette smoking and heavy coffee use are encouraged, is directly related to the powers that be. That is, many program managers, administrators, counselors and facilitators of drug and alcohol rehabilitation centers are users themselves. They teeter on the reasoning that one should not give up smoking while in treatment for substance abuse for at least one year. What do they think cigarettes and coffee are? As stated just previously, these substances are also mind-mood altering chemicals and should be discontinued as well. They only make it difficult for clients to give up their main drug of choice. To encourage their clients to nix the sticks and that cup of Joe, managers themselves would have to lead the field by setting the example. Unfortunately, many of these so called counselors, administrators and supervisors are not willing to give up their new drug of choice.

Fortunately, there are many treatment programs today that strongly encourage total abstinence from all mind-mood altering chemicals. What makes these programs attractive and very effective is that their clients receive equal or greater forms of pleasurable experiences in place of past patterns of abusing. In other words, these clients are being compensated with healthier forms of pleasure so they may successfully give up the old ones. This process of compensation works flawlessly. There's not one person on the face of this earth that is not aware of this simple process of exchange.

We have all experienced this unique and marvelous means toward improving ourselves, our lives and our pleasures. You know it! It's called replacing old shoes with new ones. It's about trading in your old car for a new and improved one. Out with the old and in with the new. People generally replace old furniture with new furniture. When we end a relationship we eventually find someone who turns out to be more exciting and interesting. At one time we wondered if we'd ever find someone who would replace our previous lover. Sure enough they eventually come into our lives. Why do we trust this process of exchange without hesitation, but are reluctant to apply it to overcoming negative addiction? Why aren't we using this plain and simple process of exchange even more?

Throughout our human lives we are always going to experience this process of compensation: replacing old pleasures with equal or greater experiences of pleasure. There are individuals who go from cigarettes to alcohol, alcohol to pot, pot to crack cocaine, cocaine to heroin and so on, all in the name of higher experiences of pleasure. It can be said that we are all a part of this evolution.

We are forever growing from one form to the next. Providing individuals who are on negative trips with the opportunity and environment to learn healthier ways to experience happiness is the ultimate means towards ongoing recovery. With happiness being our ultimate goal in life, it only seems practical to use these means towards getting people healthy and out of hospitals and treatment centers.

We often hear people say, "It takes will power to change one's behavior." My experience in behavior change is not a matter of will power. It is a matter of skill power. Learning new skills in healthier forms of pleasure is the key that promotes positive behavior change. Throughout this book, I will provide you with specific steps towards helping you develop that "skill power" necessary to overcome all forms of negative addictions.

Life is not about the power of wills, it is about learning to develop your skills.

The Need to Experience Pleasure

People who are recovering need healthy alternatives, not the condoning and encouragement of mind-mood altering chemicals such as coffee and cigarette smoking. Drug counselors, educators and treatment centers need to develop a new attitude toward their clients and the *dynamics of the optimum recovery.*

Human beings don't start out using alcohol or drugs to become negatively addicted, sick or incapacitated. Most of us start out for the experience of pleasure. Unfortunately, our desire to repeat these experiences of pleasure do not yield healthy outcomes. They only take their devastating toll on the human psyche. Regardless of the outcome of our experiences, there's one thing that we humans have in common—our need to experience pleasure. That's what motivates our behavior.

As a result of my successful recovery from negative addictions, I have spent many years researching what makes it so difficult for individuals to give up their old behaviors. The pure and simple truth is that giving up, without making up, is doomed to failure. We human beings must be compensated for our losses. Therefore, it only makes sense that we use the dynamics of the pleasure principle to encourage people to give up undesirable lifestyle habits. *Why curse the darkness when you can light a candle.*

Depriving individuals of their perceived pleasures may not be the best means towards positive behavior change. It is to provide them with those same dynamics (to experience pleasure) that caused them to use drugs, or other harmful substances in the first place. If pleasure motivates, use it to "*recreate.*" It works every time. It is called fighting fire with fire. Pleasure seeking got us into our current situation, therefore, let us use the pleasure principle to get us out, but make sure it yields healthier returns. There's not one person who has not experienced these dynamics first hand.

The dynamics of the pleasure principle states that if one pleasure outweighs another, the first pleasure will be over shadowed by the second. Why fight a dis-ease when you can promote health? Why do we human beings spend and waste so much of our time and hard earned money correcting our mistakes when all we have to do is live according to the biological laws of nature? Why would anyone take the poison then the antidote? Why would anyone take the poison in the first place? This question is very simple. It's not the poison that compels us to act, it is the effect! We human beings will do almost anything to experience pleasure. We will even give up our drugs if we know beforehand that the substance we are giving up will be replaced by an equal or greater experience of pleasure. And that, my friends, is the key to getting people off harmful substances. Not necessarily taking them away, but offering alternative means to enjoy life to its fullest. This is why it is important that treatment centers, recovery programs and rehabilitation agencies provide alternative pleasurable experiences along with the Twelve Step Tradition.

Discovery 3

Are You Minding Your Store Or Are You Taking Someone Else's Inventory?

Our wretched species is so made that those who walk on the well-trodden path always throw stones at those who are sowing a new road.

Voltaire

Have you ever heard the statement "misery loves company," or "birds of a feather flock together?" And if you dare to be different you tend to get ridiculed, hassled and put down. Our society plays one big game of follow the follower. It would be great if we played follow the leader, but there are very few leaders in our society today. Leaders lead by example and go off the beaten path to new and innovative endeavors. They take the road less traveled to success and discovery. Followers stay on the road often traveled by those before them and are afraid to explore new territory. Therefore, many of us live the same old wretched lives of those before us. In actuality, we are forever being programmed by those we choose to follow. Many of their ideas, notions, attitudes and beliefs about life, sickness, death, wellness, success, happiness and failure eventually become our own. Where else do we learn what we know today except from the environment we are exposed to and the company we keep. When we follow the traditions and customs of others, we continue the process known as "Social Reproduction."

There are two kinds of people in the world—those who think they can, and those who think they can't. What makes this statement so ironic is that they are both right. And neither have the right to impose their opinions on the other. Your beliefs are your own and can only be changed through your own personal experiences. Others may be a factor in your decision making, but they should not be held responsible for the decisions you make. You see, we are all the product of our environment and the result of our choices. In other words, we can only choose that which the environment has to offer. This is similar to choosing food from a food line. You can only select what's being offered. In some societies, we may not be offered the best, and in most situations, we're limited by what that environment is providing. This is the situation in many programs.

In many cases, if something doesn't work you try something else. But many programs will beg to differ. They would insist that it is something that you're not working instead of the "program" not working. I believe if you can find or build a better mouse trap, so be it. As long as it is working in a positive manner and meeting your wellness objectives you should continue that process of choice. There are many individuals who are suffering because they are led to believe that the reason why they are not successful in reaching their objectives is because of a defect on their part, not the program.

In his book, "The Everyday Genius," Peter Kline points out that results are more important than behavior. He states:

> *"In situations where particular goals are desired and understood, it is clear that behavior as such is far less important than results. Yet frequently parents, teachers and managers are more interested in how something is done than what end results it achieves. The point is, we shouldn't have to do a thing any particular way, provided we get the results we want. Left to develop our own methodology, we're more likely to find some joyful and uniquely personal route to our destination."*

There are not very many people in the "program," if any, that would agree with this common sense belief. If anyone were to try, the offender would be cast out—just as I was. It wasn't that I didn't work the program, the program just didn't work for me. That's obvious! When I made my decision to try a different approach to sobriety, I was bombarded by the recovering community for not following tradition. I was told in no uncertain terms that I was going to fail without the Twelve Step program. I wasn't given any options and there were no well wishes, just threats, warnings and negative predictions. Fortunately, not only was I successful in maintaining my sobriety, but in discovering true happiness as well. I was taunted with the same old statements such as, "Oh! So you're cured now? If you're not working the *program* you're going to relapse. The program is the only way." It is not the only way. *It's just one way and the average way.*

It is statements such as these that encourage some people to do just that—relapse. But what these hecklers were not aware of was that they were not defining me, they were *defining themselves*. Remember, a person cannot impose their opinions, limitations or failures on another.

The Twelve Step program works for many individuals seeking to get off harmful substances, but not everyone. "One size doesn't fit all." To think that one way of doing something is the only way is *dysfunctional in itself.* The personal attacks that I endured for discontinuing AA meetings were horrendous. Instead of people asking if I was happy or how successful I'd become, I was shunned and alienated. I knew I couldn't involve myself with the traditional programs anymore because of the "cult-like" attitudes of the program and its members.

Even though I demonstrated all signs of exuberant health and greater success, I was still considered to be relapse potential. Many people that I knew in the "program" thought that I had to be on drugs to be feeling so good about myself, my life and my new way of living. All they were concerned about was that I was not working a Twelve Step program. What made matters worse was that I worked with recovering individuals and was strongly encouraged not to incorporate any of the holistic methods I used into the program towards helping other individuals develop optimum recovery and positive addictions. But I did it anyway and was very successful in helping people find new ways of living without drugs or alcohol. It was these beautiful people and the success they were achieving that encouraged me to write this book.

As a Certified Therapeutic Recreation Specialist, I organized and conducted activities in recreation, leisure, music, arts and crafts, group outings and relaxation to individuals recovering from all kinds of pathologies. As a result, many of the clients I worked with began developing better ways to enjoy their lives. They were learning that through positive addictions, they could still get high.

We human beings need to be compensated when our perceived pleasures are taken away. Unfortunately, I find that many drug and alcohol counselors do not see recreation and leisure activities as a viable means to optimum recovery. It is my experience that many of them are not trained and qualified to provide this unique and innovative approach to treatment. Many have strong allegiance to the Twelve Step program that prevent them from developing these new approaches to sobriety, irrespective of how effective they may be. This is not only one-way thinking, but also prejudicial in nature. It is for these reasons that the traditional recovering program cannot, will not and refuses to believe in any other means to acquiring optimum recovery outside of their "program."

You are what you think. Everything you have become is a function of what you have learned and how you think. No one has the right to impose their thoughts on others. Yet it happens quite often. We all have a mind of our own but some people just won't let us be. Especially if we want to get away from the same old crowd.

Christopher Columbus received quite a lashing for expressing his desires to venture out into the unknown. He had a vision to find a better world. Even during his voyage, his men plotted against him. He maintained his ground and succeeded in accomplishing the goal he set out to accomplish. In spite of the strong disagreement, he pressed on. Although he was supported by a few of his men who believed in him, his true strength came from within.

It is my personal belief that a person should be given the opportunity to explore alternative means towards accomplishing their goals. If a program is not working for someone you're providing service for, offer another option and wish them well. That's the dynamics of good customer service. For example, if you were not receiving quality service from a merchant, would you continue to spend your hard earned cash at their establishment? Even though others may feel that they were being served properly by that establishment, it may not be the same for others' specific needs. This happens all the time. We all have choices, and they all should be honored.

It is not my intention to say that programs don't work, they do. But we must remember that one size does not fit all. We cannot place people into a cookie cutter system and expect the same results that others have acquired. Furthermore, I find it cruel to give those who are not following status quo a difficult time for not working something that's not benefiting their cause; especially if that cause is to get well, recover and get on with their lives.

If people would mind their own store, they just may be able to learn from those who are way ahead of the crowd. It's like running a marathon race where the people far behind are insulting the lead runners hoping that they will slow down so that the laggers aren't left so far behind. I say give those behind you encouragement to reach your level of accomplishment and allow those ahead to plow a fresh new path. Putting those in front of you down may prevent you from finding a better way through the brush. This is how we learn. In my experience, I have found that staying open to fresh ideas and new sensory experiences paves the way to a new tomorrow and a brand new day.

Life is a never ending adventure. We human beings should allow ourselves to stay open to new ideas and not get stuck in one discipline, especially if it is not working for us. If it does work for us and not others, we should wish them well and offer our support. The idea of getting better is to keep finding ways to live as healthy and productive as possible. Don't give way to thinking that one size fits all. We all have a choice in our recovery and discovery!

Discovery 4

Choices - It's Your Move

We are 100% Response-able (able to respond positively) to whatever happens in our lives.

Oliver Rhodes

When it comes to taking control over my life, I find it necessary to affirm the readings in Box 1 on page 54. "What makes me happy and free of worry is understanding and knowing that everything that happens to me comes as either a negative consequence or a wholesome reward. Knowing that I have that choice empowers me to do something about changing my life. I can also differentiate one outcome from the other. That is, I don't expect positive outcomes from minimum output, or negative outcomes from maximum performance." You see, rewards are the result of our efforts, and consequences are the results of our lack of responsibility. Until we all realize that the onus of responsibility lies within each of us to recreate ourselves anew, we'll always find reasons to blame other people, places and things for our misfortune. This is not to say that there aren't other circumstances that happen to us. Surely, there are things that happen that we didn't cause, didn't ask for and definitely don't care to have. I don't think any of us wish for misfortune. The point that I'm trying to make is that there are always going to be things happening that are beyond our control. The important point is, "WHAT ARE WE GOING TO DO ABOUT IT?" Are we going to be able to respond? That is, be *Response-able?*

In spite of what happens to us in the environment, we are all endowed with the power to respond positively to whatever happens. We may not like what happens or have a choice about what happens to us, but we do have a choice about how to respond to that which does happen.

> ***Responding positively does not mean we should jump for joy during the event of a crisis. It means acceptance, not agreement, challenge, not surrender, and growth, not failure.***

There is no such thing as a failure. In surveying some of the most successful people in the world, I have found that the secret to their overwhelming health, wealth and happiness was due to the mistakes they made. When we make mistakes, it positions us closer to our target. Therefore, the more mistakes we make, the closer we get to our goals. If you are afraid of making mistakes, then you are afraid of making success. If you make 5,000 mistakes, that means you are 5,000 times closer to getting it right.

Surprisingly, there are many people who have made far more mistakes than others before reaching their goals. The important point is getting there. Time is irrelevant considering that some people get there sooner than others. When it comes to time, many have often asked me, "How long does it take reach an optimum level of happiness?" And I always respond the same, "until you get it right."

Successful people don't see mistakes as failures. They see them as stepping stones, lessons, and opportunities, to develop, prosper and grow from. Unfortunately many people don't see these *factors of life* as a way of *maturing*. Many people look for a *cause to blame*. Blame takes the responsibility from the subject at hand and passes it on to an object in the environment. Millions do it every day. They profess that they came from an abusive home where the father was an alcoholic. Many people state that they were sexually molested, physically abused and verbally put down most of their life. Sure these factors may have had a big influence on how we behave today, but it doesn't have to go on that way. It may seem unfortunate, but those influences are what made us who we are today. However, today we are fortunate to have the power to make better choices in spite of what has happened to us in the past.

Yes, we are the product of our environment, but we are also the result of our choices!

It hurts to think about the difficult times in our lives, but it hurts even more if we stay the way we are. We can change by seeing our misfortunes as directions to correct what it is we are doing wrong. If we listen to our instincts, we won't fall victim to repeating our mistakes. Repeated mistakes confuse many into thinking that there are no solutions. The common statement that I hear from many people who have given up on themselves is, "I've tried everything, but nothing seems to work." Surely we have all spoken these words at one time or another in our lives. In actuality, many of us just keep making the same mistakes over and over again. Doing more of what doesn't work doesn't make it work any better. If you keep doing the same old thing you'll keep getting the same old results.

We have to be open to fresh ideas and new sensory experiences. We have to be willing to cross the *QRLP* Transition Zone (See Figure 4.1).

In a traditional treatment program, the idea is to follow certain steps to recovery. The goal is to obtain sobriety. Unfortunately, many people find this approach to sobriety difficult, boring and unproductive. Sure, the "steps" have worked well for many people, but there are many more people it hasn't worked for.

This program supports the notion that the Twelve Steps is the only way. It is not the only way; it is only one way.

There are many people who think that they have failed at whatever it is they are trying to accomplish. They haven't failed, they have just given up. There's a real big difference here. Failure can lead to success. As long as you keep moving

Action taken in a holistic approach to Discovery leads to an increased quality of life & desirable lifestyle values!
Recreation • Nutrition • Meetings • Leisure • Steps • Fitness • Sponsor • Relaxation • Hobbies • Employment • Arts • Worshipping • Vocation • Volunteering • Big book • Wilderness • Personal Gro with Program
Clockwise
QRLP Discovery Program (New Paradigm)
QRLP Transition Zone
Traditional Recovery Program (Old Paradigm)
Stinking thinking • Relapse • TX • Boredom • Frustration • Sponsor • Big Book • Meetings • Steps
Counter Clockwise
Doing more of what doesn't work doesn't make it work any better. You've got to do something different and more effective.

Figure 4.1

towards a successful and productive end, you will reach your goal. Giving up leads to nowhere.

As you move towards reaching your goals, remember that things are always going to happen that we have no control over. The only control we do have is within ourselves. We can control how we respond to people, places and things. Many people would rather blame than to claim responsibility for the choices they have made. For example, traditional recovery programs tend to condone relapse that was sparked by a recent tragedy. This could have been a divorce, death in the family, loss of employment or personal injury.

This program allows them to "Keep Coming Back" where much of their time is spent talking about what made them relapse instead of focusing on the numerous choices that were available to them. Very few people who relapse ever confess, "I just wanted to get high." It's much easier to find fault in the system. What's so scary about finding fault is that there's always going to be something happening beyond our control.

Blaming objects in the environment for our relapse leaves little chance for hope or continuous sobriety. In the first sign of a crisis, many people in recovery tend to head for the nearest drug. That's similar to grabbing onto ankle weights while abandoning a sinking ship—you go straight to the bottom.

Excuses for relapses are unfounded. With so many alternates to choose from, using is not a viable reason for dealing with the things that happen to us. Using is a choice not a solution. When someone states that they relapsed because.... they should be stopped right there. There is no because. The only reason why we do the things we do is to satisfy a need. Everything we do is based on *want, desire, passion* and *pleasure*. Life's events don't cause us to relapse, many of us *choose to use.*

The Best for Stress

If someone is under pressure, they seek to balance that pressure with pleasure through eating, drinking, resting, sleeping, medicating or fornication. We want to experience pleasure and at the same time avoid pain. And since we are *"hedonistic"* in nature, our main reasons for choosing certain behaviors are based on those hedonistic principles — The Dynamics of the Pleasure Principles (DPP).

Realizing that we make our choices based on our own specific needs, nullifies our cause to blame. Although events that occur in the environment do play a factor in our behavior, we must remember that in multiplication, there are many factors that yield numerical outcomes. As in the game of life, you too are a factor that can control your outcome. For example:

$$2 \times 3 = 6$$

The 2 and the 3 are factors. The outcome is 6. If you were a factor in this equation, let's say the 2, and the events that happen in the environment are 3, together you'd come up with 6. When you change (from a 2 to a 4), the outcome will change which means *you are the controlling factor* in your equation of life. For instance, if you change from a 2 to a 4 in the above example, the outcome will be 12. Therefore, you can make things better by changing yourself, thus resulting in better choices.

Now, if you believe that the things that happen to you are beyond your control and that you're not a factor in this equation, you'll have an equation that looks something like this:

$$0 \times 3 = 0$$

As you can see, nothing, times any factor, is nothing. Therefore, if you are doing nothing in your life (you being the 0) but blaming others, you are going to wind up with zero every time. You must do something (take responsibility) if you want to acquire a successful and happy outcome. You can become that successful person by first realizing that you are a *big* factor in the outcome of your life. Realize the choices that you make, whether good or bad, will yield good or bad outcomes. They can either be blissful or miserable.

It is without a doubt that we all have choices. As a result, I have developed the following flow chart (Figure 4.2) that I call *"Choices."* The illustration on the next page will help you understand that there are many and better ways to deal with the things that happen to us in life.

In studying "Choices" you will notice that there are certain events located all around us and the responses going up or down. As we mature, these center events become more and more prevalent. This is what I call *"leaving home."* Obviously, many of us don't take on these demands until after we are out of the house and on our own. Also, "Choices" represents the multiplication analogy that was discussed previously. These are events that generally occur in the environment and just don't happen to a selected few, they happen to us all. No one is immune to outside forces that we have no control over. So let's throw out the victim role. We can play the victim role all we want. The bottom line is, we're all *responsible* for our actions and reactions. The sooner we realize that, the better choices we can make.

These occurrences are not what cause our problems, our "Choices" (responses, reactions, actions) are what cause our problems.

Since we make the choice, we create and control the outcome. We cannot control other people, places or things. We can only control how we act and react. Therefore, if your parents abused you as a child, *they are* responsible for

CHOICES
Sound in Mind & Body
Employment & Volunteering
Relaxation & Meditation
Recreation & Leisure
Counseling & Therapy
Exercise & Nutrition
Education & Worshipping
Self-help Groups
Problem Solving
Acceptance
Bliss
Pain & Misery
Denial & Blame
Substance Abuse
Crime & Violence
Lying & Resignation
Dysfunctional Relationships
Smoking & Sedentary Living
Poor Nutrition & Self-Demoralization
Homicide & Suicidal Ideation
Mental illness

Figure 4.2

the former abuse. If you carry on that legacy, you will be accountable for any further abuse. Your parents are no excuse for your present abuse. You cannot continue to blame them for what has been done and is now over. Now, what you do here on out is strictly up to you.

Similarly, if someone were to insult you, do you respond with anger? Would you choose to blow them off or react with violence. If so, why? Is what they're saying true? Even if it were, do you let it get to you? Realize that they are not defining you, they are defining themselves. As Eleanor Rooselt once quoted: *"No one can make you feel inferior without your permission."* Guilt, distress, fear and anxiety are all subjective. We create our own hell or heaven based on our biases and limitations.

The difference between happy and unhappy people is not what happens to them, it's how each individual "Chooses to Respond" to those occurrences. We have got to wake up and realize that it is not these occurrences that are responsible for our reactions. They may influence them, but we make the final decision.

Labeled throughout the flow chart, "Choices" are lifestyle factors that are common to us all. Much of how we respond to life can be based on how we define these life situations. We can see them as:

- *Problems* • *Events* • *Situations* • *Lessons*
- *Circumstances* • *Factors* • *Hardships*
- *Occurrences* • *Incidents* • *Challenges*

How we see these events are directly related to how we will respond to them. If we see them as problems, we may feel that these situations are beyond our control, and we might have some difficulty *accepting* what has happened in our lives. On the other hand, if we see them as challenges, we may take to it with inspiration and determination to overcome these events.

To some people, these situations are also known as

stressors. Stressors can be positive or negative. For example, marriage to most can be a happy occasion, but can also be a factor for distress depending on how one responds to it. Emotionally, a marriage carries with it more responsibility and team work for the couple joining hands. While the parents may be happy, they may also become distressed by losing a family member through marriage. It is not so much what that *factor* may be, it is how we *respond* to the *demand* made on the body. Therefore, it is immaterial whether the agent or situation we face is pleasant or unpleasant; all that counts is the intensity of the demand for *readjustment* or *adaptation*.

The illustration "Choices" also represents the universal law of cause and effect. For example, the responses going up represent healthy choices. The responses going down represent unhealthy choices. The responses going up are good causes and the responses going down are not so good: Good cause — good effect, bad cause — bad effect. If you study it further, you will see that it uniquely delineates the meaning of the *"Serenity Prayer."* God grant me the Serenity to *accept* the things I cannot change (surrounding events), the *courage* to change the things that I can (responses going up), and the *wisdom* to know the difference (the surrounding events vs. the responses going up).

"Choices" clearly illustrates that there is no one now, in the past or in the future who is not able to respond positively to the events that occur in life.

> ***There is just no reason for anyone to be living in the darkness when they have a definite choice to light a candle.***

No one can honestly say while looking at this flow chart that violence was the only choice they had when dealing with difficult situations. It is the same with substance abuse, crime, smoking, lying, poor eating habits, dysfunctional relationships or suicide.

No one creates your pain and misery. They may add to it, but you have the power to stop it.

You don't have to put up with the abuse and misuse from anybody. If someone is mistreating you, you have two choices. Put up with it or get out. I know what you're thinking. "But it's not that easy." Please understand that everything we have ever accomplished in our lives came about through the following equations:

Difficulty = *Practice* = *Ease*

Realize that construction of any great building will not spring up overnight. But if you *practice* living responsibly, you will develop the skills to make better choices. Your work will be done, one brick at a time until a massive structure has been completed. What I am saying is, although you may not be able to change your situation immediately, you can change your attitude. So, get busy working on it. Do your research, ask questions, call around, by all means plan your day for a better way to live. Above all respect yourself and others will respect you.

There are many people who panic when faced with a crisis. Now there's nothing wrong with a little panic. In fact, it's quite normal. It only becomes a problem when we allow that panic to cause us to see nothing but *red.* In this situation, we honestly believe there are no other options except to fall victim to lost causes. The *power* of the mind can be lost making poor choices. But the sooner you come to grips with reality and *accept* (not agree) what has happened, the sooner you can begin to *heal*.

If the mind has the power to make you sick, it also has the power to make you well.

Your *mind* and body have the *power* to deal with the truth of *reality* (center events) that results in *healing*. For example:

Mind		Reality		Healing
Power		Truth		Results
Spirit	=	Environment	=	Harmony
Action		Events		Values
Self		Health		Wealth

Figure 4.3

Everyone has this *Mind, Reality, Healing* process contain within self. This is where your mind has the power for the spirit to take action. This action reveals the truth of life and the events that go on in the environment. As a result, everyone can produce *harmony, values* and *wealth* if they believe in self and the *power of the mind (Goose = Labor of Love = Gold Egg)*. Everything in nature begins with nourishing the roots (self). To get a better understanding of this natural process, consider how a tree produces fruit: Roots = Tree = Fruit. If you don't nourish the roots, you will not, cannot produce the fruit!

On many occasions, the difficulty in making positive choices are associated with feelings other than our own. Many of our choices are the result of *societal expectations*. We tend to respond in the same manner as our friends, relatives and associates, and find ourselves living under the hypnosis of societal conditioning. As a result, we develop this ideology that this is how things are done. Just because everyone else does it that way, it must be the best way. It is not the best way, it is the average way.

Making positive choices becomes even more difficult when people we respect and look up to are making poor choices. If our associates are making poor choices, there's a high probability we'll make them also. Most of us know better, but we choose not to disappoint those we care about—even if it is wrong. Other reasons why people choose to make poor decisions are because they are afraid of the consequences that may result from family traditions, work situations (organizational co-dependency), peer groups and other controlling environmental factors.

The collective expectation of our society starts when we're first brought into this world. As children, we observe and learn that children play and are more active than adults. At this very early age, children take in valuable information about themselves and what it's like to be an adult. We don't wait until we're adults to decide if we're going to smoke, drink or do drugs. For many of us, we *unconsciously* make these decisions well before our adolescent years. Although we may not be aware of it, the sensory experiences we pick up from the environment are already being planted into our central nervous system. It's not definite that children will follow in societies' footsteps, but it is highly probable. In actuality, a child can become no better than its surroundings and what it picks up from the environment. We are basically being programmed.

Also, many of us are in *denial* concerning the responsibility for a child's development. It has long been thought that parents are responsible for their children's development, actions and behavior. Realistically, children are not raised by parents alone (if they are to be so lucky to have parents), they are also raised by a society. We are still confused and the jury is still out on who's responsible for our children ("children are our future and greatest resource" as we so proudly profess).

We blame the parents, the parents blame the schools, the schools blame the police, and the police turn it back around to the parents. It doesn't take a rocket scientist to figure out that as a society, we are all responsible; every last one of us.

We as a people in this complicated world have to improve our ability to respond positively to the things that happen, *than to expect things to happen in our favor*. In this way, we'll stop playing the victim role, and for the first time in our lives we'll understand that it's not what happens to us that matters as much, it's how we are going respond to that which happens. Making better choices rather than resorting to distortion makes life less cloudy, plus leaves you *"sound"* in mind and body.

When you're faced with some of life's greatest challenges, use the flow chart *"choices"* on page 126 as a guideline to help you respond positively to what happens in your world. There are *sixteen steps* on this flow chart, eight going up and eight going down. You make the call whether to go up or down — no one else!

You have a *choice* to go either way. These steps are not preset chronologically as in some other programs (step 1, step 2, step 3,...). However, there are *TWO FIRST STEPS, one for each direction* that we generally take on our way up or down. *Acceptance* is the first step going up, and *Denial* is the first step going down.

What makes this process so unique is that you only have one first step. This prevents being forced into a "cookie cutter" program where everyone is encouraged to follow "cult like" steps. You have the choice to start anywhere on your way up. There is no particular order going down, so why should there be a particular order going up?

> ***When people respond negatively to events that happen in the environment, some may "choose to use" while others may decide to choose suicide.***

No two people make the same choices. Everybody is unique and different. We have different needs and different ways of seeing things. For example, in my experience many people have done well in self-help programs, whereas others have done well following an exercise and nutrition program.

Others have joined a church where they gained great support and spiritual healing from a religious congregation. Furthermore, you are not restricted to one step at a time. It is similar to how people go up regular steps. Some may take one step at a time, while others may decide to take two or three steps at a time.

There are many people who are involved in several health promoting activities (HPA) simultaneously, such as exercise, school, worshipping, relaxation, employment, meditation and recreation. The more HPAs one is involved in, the more "skillful" (skill power, not will power) they will be in warding off illness and dis-ease.

The number of steps one takes can be based on their strengths and limitations and not on the expectations of others.

Choices allow options based on one's personal needs, feelings, and desires. It's like having a tailor design you a suit with the perfect fit. You are not hustled into a "standard brand" where one size fits all. Maybe that works well with garments, but not with human beings. We're special and should have special tailoring that's going to significantly enhance our health and personal needs for growth and continued development.

Since it is better to work on lighting a candle (promoting health) than cursing the darkness (fighting an illness), I would like for you to focus on the *Eight Steps* going up. Many professional organizations spend exorbitant amounts of time working in the dungeons of our minds. We know what it's like to suffer. Why should we study that which we are trying to overcome? Pain and misery cannot exist if we are following *Qualitative Recreation Lifestyle Principles* (the eight steps going up).

The reason most professional organizations put energy and time into the lower steps is that it's predicated on profitability. Many of these multi-million dollar conglomerates cannot maintain their "cash flow" if patients are not down in the *red*.

If doctors and hospitals healed two patients a day (and they can) they would be out of business within a year.

Doctors can't work if you're not sick! I would suggest you find that candle and live going up as opposed to struggling in the darkness. In times of difficulty, pain, indecision and despair, here are the "choices" you can follow to *see* your way through:

Acceptance:

After the initial shock of panic and fear, allow yourself to *accept* what has happened for now. This doesn't mean that you condone or agree with what's going on, only that an event has happened and is now a *factor* in your life. This is the time to make *positive choices* to do something about it. At this point healing can begin. Certain events in our lives can cause us to become extremely alarmed. Sometimes the pain can be very devastating. The loss of a loved one, personal injury, divorce, pregnancy or being fired from a job are only a few of the events that can significantly leave us feeling emotionally and physically shipwrecked. For many, *Acceptance* is the first obstacle we must overcome before we can return to normalcy. Some people become so grief stricken, it takes them years to recover. The main purpose of writing this book is to empower you with the knowledge and skills to successfully overcome these events in your life. Let's face it, there's always going to be something. Everyone must pass through the turnstile of life. There's no escaping it. Again, the important point is not so much what happens, it's our reaction to what happens. A part of being truly happy and healthy is in learning from these experiences and to successfully recover from them. Life is a college and we're all in class. We are all recovering from one thing or another, some more than others. It is my hope that the flow chart *"Choices"* will help you achieve optimum health that is *Sound in Mind and Body.* By following these steps you will develop the skills to go *"Beyond Recovery."*

Problem Solving:

Now that you have accepted what has happened, see it as a platform to grow. The event now becomes a challenge to overcome in your life. Bring together all of your resources. You have a brain to think with, not sink with. Write down on a note pad as many solutions as you can come up with. Try them out until you find one that works. Be patient and allow your wonderful mind to go to work for you.

Allow yourself to reach out. Ask for help from a friend, neighbor, colleague or family member. One of the biggest problems in our society today is that people think that they can solve all of their problems alone. Maybe so, but sometimes it just may be more practical to ask for help.

Self-Help Groups:

This is another excellent choice. You can find a list of self-help groups in your local directory. Many of these groups are free of charge and generally meet on a daily basis. You will find that everyday people attend these groups and share similar experiences you may be going through. You can also call your local Public Health Service for a listing of these organizations.

Education:

What can I say about education other than *"knowledge is power."* The more you know, the easier it will be for you to get through painful experiences. Education prepares you for future skills as well as hardships. People who maintain high levels of education generally have a better understanding of life's ups and downs. For example, if two people were fired from their jobs and were going to apply for another job, but one had more education than the other, who do you think would get the job? Chances are the one with the most education, considering all other things being equal. If you are unable to finance a formal education, read books on your interests. The local library is open to everyone. Better yet, check out your local community colleges. Many of them offer free classes, and some charge a nominal fee. Most cost between $25.00 and $60.00 per class.

Worshipping:

Believing and worshipping in a higher power provides many with spiritual and soulful healing. Being spiritual means having the ability to find peace and happiness in an imperfect world, and feel that one's own personality is imperfect but acceptable. Spiritual health stems from a conviction about the sanctity and meaningfulness of life. It can serve as a *buffer* against every form of stress, preserving hope and dignity in the bleakest of circumstances. It doesn't necessarily mean you should be a member of a local church, but for some, the support of a congregation can be very uplifting. In essence, spirituality is a connection with everything in life and the universe. We are all parts of a whole held together by spiritual love.

Exercise:

The word is out: Vigorous play and exercise helps prevent heart attacks, aids in weight control, instills a feeling of well being and enhances creativity. Medically, it has been found to help people with diabetes, ulcers, nervous tension, high blood pressure, back pain, depression, varicose veins, recurrent headaches, and menstrual cramps. It cures jet lag, constipation, and insomnia. In diabetes, for example, the reduction of body fat by exercising improves the body's ability to handle sugar. Best of all exercise can improve your sex life. If life has you by the throat, get out and go for a walk. If you need some motivation, ask a friend or two to go walking with you. Walking is a joy! But whatever activity you decide to get into, start out slow. Studies indicate that people who begin with high-intensity workouts are more likely to quit than low- and moderate-intensity exercisers. Play exercise is the quick elixir that's more powerful than any drug. Do your research! Get out and play.

Nutrition:

Good nutrition means giving your body and mind the fuel they need to run efficiently. But during times of stress and crisis, when we most need nutritious foods, we often pay little attention to what we're eating. We skip meals; and as our blood sugar plummets, we feel irritable. We down cup after cup of coffee and wonder why our nerves are on edge. We snack on sweets that give us a surge of energy and then leave us feeling hungrier than before. At the end of the day, we pour ourselves a few stiff drinks to unwind. Behaviorally and nutritionally, we become our own worst enemies. A well balanced, nutritious diet is essential to help your body cope with stress. If you skip breakfast, snack compulsively, and go on and off crash diets, you're undermining your body's stress defenses and a stress-vitamin supplement is no substitute for wise *food choices.* Furthermore, good wholesome foods contain the elements from which health is built as well as to safeguard us against dis-ease. The human body is under constant attack from free radicals from both inner and outer environments. Give it what it needs to compensate for the demand that's being placed on it.

Counseling & Therapy:

A good counseling and therapy session does not necessarily have to be professional. You can receive good therapy from a friend or family member who is understanding and willing to listen. The reason why many people have difficulty talking with friends and relatives about their concerns is because most of the time they try to be too controlling. Friends and family try to correct their loved ones by telling them what they should be doing. On many occasions, family can be too aggressive and may resort to humiliation, insults and put downs. On the other hand, an understanding relative or friend can add support, compassion and empathy in times of chaos. Therefore, if you have someone you can confide in, seek them out and dump. Otherwise, get professional help somewhere.

Recreation & Leisure:

When stress turns into distress, do as I do, take a mental health day off to go out and play. In my poem, "The Power of Play" one verse reads, "Play is essential and has great potential for mind and body restoration, for the holistic way is work, rest and play, now that's the ultimate health care combination." I would like for you to review that poem *(Discovery 6, page 165)* as often as possible. In our modern society very few people take time off to just do something for fun. Going to the gym and working out is literally work. Play is that spontaneous participation in some form of activity that is fun, exciting and challenging. In addition to providing pleasurable exercise, it also acts as a buffer in times of trouble. It takes your mind off your troubles momentarily. It doesn't get rid of them, but allows your mind and body to recreate itself. You see, there are many things that you can do to keep your interest high, for if you do you will learn too, that good health will not pass you by. So get out today and stay in shape, get into play and recreate.

Relaxation & Meditation:

Making decisions to change is generally accompanied by stress. Because stress can be deadly, you should be mindful of when you sense stress becoming too great. Screen yourself for signs of excessive stress, including anxiety, depression and anger. In facing and coping with stress, we can be our own worst enemy. However, we're also the ones who can do the most to transform distress into eustress (good stress) in our lives. Relaxation produces a state that is opposite to stress. Rather than gearing up for "fight or flight," our bodies grow calmer and work more smoothly. Deep breathing relaxation, imagery relaxation, and progressive muscle relaxation are effective techniques in reducing stress and inducing the relaxation response.

How to Relax

1. *Find yourself a quite, peaceful space free of noise and distractions. Plan on 30 minutes to one hour to fully experience the benefits associated with progressive relaxation exercises. It is recommended that your relaxation session include music that is slow, soothing, and has a calming effect. Strings and woodwinds are much better for this than trumpets and trombones and should be free of lyrics.*
2. *Now sit or lie down in a comfortable position with your eyes closed. Loosen any tight clothing and breath deeply focusing on the music and your breathing technique. With each exhalation, concentrate on feeling the body sinking down and loosening up, becoming more relaxed on each exhalation.*
3. *Imagine yourself in your favorite surroundings such as on a tropical beach, ski slope, or before a glowing fireplace during a cold winter night, or create a scene that you would feel most relaxed in.*

4. *Beginning with your feet, tense and then relax each muscle group in your body, working up your body until you end at your hands. Imagine the tenseness flowing out of your body through your finger tips while listening to the soothing music stimulating each muscle group.*
5. *Scan the body from one end to the other, looking for sensations – hot or cold, tension or relaxation, comfort or discomfort. Find out what is happening and allow your body to release the pain, tension, or discomfort while continuing to breath deeply, regularly, and rhythmically.*
6. *Concentrate on positive and productive thoughts such as a focus word or phrase with each exhalation. The focus word simply acts as an anchor for your attention and can be a prayer, an affirmation ("I'm a beautiful person") or something as simple as the word "one." Use the same word each time to build an association in your mind between relaxation and repetition of the word or phrase.*
7. *Finally, use visualization and imagery to heal the body and bring about positive results from the goals you want to accomplish. See yourself getting better in oneness of body and mind. Drift with the music throughout this session feeling refreshed, energized, and thoroughly relaxed afterwards.*

Employment & Volunteering:

We recreate ourselves through our jobs, projects and activities. Service to others, whether it is employment or volunteer work, provides a feeling of accomplishment, self-worth and personal gratification. When we're not involved in some form of recreational activity, we can easily become bored. There's something that you should know about boredom. It carries a very painful price. Your own brain can turn into your biggest enemy. The brain hates boredom so much that it will do just about anything to provide itself with the thrill of challenge. And that can include inflicting pain on the body. In its quest for stimulation, the brain will first increase the level of REM (rapid eye movement) sleep so that dream capacity is boosted. If that doesn't do the trick, the brain will then increase physical restlessness, which may take the shape of impulsive behavior. Finally in a last-ditch effort to change the circumstances and provide itself with a new challenge, the brain will even create physical problems such as back pain, high blood pressure, eating disorders, drug addiction and a host of other ailments. Meaningful employment and volunteerism can boost your brain power, self-esteem and creative skills. Many people think that there are no benefits in offering their services as a volunteer. But actually, the world of volunteerism offers many exciting opportunities. As a matter of fact, many top level publishing, public relations and advertising executives *cut their teeth* (get a taste for that line of work) through volunteer work. Combine the good feeling you get from helping people with the opportunity to earn yourself some experience (and possibly a paying job), and you've got a package you can't beat.

Even people who are homeless and work recycling aluminum cans, newspapers and plastic bottles, have a much healthier glow than those who stand at intersections asking for handouts.

Remember, if you can breathe you have potential, if you can breathe then you are alive, and if you are alive you can think, feel, act and respond. Now if you're thinking that you can't teach an old dog new tricks then you're in trouble, because the only dog that's not teachable is a dead dog. Since you are reading this book, you are definitely not "dog gone." You see, you are alive and must remember that there is no such thing as the living dead, unless it's in your head. We all have capabilities to respond with some form of service to our community and ourselves. Make sure that you find something to do and make it fun. The ultimate goal in life is to be happy. That happiness can only be found in work you feel good about doing.

A Poem to Remember

Choices

Life is unique and can make living so sweet.
It can bring plenty of joy and oh boy what a treat.
But things can get flaky and may make you feel shaky,
It's called the "wrench" that tends to give life its stench.
What do you do when it happens to you?
Do you find cause to blame, and curse out His name?
Or sit and complain about life being a drain?
Life being a drain, that can't possibly be true,
For it may not be life, it just may be you.
It's easier to blame than to own up and claim,
That the anger in our voices, are the result of poor choices.
But you can change your plight with a little insight,
That there are better choices to change wrong into right.
To stay in the blue here's what you can do,
Don't let the red get the very best of you.

Shut out the noise of those negative voices,
That just may force you to make some very bad choices.
Work through your pain and try to maintain
An optimistic outlook and a positive aim.
Now, there's no evil plan so try and understand
That life isn't against you so keep your best at hand.
These events in life just don't happen to a few,
They happen to us all and not only you.
But it's not what happens that cause us to stall,
It's how we recover from that initial fall.
After the initial shock-wave of panic and fear,
Climb up that bliss ladder and put it in gear.
As your choices get better you'll be turning the table,
And say, "no strain on the crane because the cable is able."
So lift up your voice and dump the remorse,
Because you do have a choice to live and rejoice.

Discovery 5

Awareness - Time To Wake Up And Smell The Roses

Sometimes we have to experience great pain to develop an awareness, but is it necessary?

Oliver Rhodes

Many people feel that in order to develop a new awareness they have to hit bottom. Nothing could be further from the truth. When people feel this way, it becomes a self-fulfilling prophecy. We get what we expect, and usually what we are thinking is a creation of our own imagination. We are the creator of all our experiences and our interpretation of those experiences. Somewhere during our existence someone has gone through the pain for us. All we have to do is to *learn* from their experience of pain without having to experience it for ourselves. In many situations of health, sickness, addictions, success and failure, the groundwork has been laid. The ball is already on the fifty yard line. All we need to do is take the ball and run with it. It doesn't make sense to go all the way back to the one yard line and run it from there. Pick-up from the present and move forward.

Many people who are struggling to recover feel that the only way they will get a wake up call is to hit the very bottom. This "stinking thinking" is very destructive and has no place in any recovery program. Wherever you are—emotionally, physically, socially and spiritually—is your bottom at this time and space. *Don't expect to fall any further.* You just may not be able to get back up. And this happens quite frequently to those who feel they must go through such extremes in order to develop that awareness.

The discovery I'm about to share with you is, in a sense, passing you the *ball of empowerment,* strength and awareness so that you may acquire true happiness, success and a zest for life. One of the requirements necessary for moving forward from this point would be to relinquish any need to defend your current point of view, acquired traditions, old concepts and beliefs. This measure is important for developing fresh ideas and new sensory experiences. It does not mean that your ideas and beliefs are not important, they are important up to this point in time. But you must be willing to open up to fresh ideas, concepts and teachings that will pave the way from here on out. Today is the first day of the rest of your life, but live it like it's your last.

This innovative approach to increased awareness is just another incredible way of maximizing your potential toward infinite possibilities. Otherwise, old thinking patterns may prevent you from developing these innovative approaches to optimum health and overall well-being. It is a proven fact that what may have worked for many of us at one time may not be valid today.

Life Is Not About A Powerless Self; It's About Re-creating The Power Within Self

Human nature is captured, in part, by the notion that the significance of our existence is never fixed once and for all; rather, we continuously "recreate" ourselves through our projects. Humans are in a constant state of transition, emerging, and becoming. As long as we are sowing, we shall reap the harvest of success! Be patient and believe in yourself. Life is not static, it may only appear to be that way to some. We are either growing or decaying. Growing is the result of continuously challenging ourselves to look, learn and listen. Decaying is the result of constantly allowing ourselves to live in a state of rationalization, resistance and denial. We make vain and arduous attempts to stay right where we are instead of taking on new ways to live our lives. We can only make progress if we allow ourselves the opportunity to experience new concepts and innovative challenges. We have always learned in this fashion and always will.

From the time we were children in kindergarten to the present, our contact and interactions with the environment and others have had a tremendous effect on our self-esteem, self-confidence and self-concept. If our projects are positive and health promoting, we develop positive and thriving human qualities. When you perform a job and get excellent praise, the foundation for inner strength results from the projects you perform. The praise is what nourishes your inner spirit. Are we not inspired when our efforts are recognized and appreciated? Isn't it true that our heads are held high, shoulders pulled back and chest stands out when we are accomplishing worthy goals?

And are we not at our best when we are actively engaged in self-fulfilling projects, work and relationships? Sure we are! People who are in touch with their inner spirit have become that way through the power of *"Qualitative Recreation Lifestyle Principles."*

As stated previously, these principles are positive and health promoting activities that provide pleasure, awareness, challenge, and fun, with qualities designed to help us get to know our true selves. We learn about our strengths, weaknesses and potential by taking an active part in living our lives in accordance with nature. Life is a process of learning.

All knowledge and higher learning is not only based on the things that we are doing well, they are also the result of some things we inadvertently do poorly, wrong and sometimes shameful, but nevertheless, we can learn from all our experiences!

It is these experiences that accentuate our skills so

that we become more in tune with ourselves. Our well-being should not have to weigh on doing everything right the first time around. This puts many people under an awful lot of pressure. As a result, many individuals are reluctant to engage in any activity that they feel they must perform well. Each and every skill we have acquired over the course of our lives was fashioned by inept attempts of becoming, repeated failures and countless struggles with Murphy (Murphy's Law: Anything that can go wrong, will go wrong).

Learning is a process, and at times a very painful one. It has always been that way and always will. Developing an awareness for living healthy is in understanding the notion that we are all capable of learning throughout our entire lives. Learning keeps us in touch with self and gives us the inner strength to withstand some of the most difficult times in our lives. No one is incapable of learning. When we stop learning, we stop living. When we stop living we start to die, but we get sick for a long time then we die. For example, if you are reading this book you are as alive and well capable of learning. Our learning days are only over when we say that they are over, and by no means are we destined to decay unless we say. Learning is a process of stimulating the central nervous system in our brain. The process works wonders when activated by passion, desire and conscious effort.

Now, there are some who learn faster than others, but who cares as long as you get across the finish line. When people enter a marathon, they know that everyone can't take first place. The important point here is that one should put forth as much effort and drive to finish the race. It doesn't matter how long it takes for you to complete the race or how fast you run, but what is important is that you finish. In this situation of hard drive and determination, everyone becomes a winner. Even the very last person is a winner. The only failures in any lifestyle endeavor are those who do nothing or have given up. Most failures don't stick with anything long enough to see any result from their efforts. Winning takes persistence not necessarily precision.

Many people who very seldom try to make a difference in their lives, seem to always have an excuse, but there are a countless number of people who are less capable. In spite of certain disabilities, they are passionate enough to make their lives a wonderful experience. Sometimes it takes the disabilities of less fortunate people in our world to help us realize how fortunate we are. It is my belief that the only difference between people who are successful in life and those who are not is a result of how they think. Losers actually think they are incapable of making positive changes in their lives, whereas winners feel deep within their souls that they're just as capable as anybody. They have a mind, and they can put it to work, then they allow the magic to happen.

The hardest thing than trying to get a winner to think like a loser, is trying to get a loser to think like a winner; reason: A winner thinks like a winner, and a loser thinks like a loser. If they didn't we'd all be winners, but losers don't think so, however, winners do!

It never ceases to amaze me how diverse the contestants are who enter athletic competitions. We human beings are truly amazing. In almost every competitive event I've seen, from skiing to swimming, I am always inspired by those daring and fun loving people who enter these events in wheel chairs, prosthetics, and even on crutches. I witnessed a man complete a full Iron-man competition carrying his quadriplegic son the entire three event race. He carried him on his back during the swim, in the basket on the handle bars during the bike, and in a push buggy during the run. I don't think I've ever wept as hard with joy as when those two came across the finish line. These remarkable human beings that take on such challenges may not all be equal physically or mentally but the one thing that they all have in common is that they all have incredible *drive, heart* and *spirit.*

There is nothing that we humans can't do if we are spiritually connected. Knowing who we are and believing in ourselves comes from our ability to learn through our experiences and realizing that it is the *experiences* that teach us "skill power" and not always having to get it right the first, second, or third time around. Life is like playing the shell game, but with unlimited attempts of finding the ball.

In life, there is no such thing as three strikes you're out. If that were true, we'd still be reading at night by candle light, instead of by the convenience of electric light, or traveling across country by stagecoach, instead of the airline's first class coach, or better yet communicating by carrier pigeon instead of by telephone and television. In addition, life isn't over until we say it's over. Learning is a process of life, and life is a process of learning. We all have our own personal methods of how to apply what we learn in this world. Life is one big college that provides us with lessons in self, health and spiritual wealth. The wealth in this case means non-material values such as self-esteem, self-confidence, self-pride and self-love. Therefore, happiness is an inside job. Having possessions and learning to enjoy them stems from learning to love who you are and enjoying the things that you do.

When you have a purpose in life you are rewarded for your efforts. Doing nothing yields nothing. So what are you doing with your plot of ground? Are you sowing your harvest of happiness and joy or are you waiting for something to fall out of the sky into your lap? Are you looking for mister or miss right, or are you working hard to be right within yourself? Many of us try but most of us fail because we don't understand that life is about giving and not necessarily receiving. If there's nothing special going on in your life at this time, maybe it's because you're not creating it. Life is like a potluck of giving. We all gain in life if everybody contributes something. The things that I'm suggesting that we bring into this world are of a spiritual nature.

Material possessions may be okay for some, but it doesn't

cut the mustard in respect to lasting qualities and worthy values. And if we do receive some forms of gratification in the form of material things, they are usually of a shallow nature and tend to be short lived if we don't continue to reproduce them.

In our attempt to get to know ourselves through material possessions, we can lose sight of who we are as spiritual human beings. As a result, we inadvertently become rigidly attached to drugs, alcohol, cars, homes, people, money and professional status. Now, there's nothing wrong with having nice things, surely we all like to have money and what it can buy. But, in order to survive spiritually, we need to be able to purchase the things that are going to provide for our material needs as well. The problem arises when we become totally absorbed in the importance of having these possessions. At the same time, it is quite common for people to lose sight of their humanness and spirituality in the midst of owning and relishing objects. If our identity is rigidly tied to these possessions and we lose them, we tend to take a hard fall and go down with them. It is not easy to recover from objects and symbols that represents who we are. Relying on outside resources to function properly in this world, can cause us to become lost in an ocean of material possessions, drugs, alcohol, food and dysfunctional relationships. Even the people we know will associate us with what we have instead of who we are when mentioning our name. Our self-worth becomes tied to the effect instead of the cause. A point to remember on values is:

A person is either rich or poor not by what they have, but who they are.

I often hear many disgruntled people, who blame society for their short comings, state that "life sucks." Life doesn't suck. If anything, the person who chose to make that statement obviously sucks. Isn't it their life that's falling apart? The reason that life isn't working for them, is because they're not working for life.

Our purpose in life is to contribute to the beauty of

creation and allow what we sow to be the harvest of our efforts. We are fortunate to live in a country that provides us with more than we need in order to prosper. If you really think about it, our cups runith over. All we need do is use that marvelous brain we have between our ears and learn to think! Thinking is a skill that requires effort. A little effort can often provide huge returns. For example, a little each day will create a bundle of hay. It has been said that the brain is like an undiscovered gold mine and you own one clear and free. All you have to do is make it work. Now don't get thinking mixed up with remembering. Thinking requires an active use of the mind. It involves creating new thoughts that you have never created before. Remembering requires dwelling on old ineffective methods that we diligently rely on when trouble hits. As a result, we repeat the same old actions and become ever more dissatisfied with our lives, events and the people around us. We then blame life for our inability to create new thoughts and to learn new ways of living.

In order to significantly improve our lives we need to stop complaining and start doing. In other words, stop cursing the darkness when you can use your hidden energy to light a candle of power. It's not what's happening to us that creates our problems and frustrations, it's our inability to act and the lack of effort we put out that's necessary to get us up to do something about them. When you do nothing in life but ride off the backs of others, it is difficult to nourish your inner spirit, for you have done nothing to earn praise. Billy Preston, a musician, who wrote and sang one of his hit tunes back in the '70s titled "Nothin' From Nothin' Leaves Nothing", epitomizes what our lives can become if we don't assume responsibility for who we are and how we behave.

We can become all things if we believe in ourselves. Even though we have no choice about being thrust into this world, the manner in which we live and what we become is the result of the choices we do have. Because of the reality of this essential freedom, we must accept the responsibility for directing our lives. However, it is possible to avoid this reality by making excuses for what and whom we are becoming. We need to get over the assumption that something or somebody else is responsible for who we are and what we have become or we'll go nowhere. This is called the "bad faith" syndrome and refers to the falsehood of not accepting personal responsibility. Examples of "bad faith" statements are found in blaming such as, "I'm this way because I grew up in an alcoholic family" or "I was an abused child" or "I'm that way because my parents molested me when I was a child."

There are many such statements that people get hung-up on which tends to put them in a holding or destructive pattern for years. These people play the victim role throughout life, squandering their spiritual and mental powers on invalid claims of helplessness and hopelessness. Instead of utilizing their thinking abilities in times of trouble, they give up their powers to drugs, alcohol, gluttony, medication, hospitalization, jail, dysfunctional relationships and eventually mental institutions. In severe cases of desperation, many will even turn to crime and violence, while some resign to suicide instead of going to the one thing that can help them the most; their fabulous human minds.

The human brain is what you use to think with, not to sink with. Drugs and alcohol are not viable means to a successful end unless you're looking to create a dead end.

We need to allow ourselves to break out of this destructive mode by realizing that we are the creator of all our experiences. This acceptance of responsibility puts us back in control of our lives. Although these negative and destructive forces do have some influence over our lives, we are still left with the *responsibility* to make better *choices* to straighten them out. We can re-create our lives by using the following *"Qualitative Recreation Lifestyle Principles."*

Discovery 6

Qualitative Recreation Lifestyle Principles - Defined & Applied

Principles are the biological *laws* of nature that must be mirrored if we as spiritual beings are to reach our highest *human* potential.

Oliver Rhodes

To the extent of our knowledge, we are the greatest creatures that have ever walked the face of this planet. We have abilities beyond our wildest dreams but many of us dare not explore them. We all know the vast resources of the human mind and what it can do. However, many of us will not explore its potential because for some of us, our preoccupation with what we *can't* do tends to interfere with what we *can* do. So, we do nothing more than we have to.

The shunning of our powers doesn't serve the world or our purpose in life. And in order to reach our full potential, we must be aware of that power and its potential. You see, there are three forces of power that structure all of nature. They are the *creative force*, *maintenance force* and the *destructive force*. In all of nature these three forces of power are operating flawlessly in plants, animals and human beings. For example, when trees are operating in the *creative force*, they produce fruit. This fruit remains on the tree during the *maintenance force* for several weeks or so until the fruit falls to the ground and rots, thus completing the final *force of destruction*.

Although we human beings evolve through these same three forces, we tend to refer to this process as birth, growth and then death. Ironically, as we go through this evolution of life, the trillions of cell in our bodies are going through their own. However, since the life span of our cells is much shorter than the life span of the whole body, the cells must continuously "re-create" themselves to keep us alive! And if for some reason we acquire poor health through careless and destructive behaviors, it only seems appropriate that we heal ourselves through the process of "re-creation."

As a result of this universal evolution, it is obvious to see that "Re-creation" is the single most important factor towards renewing ourselves and developing a state of health that goes far beyond the absence of an illness. What's so unique about being human is that we are the only living beings that can choose which of these three forces will govern our lives. Therefore, the power to change can be as easy as understanding how these three power forces of life operate.

Here is how you can tell which power force of life you are currently operating in. If your life is one that demonstrates peace of mind, happiness, self-confidence, healthy coping and social skills, you are operating in the *creative force.* If you are living without a purpose or meaning and not making any advances towards improving your life, you are operating in the *maintenance force*. On the other hand, If you're involved in excessive drug and alcohol use, smoking cigarettes, crime, violence, gang activity, lying, cheating, stealing, reckless driving or eating in excess, you are operating in the *destructive force.*

The concepts of *Qualitative Recreation Lifestyle Principles* are health promoting activities that provide each one of us the ability to become whole. We renew and recreate ourselves from the inside out by learning from both our positive and negative experiences. For happiness is an inside job. The ideal situation for optimum growth and prosperity would be to learn from our mistakes and not repeat them. While at the same time we should be accentuating the positive and thrive on our successes.

In October 1986, I worked as a recreation therapist in a local hospital in Poway, California. My primary function was to provide patients (recovering from eating disorders, mental illness, depression, drug abuse and alcohol addiction) with recreational counseling, leisure education, and lifestyle management training. The plan was to help patients develop healthier ways to utilize their free time and assist them in locating recreational community resources. My passion for getting people excited about taking better care of their health inspired me to come up with developing *Qualitative Recreation Lifestyle Principles (QRLP).* I call these principles: *"Standards for Successful Living."*

Many of these individuals I worked with were not aware of the community resources available to them. Almost all of them had no meaning of the word *"re-creation."* It's not hard to understand why many people tend to abuse drugs and alcohol. Obviously, it's the immediate gratification (a pay off) that their drug of choice provided, and to fulfill a basic need to experience pleasure. Addiction is at root a spiritual concern because it represents a misdirected attempt to achieve wholeness, to experience inner completeness and satisfaction.

Why do we think we need something to make us feel content: Another slice of pizza, a piece of chocolate, a cigarette, a drink, a snort, a lover, another possession? Is there a way to feel complete and whole in ourselves without reaching for an external source of satisfaction? If people do not find immediate gratification in one thing they will find it in another. For example, a cigarette addict who stops smoking and becomes an exercise addict is no less an addict but is a much healthier one. This is why we should focus on adopting *Standards for Successful Living.*

These "Principles" serve as guidelines for making healthy lifestyle choices. As we organize our lives according to these biological laws of nature, we acquire the ability to overcome those negative addictions that may be stopping us from living our dreams.

If you have struggled with other methods for finding true happiness with minimal success, I strongly encourage you to relinquish your old ways and incorporate these new standards into your life. You will be amazed at how magical your life will become. It doesn't matter what your current medical or living conditions may be at this time. All one has to do is "spread their wings." In doing so, there is only one possible direction you can go and that's up and onward to a higher level of happiness. This common sense lifestyle process can work wonders for anyone.

Without a doubt, all human beings have been endowed at birth—like uncut diamonds— with shining qualities beneath a rough exterior.

Each of these four words (Qualitative, Recreation, Lifestyle, Principles) covers the basics for successful living. Also, they each contain their own separate definition, and amazingly they are all part of the whole process for success. You can't work one without the other. In essence, the heart of this process is *Recreation* and *Lifestyle.* The body is *Quality* and *Principles.* Therefore, the *Conduct* of our *Recreation* and *Lifestyle* must be governed by *Excellence* and *Integrity* (See Figure 6.1). Read and study the following *Standards for Successful Living* and discover your true potential.

Standards for Successful Living

Quality	A Standard for Excellence
Recreation	A Restoration to Health
Lifestyle	A Process of Balance
Principles	A Code of Conduct: Integrity, Harmony, Conformity

Since Recreation and Lifestyle are the heart and soul of our existence, our highest human potential can only be ignited by excellence and integrity! This results in establishing a Recreation Lifestyle Attitude.

Figure 6.1

Quality - A Standard for Excellence

First and foremost, our lifestyles and the recreational activities we engage in should be *qualitative.* Quality means following standards for excellence. In order to establish and maintain optimum health and well being we must go to any lengths to assure our lifestyles are meeting those standards for excellence. It is imperative that we understand that what we do during our free time is directly related to the quality of life. When we are at work, our time is pretty much occupied. Therefore, it is our free time that will determine if we live our lives at ease or dis-ease. We should always make it a point to associate with quality people, participate in fulfilling work, and provide some form of outstanding service to our community. Allow yourself to soar with eagles and avoid scratching with turkeys. Make sure that the people you do associate with are motivated and maintain high morals and personal respect. Irrespective of the environment you were thrust into upon birth, never allow anyone to influence your behavior to be less than excellent. Granted, there will be times your surroundings will have negative influences on your behavior, but you are still left with the choice to select quality over mediocrity.

Qualitative recreation is a means to a successful end. There is a misnomer associated with recreation that needs to be clarified. Many people in our society refer to drugs and alcohol as being recreational when in fact nothing can be further from the truth. Affixing drugs and alcohol to recreation as in recreational drugs is an oxymoron or euphemism and does not represent *quality* in the least. Drugs and alcohol are not re-creational! But in many situations they often cause the *"wreck"* in *"creation"* when these chemicals are consumed in conjunction with our activities.

Drug and alcohol use and abuse are what I call debilitating. If anything, these drugs are potentially harmful to our physical, psychological and spiritual well-being when used excessively, and in some cases harmful if they are used at all. *Quality* must go into our projects if we expect to receive excellent returns.

The values that we place on ourselves and the activities we engage in are directly related to the enhancement of mind, body and spirit. With quality, we gain control over our lives which can help us function at our highest human potential. The power to choose constructive ways to enjoy our free time originates from an inner awareness of love and passion. We *re-create* ourselves from the inside out through the knowledge that all of nature's growth stems from inner nourishment. Any attempts to find gratification outside the self is usually short lived and become a never ending quest for fulfillment. If our reliance and importance lie outside the body, we may develop a dependence on those objects and lose touch with the perfection of the inner self and the *quality* there within. It's basically okay and only normal to long for outside stimulants that are in the form of objects, people, things, foods, and financial wealth. The important thing about what we allow into our lives is that they should be of a qualitative nature.

Becoming rigidly dependent on outside stimulants will cause us to lose sight of who we are and our true nature. Quality is a way of maintaining a *state of equilibrium* so that we don't jeopardize the beauty of our lives by overindulging in one particular substance. In other words, even too much of a good thing can cause problems. Therefore, quality not only means enjoying the best in life, but also knowing when you've had enough. *Standards for excellence* provide for the regulation of stimulants so we do not become overwhelmed by any one substance.

Recreation - A Restoration of Health

Recreation as a whole is not only an activity, it is that incredible feeling of well-being one receives as a result of actively participating in health promoting activities. The power of recreation and the art of play are so unique, they are by far major factors towards helping people enjoy their lives to the fullest. This spontaneous and creative play helps us become more productive in everything that we do. It is also responsible for enhancing emotional strength, stress management and effective tension relief. If you look at some of the healthiest and most successful people in the world, you'll find that they are totally absorbed in some form of recreational activity on a regular basis. As a result, their personal, social and work relationships become more *salubrious* (conducive to producing optimum well-being) as opposed to *lugubrious* (conducive to causing doom and gloom).

To fully understand the awesome power of re-creation, I have provided you with its true meaning once again. Webster's New Collegiate Dictionary defines recreation as: "the refreshment of strength and spirit." In its original Latin form, the word meant *"the restoration of health."* Recreation is time out from the routine of our daily affairs. Play keeps us from getting stale and gives us the opportunity to discover our true selves. The *"Power of Play,"* as the following poem explicitly addresses, gratifies the importance of play, and why we should play all the days of our natural lives.

A Poem to Remember

The Power of Play

If we can all work and live in a stressful world,
plus make some time for play,
We can enhance our health and improve our
lives in a very special way.
Play is essential and has great potential, for
mind and body restoration,
For the holistic way, is work, rest and play,
Now, that's the ultimate health care combination.
When we're at play, we're also at-ease, and our
lives become a breeze.

For it is that ease, that lowers our stress, and correspondingly prevents dis-ease.
Suffering from poor health, is not a quest, or even a valid decree,
It's a consequence, of behavioral trends, due to gluttony and inactivity.
If it's sound mind and body you want, plus a great physique you seek,
Then the art of play and the power of recreation are unique to reaching your peak.
Now hard-core exercise and strict discipline may not always be the way,
For if you want true fun, and enjoy excellent health, I suggest you learn how to play.
There are many things that you can do, to keep your interests high,
For if you do, you will learn too, that good health will not pass you by.
Remember the rhyme "an apple a day, will help keep the doctor away,"
Well, it's more than our food, that keeps us in tune, it's the joy of rec and play.
We are unique and marvelous human beings, with the power and the means,
To create excellent health within ourselves, and go beyond those outside extremes.
We have a run on physicians, that keep us in transition, plus pharmaceuticals of every type.
Let's take back our good health, by improving our lives, and forget about all the medical hype.
These conglomerates say they often mean well, but why does our health continue to fail?
We sacrifice our souls without reservation, to an industry for profit that has no limitation.
They peddle their elixirs, that have made them so wealthy,
All due to our irresponsibility, for not living

as healthy.
And if you have money, and don't take time
for play,
You may find yourself without health or wealth,
some dreadful day.
But if by virtue you maintain your wealth, it
doesn't necessarily mean you'll retain your health.
Because as you get old, you begin to fold, just
like that money we intensely hold.
But if that's okay, you'll be able to pay for a room
With a phone in some cold and lonely nursing
home.
But I don't think that's what you really want to do,
Or wait for the medical establishment to come
to your rescue.
So, come out of the darkness, and see what's
for real,
Don't sacrifice your good health, for some
outrageous hospital bill.
Get into play and sound recreation, and don't
fall victim to unnecessary hospitalization.
We are special human beings in each and
every way,
Let's learn to take better care of our health,
beginning with today.
People who play are totally healthy, and don't do
it for a specific goal,
They play for fun, and don't wait around, for
dis-ease to take its deadly toll.
You can be a calorie counter or join a gym,
Where you work your buns off with hopes on
getting slim.
But why go through all this work, stress, strain
and hustle,
Just to take off a little weight and put on
little muscle.
When all you should do is play, not work, it's

simply much better for you.
And if you think that play is not for real, you're
missing out on a real deal.
For if you want proof, of its zeal, just check out
those guys and gals with the real sex appeal.
They're the ones that play, each and everyday,
And it's their play that keeps their boredom away.
Their play is real, and filled with passion,
And they earn great pleasure plus high
satisfaction.
For it's fun done that's bold, with no direct goal,
But to enhance their mind, body and soul.
So, create balance in your life, each and
everyday,
With fun and excitement in a very special way,
And, be good to yourself, and reap that good
health,
It's the fountain of youth, it's "The Power of Play."

Those who reap good health always make a habit of participating in their *"labor of love."* That's the unique thing about play. It's not a *"have to,"* it's a *"want to."*

Recreation is an attitude that teaches all people how to live and achieve fuller, happier and more harmonious lives. A positive attitude towards life is a prerequisite for physical, mental, emotional and spiritual well-being. Therefore, recreation takes into account the whole person. For example, the condition of any one element of your health directly affects the health of the other elements as well as the personality as a whole. To draw an analogy—a fine tuned automobile runs smoothly because of the quality of its individual parts and because of the precise fashion in which the parts fit and work together. Up to this point you should have a better understanding of the importance of making your lifestyle qualitative and recreational. The power of this process can be further illustrated by correlating quality and recreation with lifestyle. Therefore, a healthy lifestyle requires balance.

Lifestyle - A Process of Balance

Although it is important that what we do is of a *qualitative* and *re-creational* nature, we must also make sure that the ways in which we live our lives are in accordance with the biological laws of nature itself. This requires finding balance in our everyday living. For example, it would be inappropriate to put on your Sunday best to play slow-pitch softball. Or at the opposite end of the stick, you wouldn't want to wear cutoffs and a T-shirt to an interview for an Administrative Assistant position. In other words, your dress should fit the occasion just as sound eating habits should complement an active "fun first fitness" program. There are some people who exercise, eat well and take vitamin supplements, but on occasions they tend to drink excessively, drive recklessly and smoke cigarettes. This is an example of people who are not living totally within the biological laws of nature. Another example of lifestyle sabotage is how people in a Twelve Step program continue to use mind-mood altering chemicals such as cigarettes, coffee, and over the counter medication. This behavior is not in accordance with an optimal recovery program. Sobriety means to abstain from all mind-mood altering chemicals even the soft addictive ones.

Sometimes soft addictions can be our worst enemy because of the gross misconception that they are somewhat safe. On the contrary, they can be deadly. If one should over indulge in these soft chemicals they can possibly cause as many problems than if they had not stopped using drugs at all. This becomes another form of denial and addiction that goes unnoticed because it is widely accepted by the recovering community. Even though it is accepted, the damage continues to go unnoticed and those who are being affected by this behavior are basically living under the hypnosis of societal conditioning.

It is my understanding that a drug free lifestyle should not include unhealthy risk factors such as smoking cigarettes, excessive coffee, taking addictive medication or consuming large amounts of sugar. It does not matter what rationale or justification one gives this behavior. If it violates the biological laws of nature, it is not conducive to good health and optimum recovery.

A *Qualitative Recreation Lifestyle* is characterized by being true to thyself in every aspect of living. Knowing and understanding that our human bodies were designed to function at its best on a wholesome, well-balanced diet are the basis for optimum well-being. This would include such foods as fruits, vegetables, grains, pastas, whole grain breads, fruit and vegetable juices, plenty of water, moderate amounts of meat and occasional servings of some dairy products.

Many people in drug and alcohol programs maintain some of the worst eating and living habits. Although they may have discontinued their drug of choice, they are far from optimum health and total recovery. Therefore, to establish and maintain optimum recovery in all that you do, you must understand that it is not what you do, but how you do what you do. Optimum health results from following a *Qualitative Recreative Lifestyle.*

Now that we are aware of how *quality, recreation* and *lifestyle* pertain to total well-being, it is time to explore the final phase of this unique process which are *principles.*

Principles - Code of Conduct

To reach our full potential we must apply these *principles* and make them a part of our *lifestyle.* Up to this point, we now understand the meaning of quality, recreation and lifestyle, but without following certain principles we cannot complete the formula for optimum health, wealth and happiness. *Principles* are basically a *"code of conduct"* that allow us to exercise and perform our daily activities with three very important rules for acquiring a Re-creation Lifestyle Attitude:

Integrity • *Harmony* • *Conformity*

First, let's look at *integrity* and how it relates to *Q.R.L.* We can live our lives following all the right wellness guidelines, but if we are not true to ourselves, how can we be true to others and vice versa? Integrity carries with it a sense of unity within self as well as everyone that you meet. Individuals who practice integrity always see themselves as an extension of the universe and everything that's in it. Therefore, in order to love yourself, it's important that you love life and your fellow humans. This is a sound state of mind that shows we are operating with high morals, firmness, completeness and universal conviction; thus, we are whole. For example, if you view yourself as a part of the whole and are responsible for how all the other parts are functioning within a community, you can pretty much expect for that community to thrive in healthy human relations, productivity and prosperity. This is called *oneness!*

The second important aspect of principles is *harmony*! Without harmony we as a community or society wouldn't be able to get along very well together. The reason why crime, violence, and mayhem run rampant within our communities is because of a lack of spiritual harmony. It is my belief that the reason we are all here on this great earth is to be here for each other and to interact harmoniously together as one. We are a world of diverse population.

Diversify means we should live to understand, respect and appreciate different cultures, customs and attitudes. Although we all have physical and cultural differences, it is imperative that we understand that we share one common bond. We all have the need to be recognized and appreciated for our own individuality.

Solidify means to incorporate the strengths of diversity into a power team of one. Respecting individuals' differences and being sensitive to their needs, feelings and abilities makes them feel special. In doing so, we significantly increase personal communication, human relations and productivity in all living and working environments.

Finally, there is *conformity*. This does not mean we can't become individuals. Quite the contrary—we are individuals. Conformity means to utilize our own individuality to enrich and share with the world our skills and talents. It means contributing to the world instead of expecting life to give to us.

Life gives you exactly what you give it. If you bargain for a penny, life will return to you a penny. This is called the laws of cause and effect. Whatever *effect* is happening in your life at this time comes directly from your *cause*. Trying to get something from life without giving of yourself is like that man sitting in front of the fireplace asking for heat without first putting in the wood. Remember it doesn't work that way. Before we can enjoy all the fruits of life we must first understand that we must work the fields of life before we can reap the harvest of optimum health, wealth and happiness.

Constructive and productive codes of conduct suggest that we must all strive to live together as one. Never in the history of the world have we human beings been so interdependent. We practically can't live without each other. And contrary to what many of us may believe, we are all connected. Just as we may perceive a rock as solid matter, it is mostly empty space with forces of energy flowing around its molecules. And it is the same way with humans. If the forces of energy that flow between human beings are negative, it is very likely that our social interactions will be less than favorable, possibly hostile or even violent. On the other hand, our relationships, health and lives can become magical, if we see ourselves as one. As you can see, principles require a vast amount of responsibility. And if we all share this responsibility for creating peace and harmony, the world will be a much better place for us all. Think of principles as your way of exercising your new found skills in healthy living. When interacting with others, make sure you leave them with fond memories of yourself. Remember, the way people treat you is a representation of who you are. When you point the finger watch the hand that's doing the pointing and I guarantee you'll see three fingers pointing right back at you.

Qualitative Recreation Lifestyle Principles Illustrated

The key to overcoming dis-ease, addictions, mental illness, negative thinking, depression, poor social skills, anger, stress, fear and procrastination is quite simple. Although institutions predicated on profitability would have you think otherwise. The human body is a magnificent machine and has the ability to heal itself if only we would give it what it needs to compensate for the demand that we place on it. Most of the responsibility rests with your ability to incorporate *QRLP* into your life. Now, if you are accustomed to allowing your body to become run down and then look to the medical profession for fast relief, it may take you some time getting used to the snail's pace of natural healing.

Doctors want your business and don't mind if you visit their office as often as possible. Even though they may provide some clues to your illness and give you a psychological boost, they're only telling you what your body has been telling you for years. Your own body can provide for itself. That's right! Your body talks to you but the question is are you listening? If you don't take orders from your body when it talks to you, you will eventually start taking orders from your doctor. Bottom line, you're going to get your orders from somewhere. Doesn't it make sense to take those orders from the primary source that can put you back on course?

We human beings are equipped with one of the most reliable test labs known to science—our minds and our marvelous bodies! When you go see a doctor for an examination, she or he sends you to a lab to go through a series of tests and then they provide you with the results of those tests. If you are in tune with your body, it can provide you with similar tests and more than likely, better and more accurate results.

You see, much has been said and written about what constitutes optimum health and overall well-being. What we hear at times is so contradictory we don't know who to believe or who to turn to. It doesn't necessarily take a Ph.D., therapist, counselor, or registered dietitian to help us understand the dynamics of optimum health. All it takes is for you to become aware of the connection between mind and body and how they apply to the concepts of Qualitative Recreation Lifestyle Principles. Anyone can improve their health by *doing* good things for their mind and body. It doesn't matter where you are on the health continuum. The important thing is that you make your way up that continuum by practicing *QRLPs*. There's only one direction for your health to go when you start to practice healthy eating and living habits and that's upward. Taking medication may be okay at the onset of a disease, but you should wean yourself off medication as soon as your practice of healthier living habits "kick in" as they say in the medical profession.

Since June of 1986, I have worked in six hospitals and treatment centers. During that time I have found that many people think that it is other people or some other situation out in the environment that is responsible for their conditions. Some of the mental handicaps that plague highly capable individuals from moving out of their "accustom zone" is what I call the "bad faith" syndrome. In other words, people basically play the blame game. They point the finger at everything and everybody but themselves and say that it's the breaks or the circumstances. This is the method that the ignorant use in an attempt to excuse themselves. Many of the excuses you hear go like this: "I was an abused child," or "I grew up in an alcoholic family," or "my parents molested me." Many people blame their lack of responsibility on differences in ethnicity, being physically disabled, being too short, too tall, too fat, too black, or too white. If we believe that something in the environment, or some condition we were born with is reason for not living to our full potential, how do we account for the thousands of people who are living productive lifestyles in spite of their disabilities? The only difference between people who are successful and happy and those who are not, is how they think. You are what you think and if your thinking is stinking, you're going to experience the result of your thoughts.

Thinking that life outside of us pretty much determines our health and destiny *could* render us "powerless." Nothing could be farther from the truth. Instead of taking personal responsibility, we'd find ourselves operating from the wrong end of the stick. We have to wake up from this hypnosis and face the fact that much of our health, happiness and personal power is an inside job. Granted there are certain factors that contribute to our situation. However, it is still up to us to make things better by taking positive action. We must work through the difficult times and control the things that we can control and not sweat the things that we can't.

The redeeming benefits that result from our taking action provide us with the opportunities to grow, develop and prosper. *QRLP* is a way of life that enhances every aspect of our well-being. The most exciting thing about following these principles is that they're challenging, enjoyable, fun and exciting. This unique process gives us a purpose in life and a joy for living. Qualitative Recreation Lifestyle Principles have been proven to be very effective in any setting, situation or circumstance.

Since most human beings would prefer to live a life of optimum health and vitality, *Principles* have no boundaries when applied to anyone's current physical, emotional, psychological or spiritual condition. Qualitative Recreation Lifestyle Principles are basically Health Promoting Activities (HPA) that when applied to one's life produce Desirable

Lifestyle Values (DLV). These values are non-material qualities that are directly responsible for the enhancement of mind, body and spirit. Developing DLVs through HPAs is the granddaddy of all methods towards enriching our lives and enhancing the human spirit (Figure 6.2). Health Promoting Activities (Figure 6.3) are within your circle of influence. The process of acquiring these valuable qualities rests with each and every individual. Initiate steps towards exploring these activities and incorporating them into your lifestyle. These activities are also known as healthy habits. Your main interest should be based upon enjoyment, challenge and fun. It is not important what activities you participate in, as long as it's something you enjoy doing. Again, we "re-create" ourselves through our projects.

Just check out the list of QRLPs listed in Figure 6.3. These are just a few of the vast numbers of projects that one can indulge in towards enhancing mind, body and spirit. Health promoting activities are tasks, games, projects, challenges, work, skills, crafts, play, assignments, duties or chores that one participates in that provide redeeming values. Every time you take part in HPAs you are nourishing and building the superstructure of your inner self. You are creating *personal power* every time you read a book, complete a course, pass an exam, wash your car, make the team, fulfill a worthy goal, create a work of art or enter a race and finish. It doesn't matter whether you win or lose, or always come out on top. All that matters is that you allow yourself to participate. Perfection and excellence come with repetition. One of Dr. Martin Luther King's most prominent statements was, "If you can't be the tallest pine on the mountain peak, be the best little shrub in the valley."

The feeling of well-being and optimum health that one receives can only be accomplished through the joy and efforts we put into our projects. These rewards that build inner strength are new to no one. For example, think of a time or situation in your life where you performed at your best, where you received positive recognition for a job or

Desirable Lifestyle Values

(Process Oriented)

Qualitative Recreation Lifestyle Principles (QRLP) are captivating Health Promoting Activities (HPA). Active participation in these principles results in the production of Desirable Lifestyle Values (DLV). Values are non-material qualities that are conducive to the enhancement of **mind, body,** and **spirit**. Enhancement of your inner spirit leads to optimum health, happiness and well-being as indicated by the arrows leading out from your center creating lifelong Values.

Figure 6.2

Qualitative Recreation Lifestyle Principles

Excellent Health is a product of being totally involved in some form of specific behavior that is positive, active, stimulating and challenging and should be the rewards of our passion for living an active fun-filled lifestyle.

1. Athletics
2. Sports
3. Sound Eating
4. Photography
5. Employment
6. Arts
7. Education
8. Hobbies
9. Creative Writing
10. Table Games
11. Music Lessons
12. Sight Seeing
13. Volunteering
14. Reading
15. Languages
16. Crafts
17. Pets
18. Socializing
19. Worshipping
20. Fitness Walking
21. Nutritional Cooking
22. Travel
23. Public Speaking
24. Wilderness Ventures
25. Aquatics
26. Flying
27. Mall Walking
28. Meditation
29. Public Service
30. Bungie Jumping
31. Creative Imagery
32. Skiing
33. Horticulture
34. Singing lessons
35. Mountain Climbing
36. Working With Children
37. Writing Poetry
38. Teaching
39. Law Enforcement
40. Running For Public Office

We do not deliberately or directly set out to develop poor health. Poor health is a consequence which results from poor behavior. By the same laws of cause and effect, acquiring better health should not come as the result of strenuous effort or strict discipline. It should be the rewards of our passion for following QRLP!

Figure 6.3

project you did well. Do you remember the feeling? Wasn't that feeling incredible? The rewards we receive for our personal and team accomplishments are called strokes. If these strokes are positive and received often enough, they can become overwhelming to the point where we'll strive to produce them over and over again through our work, play and relationships.

This positive reinforcement perpetuates our ability to act more in the direction of setting future goals. The more we do, the more we become in touch with our inner strengths and abilities. It is similar to having a sports car that's built for speed. You know the car possesses speed and power, but the only way we can find out what it can actually do and be absolutely sure of its potential is by regularly putting it to the test. You drive that baby!

The true nature of human beings is that we are all pure potentiality. If we human beings don't test our potential through our activities, we may have difficulty discovering our true nature, skills and talents. Life experiences, whether good, bad, right or wrong, help us bridge the gaps from being nobody to becoming somebody, no potential to high potential, and destruction to construction. This is progressive learning through the process of trial and error. If you aspire to develop high levels of *self-esteem* and *self confidence* it is necessary that you allow yourself to shine! Self-esteem and self-confidence are two of the most important *desirable lifestyle values (DLV)* and are essential for optimum mental, spiritual and emotional health.

It is important to remember that every time we test our potential, it doesn't necessarily mean we're going to be successful the first time around. The successes of accomplishing our goals are the collective efforts of our attempts. In other words, each attempt we make towards accomplishing our goals brings us one step closer. So remember that there are no failures in doing, only failing to do. If we misfire, we re-load and fire again. We fire as many times as necessary until we hit the target. With this in mind, we should not give up on ourselves because every step we take — whether it is a hit or miss — gives us the physical strength and mental power to succeed further. This is called "*sharpening the saw.*" Some people mistake the disappointment of not hitting the target the first time around as failure. This is not failure, it is learning. Although misfires happen quite often, we sometimes have to experience the little failures before we can tackle the big ones. Failing is a part of growing. You can't grow if you don't recover from your fall.

Part of being truly happy, healthy and wealthy is learning how to recover successfully from our experiences. Again, it doesn't matter whether they are good, bad, right or wrong as long as you come out of your corner swinging again after suffering a grueling bout with life. Successful people in life are the one's that come back out swinging. They consider learning from their failures to be more productive than throwing in the towel after a few mishaps.

Gradual learning experiences of becoming successful are the most effective means of developing lifelong values. People who are successful in just about everything that they do know that: "if at first you don't succeed, try, try again."

We human beings have potential beyond our wildest dreams. Many of us are not aware of it because we have not discovered it yet. The discovery comes from doing, working, acting or learning about ourselves and our true potential. Remember, we humans are pure potentiality seeking manifestation and more. This goes back to the analogy of the high speed sports car that has to be test driven again and again before we know its full potential. This goes for you and everything else in life.

Tapping into Your Full Potential

How do we tap into our full potential. First, let's establish that we are highly effective beings with powers to spare.

Remember this statement from *Discovery 4?* "If you can breathe you have potential. If you can breathe you can achieve. If you can breathe you are alive, and only the dearly departed are without potential." Consequently, there is no such thing as the living dead unless it's in your head. Your ability to breathe means you can think, feel, act and respond. If you can do these four simple human tasks, there should be no doubt in your mind about your ability to significantly enhance your life, health and overall well-being. What are your strengths? Everyone has the ability to perform these four simple human tasks of thinking, feeling, acting and responding.

Tapping into your full potential is about using the tools that you have and not worrying about what you don't have. It's about what you can do, not what you can't do. It's about moving forward and not backwards. It's about looking ahead as you drive the bus and not look to the rear for this would be an awfully dangerous practice. Unfortunately, many people in our society overwhelmingly practice looking back.

Quite often, we are encouraged to look back over the road from which we have come by the psychotherapy and psychiatry profession. We are told by these professionals that we need to go over the past to find clues to our present dysfunctional behavior so they can be resolved. In my experience working with individuals who are having difficulties resolving their problems, I find that many are totally absorbed in issues that have already happened. Instead of focusing on actions that can help them move forward in their lives today, they squander valuable time looking to the rear. I personally and professionally see reviewing past events as a "hind-rance."

Many appear to be stuck as if they were lost in a fog trying to find their way when all they have to do is open their eyes. The profitability in looking back is staggering and people who are searching to find themselves by exploring their past have spawned a multi-billion dollar industry that cater to those who are trying to make sense of their lives. The reason for looking back may be okay to prevent a person from repeating an unpleasant experience, but often we spend *too* much time exploring the past and not enough energy exploring our present.

It has been estimated that a person spends between two to five years in therapy before they recover from traumatic past experiences. Considering the time factor involved, that's a lot of time, energy and money. Is it really that necessary for a person to sift through their "garbage" to find answers when all one has to do is to process their past issues, learn from them then, forgive, forget and then move on.

While examining your past "garbage" you may want to be careful just how deep you dig, because you just might find something that smells worse than what prompted you to dig in the first place. Do you really have time for all the superfluous pain and aggravation?

Like any lesson in life, the past is a review not a major study. The only thing major about the past is profit, and often it is the institutions that stand to gain more than the clients. If it were in your best interest, you'd be the one driving around in the Mercedes instead of the doctors, psychologist, lawyers, psychiatrists and administrators.

These facts are evident based on a 75%+ recidivism rate in hospitals, jails, recovery homes, treatment centers and mental institutions. Our wealth, health and prosperity rest in the present. Accordingly, it is working with our present that significantly defines our future. Now refer back to Figures 6.2 and 6.3 as I take you through the magic of developing those *desirable lifestyle values (DLV)* and true happiness.

We are all Recovering From One Thing or Another, and Some More Than Others

It's not important whether you are skilled in any one activity. Your skills will develop as a result of the "*practice*" you put into your activities. Since practice is the mother of skill, you'll be well on you way to a life of enjoyment and magic. As a Play Specialist, I often hear many people state that the reason they don't play is that they don't want to look foolish or make mistakes. But mistakes are how we learn during practice.

If practice is the mother that gives birth to our skills, then looking foolish and making mistakes is early morning sickness. Early morning sickness would be nice to avoid, but without it you can't give birth to excellence. No matter how hard you try to avoid it, if you want to dance to his music, you must pay the piper!

QRLP is an open process that leads to an infinite number of values that you acquire as you continue to participate in activities that nurture the soul. In doing so, you live in accordance with nature instead of violating the laws of spiritual health. When you are living from the inside out such as in *QRLP*, your whole perspective on life becomes a *process-oriented* experience where much of how you think and feel is self-directed instead of object-directed. You become totally aware of the perfection of the inner self and the infinite possibilities that are available to you. You don't completely give in to outside stimulants, and you don't become consumed by the lure of drugs, alcohol, mass amounts of medication, or other stimulants that tend to rob your mind and body of its power. The important thing to remember is that these values don't fall into your lap from out of nowhere. They have to be earned, and come as a result of the praise that you get from your efforts. These values are a product of your strong interest and participation in qualitative fun! Again, this goes back to the law of the universe, *cause and effect.* A farmer will not reap his crops if he does not till the fields. A miner will not discover diamonds if he does not work the mine.

It seems as if people complain all the time about how difficult it is to change or develop new behavioral habits. But what many of us fail to remember is that the day we set foot on this earth, we have been tasked with the challenge of learning new skills, and it will be that way all the days of our lives. If we don't allow ourselves to continuously learn new skills, how do we expect to continue growing? Are our learning days over? Everything we have ever attempted to accomplish throughout our lives has been acquired through this learning process. Much of what we know and have learned to this day requires some effort on our part. Why would it be any different now? Do you really think we should get off without paying our dues. Many people try that route, but usually wind up frustrated, angry and disappointed. Thousands of people take the drug, violence and crime trail and end up in jail, institutions, hospitals, recovery homes or find themselves living down and out on the streets.

We human beings have to realize that in order to experience true happiness, everyone must venture through the turnstile of life. There is no free ride. Many people recovering from their addictions moan and groan about now having to face reality and work a program. But they seem to forget that when they wanted to get high, loaded or wasted, the difficulty in acquiring drugs, alcohol or medication was no big deal. They went through hell and high water to get their drug of choice. The reason they achieved their goal was that they had a burning desire to acquire.

I know people who have gotten up in the middle of the night to get stoned on drugs, have another piece of cake or call their drug dealer to make a date. Their passion is what caused their fast action. When we want something bad enough, we can always come up with a plan. The process of following *QRLP* takes a holistic approach towards developing total well-being.

We don't lose our health all at once and we don't gain it back by doing just one thing. However, by doing a variety of life supporting activities we can pull ourselves back together again.

It never ceases to amaze me why many people refuse to provide their soul with what it needs to compensate for the demands that we place on it. More than most, it is people who are experiencing an illness that need super nutrition, fun first fitness, recreation, leisure, hobbies and gainful employment. Our main objective should be total health and should not rest with just acquiring sobriety alone.

In a traditional Twelve Step program, the main focus is on sobriety. It is goal oriented. Compare *QRLP's* approach to optimum health (Figure 6.2), to the Twelve Steps program's approach to sobriety—*goal-oriented* (Figure 6.4). You will notice that *QRLP* is *process-oriented* in which sobriety is not the whole, it is a part of the whole. Because of the strong *value system* associated with this process, sobriety can be established and easily maintained when practicing and living a healthy and "holistic" lifestyle (See page 177).

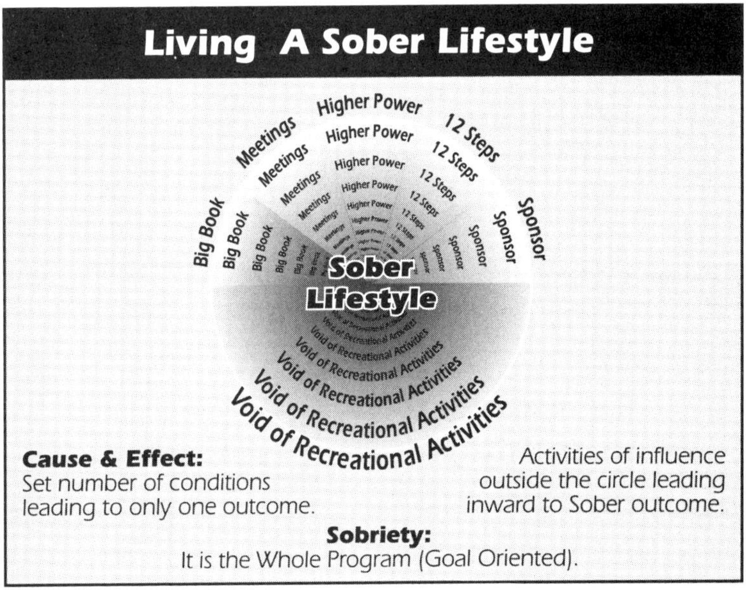

Figure 6.4

Adopting a strong value system that consists of a variety of health promoting activities that yields positive outcomes, can help develop an attitude that will not allow us to sacrifice one outcome for another.

In other words, we are not going to allow any one activity to destroy the whole; especially if our value systems are created out of self-love, respect and personal appreciation. For one activity, such as alcoholism, to progressively destroy our value system is similar to how cancer cells attack and destroy the healthy cells in our body. For example, if we over indulge in alcohol, we forsake other value systems. If done long enough, our remaining values become less important and begin to die. This is why we should maintain a *balance* in all systems outside and inside the human body.

Happiness is knowing and understanding that life is a balance between opposites of pain and pleasure, good and bad, right and wrong and hot and cold. Disrupt that balance and you create an environment for dis-ease.

Part of being happy and successful is in our ability to recover from those opposites. In order to experience warmth, we sometimes must experience a little coldness to balance the heat that occurs in our lives. I'm not suggesting that we must demonstrate being cold hearted, but that life sometimes adds a little coldness of its own. Also, too much of a good thing can cause obsessive compulsive behavior. Maintaining balance in our lives is the result of actively participating in a variety of health promoting activities. Any attempt to side step this unique and wonderful process of *re-creating* ourselves will end in frustration, anger and eventually demoralization.

It was stated earlier that we re-create ourselves through our projects. The feeling of praise and the joy of our efforts have a tremendous effect on our physical, mental, emotional and spiritual well being. Anyone can improve their health and their life by incorporating these activities into their lifestyle. Why do we have to wait until we are hospitalized, or have to be bombed with chemotherapy, or drugged to capacity before we take a *proactive* approach in preserving our health? Our society promotes and perpetuates this "hit bottom," *insane* approach to recovery. Many of us tend to blindly follow doctor's orders without question or concern for healthier alternatives.

Anytime the wants of our personality override the needs of our soul, we create an inner environment for further pain and suffering.

We develop the attitude that says, "If it's not broke, don't fix it." This is a reactive approach to health care. Often, by the time we do end up in the hospital, it's generally too late and then we find ourselves left with very few options. Some of us begin to live under the superstition of materialism and become oriented to the *medical dependent syndrome* of health care as opposed to following our own program of *health prevention.* We tend to become emotionally, physically and spiritually imprisoned by the notion that the medical equivalent of all the king's horses and all the king's men will be able to put you back together again. Remember what happen to "Humpty-Dumpty?"

When we depend too much on the medical establishment, our lives can become a wretched process of consuming multitudes of medication, stringent living conditions and chronic pain due to both dis-ease and the uncertain side effects of medication. If what we do in life is of a worthy *cause*, we will receive a worthy *effect*—total well-being.

The process of following *QRLP* and actively

participating in health promoting activities (HPA) is what creates a feeling of wholeness within self. You will often find that people who experience feelings of wholeness do not have to search for solace in objects to feel complete. They don't need or require drugs, alcohol, cigarettes, medication, therapy or counseling in order to cope. It's not that people who feel whole don't need to experience pleasure, it's just that they aren't consumed by these experiences to the point of obsession. They receive pleasure from both internal and external sources and realize that life is a balancing act between the banks of pain and pleasure. Some of the healthiest people in the world can enjoy most pleasures in life but don't get stuck in them. People who generally get stuck are those who feel lost if they are not experiencing pleasure in that one thing. People who feel whole are actively engaged in some form of re-creating activity. That feeling of well-being that comes from being totally absorbed in something positive is so exhilarating. It's unlikely that you'll allow anything to interfere with the value you place on yourself.

> ***People who do nothing in life generally have nothing to feel good about unless it comes from objects in the environment.***

So, they attempt to find wholeness in illicit and life destroying activities such as drug and alcohol abuse, crime, violence, and smoking. As a result of being stuck in this type of lifestyle, many people diligently try to justify a lifestyle of pain and misery. These are the people that end up under the care of a physician, go under the surgeon's knife, require psychiatric counseling, live in recovery homes, on the streets and in jails. They generally complain about almost everything or blame life or God for their own doings. Although happiness is within their reach, they deny that happiness and choose to believe that something or someone else is responsible for causing their problems.

The most depressing thing that I have seen during the last twelve years of working in hospitals, drug and alcohol treatment centers and mental institutions, are people who have thrown their lives away to the belief that external forces are responsible for their poor physical, mental and emotional conditions when they themselves are responsible.

Feeling that outside forces are responsible for our current health conditions is like giving up our personal power to the object of reference and feeling helpless to do anything about it. Our society perpetuates the attitude that we are powerless to act responsibly. The mind set that we cannot function without external factors is predicated on profitability. In many of my experiences working in hospitals, I continually hear patients justify why they can't free themselves from situations that are causing their pain. They do this by blaming everything and everybody but themselves. Some of the negative affirmations that many people reiterate are:

- *I don't know how*
- *It's my disease*
- *Life sucks*
- *I came from an abusive family*
- *Somebody pulled the rug out from under me*
- *It's the system*
- *My significant other won't listen to what I say*
- *I'm too old*
- *I was dealt a bad hand in life*
- *I'm afraid of the unknown*
- *I'm ugly*
- *It's too hard*
- *I was born that way (predisposition)*

- *Life's not fair*
- *My gold fish died*
- *They don't want me to succeed*

This is not to say that these are not predisposing conditions. What perpetuates many of these people's problems are that sometimes they may feel that they have little or no control over their ability to cope or to make better choices. Many are quite comfortable with where they are in life and don't want to take responsibility for making things right. Many refuse to accept the fact that they themselves are responsible for not only being where they are, but also for not doing anything about it. Many people wait around hoping someone or somebody will come into their lives and rescue them from the fate that they themselves caused. Many find that it is less difficult to deal with the painful situation when the blame is on external forces.

The people who experience these negative attitudes only find relief in the presence of those who are worse off than they are. They feel the only way to exhilarate themselves is to find someone else they can verbally or physically put down. The reason many people with such low self-esteem resort to this behavior is because they can't move up on their own merit. As a result of their choice to do nothing with their lives, they have nothing to fall back on. They fall deeper and deeper into depression and find it almost impossible to find their way out of this *cataclysmic* mind set. The reason: they have not practiced following biological laws of nature. Therefore, they have acquired no skills, talents or any redeeming values. Is it any wonder why these people are hurting? But there is always hope towards recovery from a life of hopelessness and helplessness. It's called get yourself up and get busy *practicing QRLP*.

Putting the Spark Back into Your Life

An exciting and healthy lifestyle is based on doing exciting and health promoting activities. Our society has become so relaxed and ill-responsible with stuffing medication into our bodies when we become sick, that at times we may not be aware of the perpetual damage we are causing ourselves. We make these commitments to using medication without reservation and see it as a way of life. We consume foods that poison our bodies and then take the antidotes of medication. That's what happens when we consume the wrong kinds of foods. We wind up taking antacids and other digestive aids to remedy our eating problems.

Figure 6.5

We lose touch with self and avoid the reality that poor health is a result of poor eating habits, gluttony, inactivity, negative thinking patterns and resistance to change.

Medication may provide many with some relief, but generally it tends to mask the symptoms of our behavior temporarily. However, as long as the dysfunctional behaviors persist, the damage from poor lifestyle practices can go unnoticed and could possibly result in more serious disease later in life. Diseases such as cancer, high blood pressure, psychosis, arteriosclerosis, colitis, diverticulosis, arthritis, and other degenerative diseases could possibly result from a perpetual dependency on pharmaceuticals. It is ironic that with all the technology that has been discovered to fight disease, we are still seeing a rise in sickness and death.

It appears that the more advanced we become in fighting a disease, the more diseases we have to learn to fight. Anyone with the ability to see things as they are would know that all we have to do is stop fighting the diseases and start promoting health!

It's futile to curse the darkness when all we have to do is light a candle. Now, it doesn't take a rocket scientist to understand the laws of cause and effect.

Much of our illness stems from ignorance perpetuated by the pharmaceutical establishment, fast food industry and medical practitioners such as hospitals, pharmacies, treatment centers, mental institutions and psychiatric counseling centers.

They are all competing for our insurance dollars. Your health is very precious and should be treated with care, love and respect. I am appalled when I see the astronomical amount of medication of various brands lining the store shelves with their little funny names that are supposed to make them sound scientific and appealing. This industry performs their "drug pusher" type methods on the public to impress or to entice them to buy something that their body and mind can do on its own. The mind and body are designed to heal more efficiently and can do a much better job without the help of many pharmaceuticals.

These medications are supposed to make our lives more manageable and convenient. Many of us are unaware of the connection that much of how we think and feel is directly related to what we put into our bodies. Most of our ills are a result of diseases of the intestinal track. If you keep your intestinal track clean, by eating fresh fruit, assorted vegetables, whole grains, pastas, grain breads, vegetable and fruit juices and plenty of pure drinking water, it is unlikely that you would need to take three quarters of the drugs that are available. It only makes sense that we clean the inside of our bodies just as we would clean the outside. I don't think there are very many people who would go out in the mornings without taking their daily shower. For most, the inside of the body is a lot worse than the outside. Therefore, we should at least provide our inner body with a weekly cleansing (a fruit or raw vegetable juice fast). If we cleaned the intestinal track with fasting on a regular basis, we'd very seldom experience illness, particularly ones such as the common cold. The premise that there is no cure for the common cold is a myth. The truth of the matter is that it can be cured. It's really very basic. Simply don't allow yourself to eat the kinds of foods that irritate and inflame the mucus membrane. The kinds of foods that produce this type of harmful activity are:

- *Sugar*
- *Candy*
- *Chocolates*
- *Soda Pop*
- *Rich Salad dressings*

- *Hot, spicy foods*
- *Mayonnaise*
- *Oils*
- *Alcohol*
- *Cigarettes*
- *Milk and other dairy products such as cheese, ice cream, milk shakes*
- *Meats latent with sodium nitrites, food additives, artificial colorings, waxed produce*

Although our bodies need some mucus to protect the linings of our inner skin, too much can weaken our immune system. There are many people who experience excellent health all of the time and never catch colds. We over load our body's ability to function properly when we consume too much mucus producing foods. Our system then becomes susceptible to various toxins, viruses, poisons and other types of free radicals that damage our healthy cells. Many people would be surprised to know that the taking of medication complicates the body's ability to heal itself.

When you don't clean your insides properly, plus take medication on top of it, it's similar to sweeping the dirt in your house under the rug. The dirt is still there. You forget about it, until it begins to appear as a bulge in your carpet. This is similar to the way you discover a lump in your breast.

That analogy can be compared to how tumors grow in our body. These lumps go unnoticed for years causing very little pain or complications until we get a wake up call. Ask your doctor how it works and you'll be surprised to know that the predisposition occurs when we ignore orders from our body—those internal warning signs.

The use of medication masks the warning signs that tell us when something is wrong. If you concealed your gas indicator on the dashboard of your car, you would have no way of detecting fuel expenditure. Without warning, your car engine would flutter, slow down and eventually come to a "dead" halt.

This scenario of how your car malfunctions when it's neglected is precisely what happens to you when you are experiencing a heart attack. There you are stuck on the side of the road. Our body's indicators are designed to work pretty much in the same way by telling us when something is wrong. If you don't listen to what those indicators are saying today, you'll find yourself in the same situation that you'd find your car if you ignore its' warning signs — at the service station being overhauled. The selling and promotion of the need to take medication are a scam in the sense that it is pretty much the same way people sell drugs on the streets. The major differences are that medication is government regulated and taxed. Most of the medications that we consume are unnecessary. But we are led to believe by the hype of the medical establishment that we can't live without them.

The reason why there is so much sickness, pain, suffering and death is because we are living under the hypnosis of societal conditioning and the superstition of materialism (treating the symptoms of our behavior with pills). The biggest problem is that we hand over most of our trust to doctors. Sickness is perpetuated by doctors, media, pharmaceutical companies and hospitals. The reason for this is profitability. They can't work if you don't get sick. Society promotes the attitude that it's okay to live irresponsibly, as long as doctors can provide us with a quick fix for our ills. Such statements as, "my doctor says Mylanta," is very common practice to those who choose to eat poorly.

The *junk food* industry isn't that concerned either. They work in con-*junk*-tion with the medical establishment. They get you sick and the medical establishment comes to your rescue with a pill, liquid or capsule to help you deal with the indigestion. If it gets any worse, the doctors will take over from there. And once the junk has taken its cancerous toll on your cells, surgeons don't mind cutting tumors out of your body either.

You see, many of us will go with what the medical establishment says instead of us *listening* to what our bodies are saying. Doctors go to medical school to learn medicine, not health. That's why they are called doctors of medicine. They doctor-up medicines for sick people to take. Healthy people don't need or require medication. Besides, medication has nothing to do with the healing process. The human body is a magnificent machine and has the ability to heal itself. But we must be willing to give it what it needs to compensate for the demands that we place on it.

Medicine is a practice that has many people dependent on doctors and pharmaceuticals to bail them out when poor eating habits and sedentary living weakens the immune system. It has a difficult time recovering under its own power after junking out. Granted, medications do make our lives a little more manageable, but in the process of using them, our medicine cabinets become filled to the brim with countless brands of drugs that turn our homes into mini pharmacies and many people into drug dependent junkies.

Following *QRLP* can take the medical dependency out of your life and replace it with the spark of excitement. Remember that everywhere in nature there are three forces that structure all of life — the creative force, maintenance force and the destructive force.

When we are operating in the creative force, we live in accordance with nature, producing a state of health that is positive, self-healing and stimulating. We can produce this state of health without the use of outside chemicals. This process is within our circle of influence. That is, as long as we are actively taking part in health promoting activities, we produce those desirable lifestyle values. We can produce values just like a miner mines for gold or diamonds. We can heal our lives just like a farmer farms his land. All that is needed is a passion for active participation in life sustaining projects. In doing so, we can experience the wealth and health benefits that our bodies and minds are capable of producing. If we are not willing to engage in pleasurable health promoting activities, we cannot experience true happiness that comes from diligently living in accordance with the biological laws of nature.

Similar to hard working farmers who work the fields, they know too often that "no sowing" generally means "no reaping." It is the means that justifies the ends and not the ends that justifies the means. In other words, our motivation should stem from our appreciation for who we are and what we are capable of producing. Recognizing our true nature, that we are pure potentiality, is the first step towards self-healing and happiness. When we see ourselves as the creator of all our outcomes, we develop an attitude that gives us total power over our destiny.

If we believe that objects in the environment have control over our behavior and attitude, then the power becomes a force outside our control and we become slaves to those objects and the circumstances that occur as a result.

We have talked about that outside force which takes power right out of our hands. And as long as we give those forces our power, we are always going to be slaves to these institutions. These factions that tend to have control over our lives are jails, hospitals, police, recovery homes, doctors, and the pharmaceutical establishments—one of the biggest conglomerates of them all. I have never seen such a farce in all my life. Could there be a connection with the idea that *farce* is a form of *force* related to pushing medication so heavily?

If we don't take the responsibility for living better lives, we will just continue to perpetuate the never ending research to increase drugs, surgery and elixirs. Case in point, there are now claims that a pill exists that can cure alcoholism. What brought about the need to create such a pill? The truth is in the pudding. The reason that this pill came about is due to our inability and refusal to take personal responsibility to improve our behavior. Until we develop a strong awareness of the hypnosis we are living under, we are going to continue the trend of having to rely on doctors, hospitals, mental institutions, psychiatrists and surgeons. Therefore, these institutions are always going to play the part of all the king's horses and all the king's men that will come to aid our "Humpty-Dumpty" style of living. Unfortunately in the nursery rhyme, and in many real life circumstances, they were never able to put Humpty-Dumpty back together again.

Realizing that we are responsible for our health is the first step towards freedom from pain, sickness, despair and suffering. "Suffering from poor health is not our quest or even a valid decree, It's a consequence of behavioral trends due to gluttony and inactivity." We have the power but may not be aware of its presence. Our ignorance is partly due to our belief in the medical establishment and disbelief in our ability to heal ourselves. We must allow ourselves to wake up from this hypnosis and see the reality that's causing perpetual sickness. As long as there is a profit to be made, the system will continue to work on keeping us in the dark. To a large extent, world economy is strongly dependent on a certain amount of ignorance from human beings to stay on top and keep us powerless.

The real truth is that we are not powerless. We are capable of taking back our health without the use of outside stimulants. We are resourceful, powerful and unique human beings with the power and the means to improve our good health without those outside extremes. It is not that the truly healthy people possess powers that others don't, it's just that they understand and know their true potential plus the power of self. As long as you continue to produce, act and participate in *QRLP*, you will continue to reap the valuable rewards of healthy lifestyle habits.

Recap on Qualitative Recreation Lifestyle Principles

Quality is a standard for excellence. Your life should consist of nothing but the best that's conducive to developing high morals, great taste and high spirit. By following standards for excellence, we become the best in everything we do. Qualitative standards should be our major objective when living, learning, giving, growing and loving. We also have a responsibility to the young people in our world who look up to honorable role models for guidance and understanding. The deepest craving of young people is to be just like their role models and to be liked by their peers. If we are not doing our best to be available for our young, who will? Only quality people can act as bench marks to inspire young people to develop their own standards for excellence and redeeming values.

Recreation is a restoration to health. It is not only an activity, but also an incredible feeling of well-being that comes as a result of following the biological laws of nature. We recreate ourselves through our projects by actively participating in health promoting activities. These activities should provide optimum health, fun, challenge, excitement and pleasure. Excellent health comes as a result of our passion for life and a joy for living. Through the power of recreation, we can overcome the devastating effects of disease and significantly improve our overall health and well-being beyond our wildest dreams.

Lifestyle is a process for balance and working within the biological laws of nature as an entire unit. You live your life as a whole where every aspect of your being is working harmoniously together. For example, people who practice total health would not allow anything to interfere with the value they place on themselves. Be it smoking, drinking excessively, drugs, violence, crime or dysfunctional relationships. Drugs and alcohol are not re-creational and should not be viewed as such. Finally, lifestyle means maintaining a *state of equilibrium* so that we do not over indulge in stimulating practices that could possibly jeopardize the quality of our lives. Remember, too much of a good thing can be harmful to our physical, mental and emotional well-being.

Principles are a code of conduct that allow us to exercise and perform our activities of daily living with three very important rules for a healthy lifestyle attitude; they are, integrity, harmony and conformity. It's not only what we do, but how we do what we do. In order to reach our full potential, we must apply these principles into our everyday lives. It means treating the world and everyone in it with respect, appreciation, and praise (RAP). We are all on this planet for a purpose and that is to work harmoniously together as one. In the next *Discovery* you will learn how to dissolve the *chains of addiction.*

Discovery 7

Overcoming The Dis-ease Of Addiction – What Is It Really?

It is not the disease that keeps us imprisoned; it is our mind.

Oliver Rhodes

Throughout our lives we human beings pursue, with relentless passion, the experience of pleasure through the five senses while at the same time desperately striving — with painful and strenuous effort — to minimize discomfort. *This Is Exploring And Discovering.*

We will go to any lengths to satisfy our pleasure centers even to the extent of over stimulation. In the process, some of us will use the most devastating substances with little regards to the damage we impose on our physical, mental, emotional and spiritual well-being. Today, more than ever, addiction and compulsive behavior of all kinds run rampant. Many people are concerned not only with losing control over their use of alcohol and drugs, but over food, smoking, gambling, and even shopping. But what is the nature of addiction, and how do we explain its hold over certain individuals? Smoking-related illnesses, for example, kill more than 100 people per day in Canada. Although warned of the hazards of smoking, nicotine addicts are frequently unable to kick the habit—despite numerous attempts. Or consider the alcoholic who will trade away family and career rather than quit drinking. Chocolate, exercise, coffee, work, sex, indeed *almost everything these days has been labeled as being addictive.* But when and how does a simple experience or indulgence spiral into a full-blown negative addiction?

How did we allow these casual experiences of what we used to enjoy become our masters? There are many theories suggesting that addictions and compulsive behaviors are the result of many causes. For example, in many arguments, the cause of these uncontrollable habits are so numerous that one theory strongly contradicts another. There seems to be so much confusion on the causes that very little focus is spent on the solutions. People want to get better, not research how and why they became negatively addicted.

Changing Your Behavior, Not Your Addiction

What I hope to establish throughout this book is a more appropriate expression for sobriety and addiction. The term that I think is most appropriate is *optimum recovery* instead of *sobriety*. Correspondingly, I would like to refer to *addiction* as being *"positive"* or *"negative"* because it is the prefix that we attach to the word *addiction* that tends to give it its meaning or power.

In developing optimum recovery we must first understand and realize that we are hedonistic in nature. One of our basic needs is to experience pleasure through our sensory receptors. To deny ourselves of that basic need results in frustration, anger, unhappiness and despair. There's nothing wrong with wanting to enjoy life to its fullest, except we must find health promoting experiences to satisfy our pleasure centers. Not only must we find healthy alternatives to destructive behaviors, we must also find a *balance* in the way we live our lives. We need to focus on changing our *state of mind* before we can change ourselves.

Too much emphasis is placed on changing ourselves instead of how we think. And since thought is the essence of who we are, we can change ourselves just by the way we think. We need to develop an understanding of the true meaning of addiction and what positive measures we can take to create harmony in mind and body. I refer to these measures as "three steps to recovery":

1. *Mind Set*
2. *Balance*
3. *Replace*

First, you must be willing to develop a healthy *mind set* by ridding yourself of premature cognitive commitments. In other words, relinquish your need to defend your point of view. If your ideas of how things should be have not worked for you up to this point, there's a good chance that they are not going to work any better now. Regardless of how hard you continue to try, if you are not willing to change your perspective on recovery, you'll spend much of your recovering life with anger, guilt, frustration and blame. It's the same as trying to force a square peg into a round hole. It won't go in no matter how hard you push.

Second, we have to create a *balance* in our lives when it comes to our experiences with pleasure. I'm sure you have all heard, "too much of a good thing could be destructive." That's hitting the nail right on the head. It is my belief that most addictions stem from being too far to the left or right as we go down the river of life. We get stuck on the banks of pain or pleasure and become disoriented as to how to get off. A happy medium is in developing an understanding that life is a balance between those opposites. I have found that some of the healthiest people in the world maintain their center of control by learning from each end of a continuum of pain and pleasure, good and bad, happy and sad and right and wrong. They will not allow any one side of this continuum to cause them to become *stuck* in one or the other, thus losing sight of who they are.

What makes these people so unique? They have evolved to a state of total *bliss* that allows them to bounce off the banks of pain and pleasure and will not allow themselves to be consumed in either. They are totally *centered* and will allow no one or anything to interfere with the value that they place on themselves. Happiness requires some form of material connection, but bliss is independent of external objects. Maintaining that *inner bliss* makes it easy for people to occasionally experience and "let go" of outside stimulants, dysfunctional relationships, negative thoughts and compulsive behaviors. How does one acquire bliss? Bliss is acquired by the active participation in *QRLP* and is directly responsible for helping people get in touch with the perfection of their inner self.

Once you know yourself and the beauty you possess, nothing can destroy that essence of beauty you have developed and the personal love you have nourished within yourself. Nourishment comes from giving yourself loving attention as you would give a friend, pet, plant, child or tree. Without sound nutrition, it would be difficult for anything or anyone to function at their highest level of potential. In addition, we human beings must learn to value ourselves through unconditional self-love. We must provide ourselves with challenge, fun first fitness, recreation, ongoing education, and have a specific purpose in life (volunteer work or gainful employment). Individuals who follow these principles can enjoy all the pleasures of life without giving up their souls to either extremes of pain or pleasure.

Negatively addicted people get *stuck* in one extreme or the other. As a result they must be encouraged to break free by what we know as; counseling, treatment centers, AA meetings, recovery homes, mental institutions or structured imprisonment. Positively addicted people have a unique value system that allows them to pull back after the mind, body, and soul have been nourished. They enjoy their pleasurable experiences but are not rigidly attached to those objects of reference.

The third and most important step, but probably the simplest is that we must be willing to make a conscious effort to *replace* old behaviors with fresh and rewarding behaviors.

The law of exchange states that in order for us to give up one activity or behavior for another, the new activity must provide an equal or greater payoff than the one previous. In other words, allow yourself to be open to fresh ideas and new sensory experiences until you find a replacement that's more rewarding than your last fix, but make sure that it yields healthier results.

The entire process of replacement can be summarized in the following inset on "What is Health?":

What is Health?

Health (fitness, wellness, success) is an interpretation directly proportionate to one's level of peak performance (output). In other words, it is our performance that determines our degree of health, not our health that determines our performance.

For example, many people will contest (resist, dispute) that they are too tired or don't have the energy to exercise or re-create. But being tired is a symptom of living a sedentary lifestyle (low performance) and does not excuse you from being more active. Performance is relative depending on our need to exceed our current behavior.

Only a need to exceed (improve) our current behavior (performance) will create that motivation to change, if the new behavior (activity) creates (promises) an experience of pleasure equal or greater than (supersedes) what it is we are doing now (i.e. smoking, drug use, over eating, etc.).

Change (growth) occurs only when a life-force (human being) wakes up (is inspired) to the knowledge (awareness) that change in self is possible. Only then can the noise of self-persecution (self-injury) be subdued by the excitement of self-resurrection (re-newal, re-birth, re-creation).

There are many people who are pushing against the grain by resisting to replace old behaviors. But many people are beginning to realize that there are other options—such as the case of Thelma Jones. She had tried almost everything until she met a close friend who told her about a new approach to recovery. Let's explore Thelma's victory in the pursuit of happiness and an end to pain.

Thelma's Victory Over Negative Addictions

Ten years has elapsed since Thelma was admitted to a local hospital in San Diego, CA for her drug and alcohol addiction. She had been a nurse for 15 years during which time she drank sociably and periodically smoked marijuana. To her, this behavior was no big deal. The demand from her patients, supervisor and family was a big stress factor in her life. Along with financial problems and a painful divorce, her life became even more stressful. It was all just too difficult for Thelma to handle. She began to drink more often. An easy access to the prescription medication cabinet at the nurse's station didn't make things any better. She began stealing the patient's medicine to cope with her own personal problems.

As her needs for more prescription drugs increased, so did her illicit drug and alcohol use. Thelma had become seriously addicted to prescription drugs as well as alcohol. It would take two DWI's, a broken marriage and the loss of her job before she realized she had a big problem.

After numerous Twelve Step programs and failed attempts to live a sober lifestyle, Thelma found herself destitute and hopeless. She had been in and out of many treatment programs only to relapse within four to six months each time. Tired of the same old program paradigm, Thelma took the advice of a close friend, Helen. Helen had not only been sober for the last five years but had gone beyond recovery and was now enjoying her life to the fullest. Thelma was advised by Helen to try an alternative approach to kicking the negative habits of addiction. Helen was referring to the program I developed called, *"Drug Recovery through a New Discovery."* For Thelma, this was a new approach, and she was willing to try anything.

After setting up an appointment with me over the phone, Thelma came to my office desperately seeking help with her drug and alcohol problem. As she came into the office, Thelma appeared to be emotionally drained and hung over.

Sobbing she said, "Thank you Mr. Rhodes for taking the time to speak with me about my situation."

"You're welcome. And please, call me Oliver."

Frantic with fear Thelma exclaimed, "I've tried everything but just can't seem to give up my drug use. I need to do something because, if I don't stop using, I believe I'm going to wind up just like my mother. She died of cirrhosis of the liver when I was just ten years of age."

I reassured Thelma by stating, "I understand where you're coming from. I've been there myself, and I am aware of the difficulty in trying to overcome the dis-ease of addiction."

Thelma responded, "I need to get off these chemicals because they are destroying my life. I've tried everything. I've lost my job, my family, my home, and now I feel as if I'm losing my soul and spirit. I Just don't know what to do anymore."

"Why don't you come in and sit down and let's take a look at just what things have not worked for you. Then let's *explore* what options we can take to help you find that *happy medium*.

"First of all, I would like to reassure you that there is hope. In spite of everything you've tried, there will always be options for your ills. As long as you can breathe, you have potential. As sure as there was a way in, there is definitely a way out. No door is permanently closed."

"Do you really believe there's hope for me?"

"Sure, I do. But the important thing is that you must *believe* in yourself. That's half the battle.

"You see I have a passion for what I do. And that is to get people excited about taking better care of their health and living their lives to the fullest. I've helped many people overcome chemical dependency by helping them get in touch with their true nature. That is, we are all pure potentiality."

"But what makes you think you can help me. I'm a lost cause."

"Thelma, remember what I told you about believing in yourself. In order for you to break this cycle, because that's all it is a cycle, you have to trust, not only in your counselor but most importantly, yourself."

"Okay Oliver, but I'm a difficult case. I haven't been very successful in giving up my drugs. So please bear with me, okay?"

"I'm here for you just as I have been for others before you.

"Now, getting back to whether I can help you help yourself. Remember, I have a passion for helping people, because I've been down the road of pain and despair brought on by chemical dependency. I know what it is like to suffer. I've been to hell and sifted through the ashes and I don't ever want to go there again.

"I've got over twelve years living beyond recovery and have been enjoying my life ever since. After my bout with drugs and alcohol, I vowed to help others overcome the chains of their negative addictions.

"I went back to school and graduated from San Diego State University with Honors. I have worked in several recovery homes, five hospitals and numerous residential treatment centers for adults and teens.

"Speaking, writing and lecturing on overcoming negative addictions is almost an obsession with me because it gives me pleasure knowing that I'm helping people live productive lives again.

"I'm even writing my first book titled 'Overcoming

Addictions Without a Twelve Step Conviction,' and guess what, Thelma? You're going to be in it."

"Oliver, I hear you saying things that I've never heard in recovery programs before like, beyond recovery, negative addiction and having an obsession with pleasure. What that tells me is that you're still addicted."

"That's right, Thelma. But it is a positive addiction. We all have some form of pleasure principle. You know, something we enjoy most of the time if not all of the time. It's our passion.

"Positive addictions such as skiing, biking, stamp collecting, weight training, running, beach combing, art, and other health promoting activities are good for you. I think this idea of taking someone's perceived pleasure away without a healthy tradeoff is dysfunctional in itself. What I'm saying is all you have to do to get off negative addictions is explore your options and develop healthy habits. You see, only a habit can subdue a habit.

"So what I encourage my clients to do is to develop healthier habits. You won't have to worry about the old ones. They will go out all by themselves when you find a viable *replacement*.

"The key thing to remember is "COMPENSATION." Most people give up old behaviors by finding some other form of activity to enjoy. It doesn't matter whether it's good or bad.

"Let's look at why people go from one job to the next, one car to the next, one food to the next, and surely let's not forget why people go from one drug to the next. In every situation, people all want something bigger and better. That's called compensation! In with the new and out with the old.

"There is one distinction between people who develop healthy habits and those who acquire poor ones. The people who tend to develop healthy habits also tend to develop Desirable Lifestyle Values (DLVs)! They don't allow anyone or anything to interfere with the value they place on themselves."

"If I decided to work with you on developing healthier habits, does that mean I would have to give up my old friends as well?"

"That's right! Would you take a shower without changing your underwear or putting on a fresh set of clean clothes? No, you wouldn't. If you did, you'd still stink!" Whenever you come around, people would assume that you had been eating Chinese food, because of your sweet and sour smell!"

"But Oliver it sounds so simple."

"It is simple. It took me years to figure that out. I still don't know why there are so many programs that refuse to practice this simple process of give and take towards positive behavioral change.

"The art of change suggests that for every experience that you give up, you replace it with a bigger and better experience. I have seen people change their lives and their whole attitude using this simple process.

"You see, it's much easier to get people to do something positive than it is to get them to give up something negative.

"And most of the treatment programs today run on that premise of taking their client's perceived pleasures away without "COMPENSATION."

"But what about recovering their good health as being compensation? Isn't that enough?"

"If people could change their negative behaviors because of the health benefits, most doctors would be out of business in no time. Most people know that if they would just stop the negative behaviors their health would improve. People do the things they do because they want to experience pleasure and to avoid pain all at the same time.

"This is why doctors give patients pills for their ills. That way, people can have their poisons and then take the antidote in the form of a pill. People want to have their cake and eat it too. And if the medical establishment can provide a means for people to continue certain behaviors by giving them a pill to recover from the things we so carelessly ingest, then the medical establishment stands to make a lot of money.

"And you know and I both know that many people often use drugs, cigarettes, alcohol and food as a crutch to avoid painful situations. We are hedonistic beings and are motivated by pleasure and repelled by pain.

"All we have to do to get people on the right track is line them up with positive and pleasurable activities that will enrich their minds, health and well-being instead of taking away their negative experiences. Taking away a person's *perceived* pleasures is similar to punishment.

"That's why many people refuse to go into treatment programs today because their method is based on the punishment and pain principle. No one likes to be shamed into giving something up. Especially if it puts them in front of others and has them utter negative affirmations about their character."

"That really makes a lot of sense to me. I never heard it expressed in those terms. Now I understand why you refer to health as going beyond recovery. Why didn't you promote that method in the hospitals, treatment centers and recovery homes that you worked in?"

"I have used this method in the traditional drug and alcohol treatment programs and have helped many people see the light about true health and overall well-being. The reason why it didn't catch on in many of the treatment centers is because it didn't fit or follow protocol.

"I believe people should know and want to know the truth. My concerns are with helping people find out what works for them. Not just follow some protocol. I would rather see someone happy following a program that works than to be worrying about the salary these treatment programs are paying me."

"Well, I'm feeling very excited about working with you Oliver."

"That's good, Thelma because excitement is the key to motivation and that's exactly what I want you to be is *motivated!"*

"Well Oliver, it has been interesting talking with you about discovering new options to live a healthy lifestyle. I'm ready to work with you. But I'm awfully scared. How long do you think it will take before I get it right. You know, before I am in control again?"

"Thelma, because of your past-based-conditioning, you may find this hard to believe, and it may even sound unrealistic, but it only takes one day."

"Only one day? You're right! That is hard to believe."

"That's right, Thelma. Considering you only have one day and that's all you will ever have. Most people in recovery are time oriented. But you can't accumulate time in anything. You only have this day and what you do with today's time and space will determine how you progress from here on out.

"Accumulating time means looking back and you don't want to do that. You see, the past is just a review, not a major study. So remember, beyond recovery in not about a factor of time, it's about a state of mind. And you can change your mind set in just one day. You don't need years of time to develop a positive state of mind. You can do that right here on the spot."

"Oliver, let's get to work on my new lifestyle."

"Let's do it, Thelma."

Thelma changed her attitude about recovery. She has explored her options and now lives in San Diego, CA. She has resumed her profession as a nurse, but with a new attitude and a positive value system. She attends school, trains at the gym on a regular basis and has come to realize that living beyond recovery is not without problems, it's about developing the ability to solve her problems.

She stills experiences pain and despair, but accepts her short comings as a way of life. Thelma now understands that in each person's life a little rain must fall. And it's good to hear her refer to the rain being necessary for her personal growth and development. She says, "without April showers there can't be May flowers."

During the last six years, Thelma has developed a new way of thinking and goes on to enjoy her life and her new found *Recreation Lifestyle Attitude*. She doesn't worry about living a sober life, she's thrives on living a bolder life. She now understands that sobriety is a result, not a goal, of living a productive and fun-filled lifestyle.

A Workable and Worthy Plan of Action

Our behavior must fit a workable and worthy plan of action. It doesn't matter what plan or program you enter as long as *it works!* To become hung-up on a program that may work for some and not others would be cruel and unjust by forcing people to believe it will also work for them when in fact it just may not. Traditional recovery programs give their clients very few options—if any at all—outside the Twelve Steps. They are repeatedly told that they must work the "program" if they want to *establish* sobriety. If they are not successful in acquiring some kind of ongoing sobriety, many will blame themselves instead of the program. In my experience, I have found people who fail to establish and maintain their sobriety become angry and frustrated with themselves first instead of considering that there may be a flaw in the program. It is only after they have tried repeatedly to acquire sobriety that they become disgruntled and angry with the program and eventually give up. As a result, they acquire feelings of helplessness and hopelessness. The trials and tribulations these people experience cause tremendous amounts of stress and disappointment due to their inability to fit the mold.

This method of treatment is "program" centered instead of "client" centered. Many in recovery who are unhappy with this totalitarian approach call this treatment plan the *boilerplate special.* If an alternate or optional program is not available, these confused individuals looking for help are led right back to the same old grind. Yet they are taunted and hounded to work a program that may not be particular to their specific needs.

Janet Howard is one of those patients who has lived with pain, sadness, guilt and despair most of her using years. She had been in and out of treatment centers, mental institutions and recovery homes all with the same results—no successful or long term recovery. As a result, Janet became very frustrated, angry and bewildered. She suffered from the guilt that many of these programs tend to cause people due to their lack of discipline. Feeling alone and destitute, Janet even thought of taking her life.

It is very common for members of a Twelve Step program to force you to say you're an addict and that you'll always be an addict. The feelings of guilt that are passed on to those who may be having problems adjusting is relentless. If for some reason you discover an alternate program that works better for you, you are still bombarded with: "If you don't follow the program by going to meetings, you are going to relapse," or, "what you are doing is relapse behavior." In spite of the fact that their new program is working for them, they still receive flack from devout AA members. If for some reason you discontinue going to meetings, you get the old standard, "Oh, so you're cured now?" Why do people get an attitude when you are doing so well in an alternative program? Maybe because misery loves company.

In my twelve years of working with the recovering community, I have not once observed an occasion where AA programs acknowledge that maybe their program isn't for everyone. In addition, I cannot recall any of the programs that have taken responsibility for someone who was not successful working the Steps. Individuals who tend to have trouble coping with the traditional Twelve Steps are never given options outside of the programs. In the event that they do seek alternative programs in recovery, they tend to get persecuted for not following the strict "cult-like" Steps program. These people who get hounded by the program usually blame themselves and tend to relapse because they feel they have become failures. They say, " what's the use of trying to get sober, I've failed, so I might as well get high anyway."

This program-applied guilt tends to play a big factor in causing many people to drop out due to the stringent warnings and threats they receive. That is, any attempt to rely on yourself or outside help is relapse behavior. These people who leave the program continue to blame themselves and fall further into deep states of guilt, grief and despair. They become disillusioned and resort to relapse after relapse. Many become depressed and doubt that they'll ever overcome the disease of their negative addiction. They are warned — and at times put down by program managers — that if they don't follow their program it would mean definite relapse. What this approach does in many cases is create resentment on the part of the patient and reinforces relapse behavior in people who are looking for options.

It is inappropriate to make people feel that a single program is indispensable.

We don't lose our health all at once and we don't gain it back by relying on one single approach. We gain it back by having the opportunity to incorporate a variety of health-promoting activities into our lives. People should be given these options in their treatment plans and not be conditioned that the Twelve Steps to recovery is the only way.

The psychotherapy approach is also "program" centered as opposed to "client" centered. It's ironic that both the Twelve Step program and the psychotherapy approach to treatment are at odds with each other's methods. In this situation, the clients experience feelings of confusion as to what extent their needs can be met. It is similar to divorce court cases where feuding parents battle over community property. Each is defending their own point of view with little regard for the children's best interest. Due to their own selfish interest, the children — and clients as in the case of treatment programs — are left out in the cold wondering.

Addiction: Friend or Foe?

Studying the true meaning of addiction reveals that it is not necessarily an *ominous* term. In its true meaning, addiction is basically a habit, practice or custom that one chooses to participate in based on interest, benefits, payoff and rewards. It's a mode of behaving or doing, fixed by constant repetition. It is when our addictions become obsessive that they begin to create problems. Then they become negative addictions. If we follow *QRLP,* we can develop worthy habits and *desirable lifestyle values.* If we choose to follow *unsound* living practices, we will develop unhealthy habits and destructive lifestyle values. Your habits, as well as your addictions can be good or bad depending on what areas of life motivate you to act. It is the meaning that we apply to addiction that gives it a negative semblance. Some of the most successful people in the world have practiced "positive addiction" and see it as a *means* to a productive *end.* Therefore, understanding that addiction is okay as long as it's positive can help anyone accomplish the magic of overcoming the *dis-ease of addiction*. With this in mind, we can start looking at addiction in a whole new light.

So what is addiction? Addiction is only the linking of a stimulant with a perceived pleasure or happiness. It's our perception of happiness that causes us to choose a certain stimulant we think will bring us joy. In the process of selecting our stimulants, *society* becomes a big influence on what we choose to use. We tend to choose our drug of choice based on what a large number in our society think is the cool or right thing to do for fun and excitement. Unfortunately, we play follow the follower and grab hold of the wrong substances which eventually take us for the ride of our lives, destroying our inner spirit in the process. I really don't think that's what we start out to do, but somehow many of us have ended up that way. Many people may seem skeptical about how simple it is to break an addiction. This is understandable because of the commitments we make to the societal expectation of what measures are appropriate for overcoming the dis-ease of addiction. *Is it really the substance that we are addicted to, or is it our minds that imprison us?*

Since we are motivated by numbers and the collective expectation of our environment, many of us fall under the spell of societal conditioning. To a large extent, some of us are still struggling diligently in the war against drugs, alcoholism and food disorders when all one has to do is change the *"link"* of their addiction. We accomplish this by finding an equal or greater experience of healthy activities. It appears that we are addicted to the perceived pleasure not the substance. Substances are just vehicles that provide pleasure. Virtually, there are numerous ways to experience *salubrious* pleasures without having to abuse drugs, alcohol, medication, cigarettes, chocolate, coffee or other *damaging* stimulants. Replacing the link of addiction is basically as easy as changing your *state of mind.* You've done it before and you can do it again. For example, has there ever been a time that you enjoyed a particular food, only to have your taste for that food overshadowed by another food of greater taste, or a motorcycle that was given up for a car or truck? We have also played this game of switch with certain types of drugs. Some of us have gone from alcohol to pot, or cocaine to heroin, or crystal to crack. It wasn't necessarily the substance but what it appeared to produce. This simple and workable process can be accomplished by allowing yourself to go from self-destructive activities to health promoting activities. Activities such as recreation, education, leisure, vocation, relaxation, meditation, art, music or creative visualization can be a tremendous boost to anyone's recovery program. You must first understand that the transition to a higher level of consciousness results by changing your stubbornness. Refusing to change the way you think perpetuates the negative thinking that it is the *"addiction"* that has your minds imprisoned.

The truth of the matter is that it is your mind and behavior that create the prison and not the substance. For example, the way elephants are trained in India can be linked to how most of us become negatively addicted. At birth, elephant trainers take a large chain and place it around the baby elephant's leg to prevent it from running away. Over a period of years, they replace the chain with a large rope until the elephant becomes full grown. At this time the trainers can place a flimsy rope around the elephant's leg and tie it to a small tree. As a result of its conditioning, the elephant believes it is still tied down by a large chain, when in fact it could easily uproot the tree, break the rope and run free. But in the elephant's mind it *believes* it's in a prison and unable to free itself. By the same token, many of us could break free from our hang-ups if we allow ourselves to develop the understanding that our inertia is all in our minds. Unfortunately, due to years of negative societal conditioning, many of us have become resistant to change. That is, we have inadvertently created a prison in our own minds due to the influence of our surroundings. This prevents us from *believing* that we can make positive changes in our lives.

In this state of mind, one feels helpless, hopeless and "powerless" to do anything that will improve their life. Their power to change becomes dependent on what happens in the environment as opposed to what's going on inside the individual. For these people, something in the environment has to change before they can find it in themselves to change. That's similar to the tail wagging the dog instead of the dog wagging the tail. It's easier and more realistic for the dog to wag its tail than the other way around. Many people go through life waiting to be wagged when it is their responsibility to do the wagging. They do nothing with their lives and expect to get something for nothing. They wait until they meet the right people, win the lotto, receive an inheritance or take from other hard working individuals. If anything, much of their self-worth is based on luck, hope, crime and a prayer. This kind of lifestyle requires minimal efforts and reaps minimal rewards. Being *controlled* by external forces is living your life by default.

In this situation, life is doing the living and you're doing the following. I guess when you live your life by default and it doesn't work to your advantage, you're stuck with it. These are the people who say, "life sucks." When you do nothing with your life you turn over control to the circumstances, situations, happenings and pitfalls of an unpredictable environment. Quoting Tom Hanks in his character role in the movie "Forrest Gump" he states, "Life is like a box of chocolates, you never know what you're going to get." So, if you become a coward of life, you're going to have to live with what you get. Otherwise, you can take control by responding positively and pro-actively to what happens in your world.

Individuals who live their lives by default tend to respond negatively to crisis situations. They believe that external forces are responsible for their behavior and place blame on everything and everybody but themselves. For example, many people will state that the reason they relapsed was because they lost their job, or their wife left them, or a close relative died. It's easier for them to throw the responsibility on some tragedy than to assume responsibility for their own actions. The ironic thing is that society condones this behavior. They say it's understandable that a person can go out and rape and abuse someone because they were raped and abused as a child themselves. I'm sorry, but that just doesn't fly. We are taught to plead that defense and that's all it is—a defense. It's more an excuse. It is the same way some people of color play the race card. It may be true, but what positive steps are we going to take to rise above it all?

People choose to abuse drugs, kill, rape, commit crime and offend others. If we as a society continue to allow this morbid defense to excuse our behavior, it's just going to get worse. With so many other choices to make in times of trouble, people seem to take the most familiar road instead of one that will help them develop *skills* that are healthy and life supporting.

If the road that one often takes is of drugs, alcohol, crack, crystal, heroin, pot, crime or violence, it's more likely that they're going to take that road again. In addition, many people won't take the responsibility to say, "I choose to use." Many will plead the defense that it was the "dis-ease" that made them irresponsible.

This is another method of denial, justification and rationalization. We have got to get it in our heads that we have strengths and abilities to make better choices in living positive lifestyles. Most people in any recovery program have difficulties understanding that pleasure is an okay thing. Enjoy your pleasure, but make it health promoting. If you are not creating a healthier and more pleasurable way to enjoy life, you could be setting yourselves up for problems of compulsion further down the river of your life.

The Road Less Traveled

There is much more to life than the destructive use of foreign substances. Although drugs may appear to deliver relief from our woes and provide some form of excitement, they are a total bust. Drugs tend to distort reality and the minds of those who are chronic users. Much of what people experience from chemicals are false feelings of euphoria.

In spite of the overwhelming evidence from the mounting damage and destruction from substance abuse, we human beings either refuse to or fail to see the writings on the wall. Many of us are not willing to hear what can be heard so easily, therefore, we deny hearing anything at all.

Countless numbers of people take their chance at rolling the dice of experimenting with harmful substances with little regard of the serious damage they are causing. On the flip side of this coin, they are jeopardizing the true beauty they are capable of producing within themselves. This is a classic example of lost souls who aimlessly take *the short road to a dead end* instead of *the road less traveled* for fear of the unknown. No one should ever fear the unknown because there's nothing to fear. What should be feared is the known for it is the known that has us by the throat. Fear of the unknown is a prefabrication for what some people perceive to be dangerous while others see it as an opportunity to explore fresh ideas and new sensory experiences.

Christopher Columbus' journey into the unknown is a prime example of how our perception can influence our attitudes on life and the unknown. Columbus had a vision and an optimistic perception of his venture while most of his crew perceived danger. Only a few of his crew had faith in Columbus and also saw a new world with golden opportunities and a chance for a new lease on life. Look what happened. Had Columbus been influenced to turn back by the fears and pessimism of his crew, most of us—excluding native Americans—would still be in their native home land of origin. Your personal unknown can be whatever you want it to be, for your thoughts are your own and eventually becomes a self fulfilling prophecy.

When you take the road less traveled, you open yourselves up to a world of infinite possibilities. You begin to unlock your subconscious mind that stores a powerhouse of abilities you never thought existed. It is a time for exploring your mind and the unlimited powers you possess. The reason why many people never discover the beauty of their minds is because of societal conditioning. Throughout our lives we are being influenced and told by those who control most of the wealth, that we are inferior. We are taught that we are "nothing" unless we are using, wearing, eating, driving, smoking, or investing in their products. Claims are made that our world would be better off if we were consuming their goods. Maybe so, but our society has become strongly dependent on doctors, lawyers, medication, fast foods, drugs, alcohol, and other outside resources. We turn to these knaves for sanctity rather than to turn to the one thing that can provide us with unlimited power — our own minds and bodies. It is a common ploy used by conglomerates to keep the public ignorant of their true agendas — the usurping of billions of dollars from the ill-informed.

One example of the tactics used to keep people ignorant is the cigarette and tobacco industry with misleading claims that smoking is glamorous and the taste of tobacco is refreshing. At one time, people perceived these claims to be valid because of the need to experience pleasure in their lives where there was none. The slogan, "Come up to the cool taste of Kool Filter Kings" is what got me excited and hooked on smoking when I was just fourteen years of age. Thank God I *woke up* and allowed myself to see the writing on the wall. I stopped smoking at the age of nineteen. Not because it was bad for my health, mind you, but because I wanted to do something good for my health. I wanted to live and enjoy life. I developed an awareness and understanding that smoking was not conducive to a healthy lifestyle. I did not want to be sickly or chained to the hideous dependence of cigarettes for the rest of my life. I wanted to fill a need to experience true joy by following Qualitative Recreation Lifestyle Principles *(QRLP)*. If we allow ourselves the opportunities to develop a new awareness, we will *discover* and experience unlimited happiness throughout the rest of our lives.

Our Relentless Need To Experience Pleasure

We human beings have several basic needs in order to live comfortably in this world. One of those needs that is not illustrated in Maslow's Hierarchy is the need to experience pleasure. We human beings are hedonistic in nature and will always have the need to experience pleasure through the five senses. If we don't get that pleasure from health promoting activities we are going to get it from other sources that may not be as healthy. Inasmuch, we will defend our right to do whatever it takes to satisfy that urge to feel good no matter what (relapse). Even though people are aware that cigarette smoking is a high risk factor and has been found to cause respiratory illness, heart problems and some cancers, people will diligently defend their right to experience this perceived pleasure of smoking. It is not so much the cigarettes that they are hooked on, but the *idea* or notion that smoking is a truly pleasurable experience. Little do they know that they could easily give up smoking if they understood that it is not the smoking that has them hooked, but the perceived pleasure they're experiencing as a result of the smoking. All one has to do to diminish their need to smoke is to change the *vehicle* that's providing the experience of pleasure to a vehicle that will give them an *equal or greater experience of pleasure.* But make sure it is a health promoting experience.

Anyone can do this! They just have to stop listening to all the hype and myths about being addicted to the substance when in fact they are addicted to the perceived pleasure of that substance.

This conditioning is a prime example that systematically imprisons the lives of many unsuspecting people. They believe that they are locked into the *means* when, in fact, it is the *ends* that propels them back for more. Surprisingly, the means can be replaced to produce an ends that creates *an equal or greater feeling of pleasure.* This is the key to overcoming the *addictive hold* on *destructive substances.* All one has to do is to connect with *constructive substances.* Convincing people that it is the substance *(the means)* that they are hooked on can create a mind set that the addict is chained to the cigarette, cocaine, crystal, crack, heroin, pot, alcohol or medication instead of the perceived pleasure *(the ends)*. Again, the *substance* is just the *vehicle* that can be changed to provide us with *an equal or greater experience of pleasure.*

Many people feel that it is wrong to experience pleasure so they don't look for another vehicle that could possibly cure their *addictive hold* on harmful substances. For example, many people have gone from drugs to an exercise program and may have become addicted to running. Although they are still hooked on something, they are healthier and happier. Being hooked on something does not mean we're powerless or diseased. Disease and powerlessness depends on the substance being used and the results from its use.

> ***As someone who has recovered, I am now hooked on skiing, running, swimming, rollerblading, photography and running my own business. I basically feel I've found a new form of freedom which allows me to get high on life. Therefore, I'm still addicted and I still get high, but it is a positive addiction, and I get high on life instead of the drugs and alcohol I once used.***

Does being high on life mean that I'm dis-eased, powerless or that my life is unmanageable? Must I attend meetings for the rest of my life because of my affinity to experience pleasure through the five senses? As long as I'm not in violation of the biological laws of nature I live my life at-ease as opposed to dis-eased. What this suggests is that we should not deprive ourselves of getting high or becoming addicted to activities, people, events or substances that nourish the mind, body and spirit. The monumental problems I see in Twelve Step programs and the like, are that many people are not nourishing their spirits. Sitting around indulging in addictive behavior such as smoking and drinking cup after cup of coffee and caffeine beverages are not in accordance with optimum recovery. I think that's the problem with the whole dynamics of the Twelve Step program. We should encourage individuals to maintain their addictive attitudes by getting high on life instead of encouraging them to give something up. Depriving one of their need to experience pleasure is dysfunctional in itself, and may create more problems than it solves.

If people felt that their old experiences of pleasure could somehow be replaced by new and healthier experiences of pleasure, I believe that such a plan would provide for a more successful recovery program.

It is similar to trading your old car in on a new one. You're not completely giving up your wheels, you're getting something better. Evidence shows that if programs were designed and conducted in this fashion, many people would be encouraged, more willing and able to give up their old behaviors for new ways to live their lives. This is what I call *"EMPOWERMENT."* Empowerment is much better than shoving old traditions down people's throats.

Empowerment is much more effective and has been proven to help many people overcome their physical, mental, social and spiritual problems. The reason traditional treatment methods persist is because many in the field are trained to follow traditional methods. Change generally is not welcomed in the Twelve Step program because it would mean having to do things very differently from Twelve Step tradition. Since this innovative approach to recovery is contrary to the AA tradition, it is generally ridiculed, mocked and even put down instead of being viewed as a viable means to optimum recovery.

We should look at exploring and developing other means (vehicles) towards satisfying our pleasure centers that promote health, happiness and overall well-being. That appears to be the most logical means towards overcoming negative addictions. Out with the old and in with the new is an optimum approach for replacing bad habits. We are fooling ourselves and others if we believe that successfully getting off drugs and alcohol should be based on *abstinence* (strict habitual and unusually complete self-denial in the gratification of appetites or passion) when, in fact, it should be based on *sustenance* (material that feeds and supports the mind and spirit). In comparison of the two, *sustenance* would be the most desirable and logical choice in getting people who are negatively addicted to give up destructive behaviors. Whereas *abstinence* generally creates high stress levels and places the individual right back into a cataclysmic mind set that promotes the very same behavior and attitude they're trying to change.

I have seen how people in the traditional recovery programs respond with anger and frustration at being told that they have to give up their old way of thinking and living when all they have to do is to change the link of their addiction. Is it any wonder why the relapse rate is 85% or higher in these recovery and Twelve Step programs?

We human beings are always searching for a means to an end that has no means. Many of us appear to be lost and trying to find our way back home. Dorothy, the scarecrow, the cowardly lion and the tin man went looking for answers to their problems in the fantasy movie titled, "The Wizard of Oz," only to discover that the end did not justify the means. The means was her journey to the city of Oz, and the end was the reality that the power to return home was within her all the time. In other words, the end led right back to her. All she had to do was close her eyes and click her heels. The cowardly lion who was looking for courage was never without it. He just needed to develop an awareness that it was always within him. The scarecrow was not without a brain, and "Oz never gave anything to the tin man that he didn't already have."

We human beings are pure potentiality but we are forever searching outside of ourselves for powers that we already possess. It is unfortunate that much of our conditioning keeps us ignorant to the truth of that reality.

What makes people choose to use harmful substances is not only that they may appear to provide mystical powers, it is also the ingenious methods that marketing specialists, drug pushers, and pharmacists use to increase one's excitement about their products. Since excitement is the key to motivation, such excitement can cause people to take unsound risks. Many people become so entrenched and committed toward getting on the band wagon of excitement, they'll gamble their lives away in hopes of acquiring large returns on minimal investments. If a person's excitement is extremely high, they will buy just about anything including bad insurance policies, lottery tickets, worthless junk bonds, drugs, swamp land and even the Brooklyn Bridge. But if you truly want to develop your hidden power to overcome the devastating effects of negative addictions and compulsive behaviors, prepare yourself to discover *The Dynamics of the Pleasure Principle.*

Discovery 8

The Dynamics Of The Pleasure Principle (DPP)

It is not the experience of pleasure that causes our problems; it's the vehicle that takes us there.

Oliver Rhodes

When it comes to breaking the chains of addiction very few of us ask three of the most important questions that can give us all the right answers:

1. What are the dynamics that cause our addictions?
2. If something gives us pleasure, why would we want to stop?
3. When we do decide to stop, why is it so difficult to break away from the addictions that have control over our behavior?

Answer to question number one: the dynamics behind our addictions are to experience pleasure through the five senses. That's the reason anyone does anything — to experience pleasure. We very seldom do anything for the sake of just doing it. We are motivated by the *"pleasure principle."* No one deliberately makes a conscious decision to become negatively addicted. Unfortunately, due to the commitment we make to that experience of pleasure, we find ourselves repeating the behavior. As a result, that behavior eventually becomes our habit.

Referring to the Dynamics of Development and Positive Behavior Change on page 264, (Figure 8.2) our habits are that *protective inner core* (PIC) that governs how we think. If we have been accustomed to using drugs or drinking alcohol for many years, our PIC will reinforce our current thinking that may prevent us from listening intuitively, creatively and indiscriminately to new information. In this state of mind, the only thoughts that we hear are the old ones. As a result, our minds can become so distorted that we may not be receptive to those voices that come from our ailing body, counselors, friends, parents, doctors or those who have died before us. Our automatic defense system (AutoDens) will not allow us to listen to reason from any other source, even though our dysfunctional behavior may be killing us. Simply put, we have our *own private logic* that supersedes that of anything else – even to the degree of destroying our precious health.

Answer number two: why would we choose to stop a pleasurable experience? Maybe that good thing has turned into a problem that is now too big for us. Yet we still hold on to our idea, notion, attitude and belief (INAB) that we can somehow continue that destructive behavior, when in fact it is killing us. Another reason we may want to give up a particular behavior is because we may have discovered the ultimate trade off — a more rewarding experience of pleasure to replace the old experience. This process of exchange is the basic and most reliable method for re-newal and breaking old habits.

Answer number three: Unfortunately, the motivation to stop may not be as strong as the motivation to continue. The reason is that we have created a very powerful *Automatic Defense System* (AutoDens: INAB, Memories, commitments, PIC and Old Thoughts) that is capable of shutting out any reasonable alternatives that could assist in helping us develop new behaviors and healthier lifestyle habits. If we allow ourselves to *"listen"* to new approaches to recovery, we can overcome these negative addictions. Without listening, we diligently resist any encouragement, support or guidance that could possibly bring us up from the depths of hell.

Understanding how our AutoDens prevents us from developing new ways to live our lives is a major factor towards positive behavior change. We unconsciously defend our right to experience pleasure, even those of the worst kind. But pleasure is not the culprit. It's the vehicle! The vehicle (substance) is what takes us there. "Pleasure" is the motivating force behind our behavior and our addictions. To many people, it doesn't matter whether that destination yields positive or negative consequences. Therefore, the problems with addictions and compulsive behaviors are *undesirable consequences* not deliberate pursuits.

So why do we deliberately set out to get rid of them? This approach has caused so many people anguish, despair, frustration and even confusion. We spend many years getting to that point of pleasure only to have to give it all up. Many of us who try to give up old behaviors in this fashion find it very difficult, even if the new behavior is better for our overall health and well-being.

The point is that it's much easier to do something positive than to give up something negative. Trying to give up something negative that provides for our perceived pleasure is what we call *"fighting a disease."* This is far from promoting health. It's also similar to cursing the darkness instead of lighting a candle.

Another example of this approach could be similar to a builder who builds a house and realizes that the house they have built violates city construction and housing codes. As a result, the house is unsuitable to live in. You are left with two choices: (1) you can spend energy tearing it down and then rebuilding it or; (2) save energy by leaving it and build a new house from scratch.

Having to tear down what you have already built then starting all over again can be more frustrating than starting *fresh* from scratch. How many times have we worked hard to get to an end only to discover that the end did not justify the means. For example, taking a college course we thought was a requirement for graduation but found out later it was not. The ideal approach to take in the event of a botched job or decision is to just disregard the first mess you've made and move on. You don't see chefs take apart the soufflé that fell and try to make that same one all over again. They throw it away and start from scratch.

Many of the recovery programs that are supposed to help you stop smoking, give-up drugs, lose weight and so on, use this approach of breaking you down by taking away what you have become *accustomed* to. I know it seems perfectly logical to take something from someone that's causing them problems, but the reason this approach is so difficult is because the individuals in question perceive their experiences as pleasurable. Many people can and will become angry, resentful, belligerent and down right indignant if their perceived *"pleasure principle"* is threatened. These methods are based on deprivation. It is difficult for anyone to do anything for very long that has a negative foundation, because *no one* can operate in a constant state of denial. After a period of time, the pendulum swings back and eventually prompts that person into excessive behavior (relapse).

You see, it is not the addictions that create our problems, it is the denial and avoidance of the *"pleasure principle."* The *Dynamics of the Pleasure Principle* are the mechanics that govern our quest for happiness. Since happiness is the ultimate goal in life, we choose certain behaviors, things and people that we believe will make us feel good and therefore make us feel happy. The *Hedonic Equation* is a process that every living thing follows to achieve happiness and can best be illustrated as A = B = C (see Figure 8.1, page 254).

A = Human being
B = Vehicle
C = Pleasure Principle

It is easy to understand that (A) and (C) will always be constant. As long as we are living we, (A) will always have a need to experience pleasure (C) through the five senses. It is the "vehicle" (B) that will provide the ride to our destination of pleasure, and therefore our happiness. If the vehicle in which we choose is of a destructive nature, then it is *that* vehicle that is the problem and not the addiction. Removing the "vehicle" (B) without *compensation*, will only break down the equation and make it difficult for anyone to function properly as a pleasure oriented being. Therefore, depriving someone of their need to experience pleasure is dysfunctional in itself. For example, if you gave your car keys (the vehicle) to a toddler, he would most likely be fascinated with the jingle-jangle sounds that those keys made (the pleasure). You know and I know that if we should take those keys from that toddler, the child would probably have a conniption fit — just like many people who are forced to give up their drugs, alcohol, cigarettes, food, T.V., computers, etc.

How do we get those keys *away* from the toddler after he was having so much fun playing with them? You have to give him something in return to keep him happy— *compensation!* You see, the ultimate goal in life is to be happy. Take away someone's happiness without giving them something in return will often cause retribution, resentment, anger, fear and a host of other emotional reactions. This is commonly known as the withdrawal syndrome. It doesn't matter whether the perceived pleasure is harmful to the body or not. Many people feel that it is their right to experience that pleasure even if they are destroying their mind, body and soul.

For example, take people who smoke cigarettes. You may even know someone who smokes. If we attempt to deprive anyone of their smokes without their permission, we just may be opening up one hell of a Pandora's box, let me tell you.

While I was out shopping one day, I came across an elderly woman buying cigarettes in a convenience store. She noticed that my facial expression suggested strong disapproval. It was very obvious how shocked I was that this sixty-something year old woman was buying cigarettes. In fact, I don't approve of people buying cigarettes at any age. She picked up on my vibes and responded harshly, "I smoke and I vote." I then responded, "That may be true, but when you smoke, you also choke!" The woman was not impressed with my humor or poetic antics. She growled, gave me a dirty look and continued on her way as she gave me the one finger salute.

This scenario is a prime example of how difficult the process of *change* can be when there is an unwillingness to learn. To make matters worse, the "program" person or persons wanting to see change in the user, generally do not provide any form of compensation.

The ideal method of getting people to nix their destructive behaviors would best be accomplished in the same manner in which you compensated that toddler in getting him to give up those keys. Therefore, successfully getting people to give up destructive behaviors is to work on providing them with healthier alternatives (sustenance: materials that feed and support the mind and spirit) instead of taking away their perceived pleasures (abstinence: strict habitual and usually complete self-denial in the gratification of appetites or passions).

A Break with Tradition

There are many programs throughout the world that successfully help negatively addictive people develop new behaviors. They don't waste their time on what things people should give up, they help their clients focus on healthier alternatives that can jettison them out of those old destructive habits. Let's face it, we are always going to have habits, addictions, affinities, wants and passions. It is the positive addictions and good habits that are the essence of true happiness and optimum recovery. We don't have a psychological mechanism that decides not to do something; we decide in the affirmative. It's much easier to drive forward than it is to drive in reverse. Trying to condition or convince people that they need to get rid of the human traits of addiction is futile and ridiculous. It only makes common sense to replace the vehicle instead of trying to rid someone of their need to experience pleasure. Addictions are something we live with, not dispose of.

Again, the problem is not with the addiction but with the vehicle. Common vehicles that many of us have used or may be using now are as follows:

Positive Addictions:

- *Dancing*
- *Swimming*
- *Skiing*
- *Racquetball*
- *Employment*
- *Rollerblading*
- *Arts & Crafts*
- *Photography*
- *Public Speaking*
- *Sailing*
- *Tennis*
- *Music*
- *Singing*
- *Running*
- *Wood Working*
- *Camping*
- *Biking*
- *Snow Boarding*
- *Reading*
- *Flying*

Negative Addictions:

- *Drugs*
- *Alcohol*
- *Gambling*
- *Smoking*
- *Excessive Eating*
- *Crime*
- *Violence*
- *Laziness*
- *Denigrating*
- *Poaching*
- *Sugar Abuse*
- *Chocolate Abuse*
- *Candy Abuse*
- *Negative Thinking*

These are all vehicles that provide people with the *ride of their life.* Some are negative and some are positive. If you are positively addicted, you're probably one happy camper. Whether your behavior is positive or negative, it is your *perception* of pleasure that motivates you. Although drugs can be harmful to your health, many people will indulge in these substances simply because they see them as being useful in making them happy.

As someone who cares about the health of others, I have worked with many people who testify and justify that marijuana is safe, stimulating, and a non-addictive natural herb. It may be a natural herb, but so are poisonous mushrooms, ivy and other plants that are deadly to the taste or touch. In their minds this potential deadly substance (pot) is the vehicle that provides false feelings of euphoria that also distorts the thinking and reasoning potential of millions of people.

The Dynamics of the Pleasure Principle opens up a new understanding to the underlying cause of the problems we have with certain substances. It is an innovative and unique approach towards acquiring optimum recovery and is designed to help individuals overcome negative addictions and compulsive behaviors. Not only does it provide a greater understanding of how we fall victim to disease, but it also empowers us to live our lives effectively, successfully and productively.

The DPP also helps us develop a whole new way of looking at addictions. It is not so much the addiction that robs us of our power, it's the tiger we mistakenly grab by the tail. With this new approach to recovery, we can all maintain our dignity in knowing that everyone is recovering from one thing or another. Instead of having to humiliate ourselves by stating that we are powerless, addicts and irresponsible, we can proudly stand and say we have a problem. And since everyone has problems, we are not set off like some freak in a side show who are different from the *norm.* Most people in traditional recovery or Twelve Step programs don't see themselves as being normal. Therefore, many consider themselves to be abnormal; how sad.

The fascinating thing about the dynamics of the pleasure principle is that all one has to do is replace their old behaviors with new ones. It works on the same principles as other ways we make changes in our lives. Why would getting off drugs and alcohol be any different. For example, I don't believe anyone would trade in their old vehicle to a car dealer without expecting to get a another one of equal or greater value. Why would we want to give up cigarettes, alcohol, drugs or chocolate without some form of compensation? You say, "it's better for their health." But what do you think the users would say? "I like smoking. It's my body and I can choose to do with it whatever I want."

You see, to these people, their health isn't as important as their need to smoke. At least not at this time. They just may have to be on their death beds before they realize that they should have quit a long time ago. The most important way to encourage people to give up destructive behaviors, is not to threaten them with the fact that they could possibly die. They need positive encouragement that there are more productive and healthier ways to experience pleasure.

It's the pleasure principle, not the threat of death that motivates our behavior.

Replacing the "Vehicle" of Addiction

In his cassette series, "Magical Mind, Magical Body," Dr. Deepak Chopra states, "Addiction is only the linking of a stimulant with a perceived pleasure or happiness." It seems clear then, that it is that *link* not the *addiction* that causes our problems. A person who spends their life trying to rid themselves of an addiction is barking up the wrong tree. For anyone, be it a psychologist, doctor or drug counselor, to make one feel that they should rid themselves of their addictions, may not be providing sound advice. A new awareness in the treatment of disease would be to look at the vehicle (the cause) that the person is using instead of his need to experience pleasure (the effect). How can this sound approach be applied? Let's start with the *Hedonic Equation:*

$$A = B = C$$

In this equation, (B), the vehicle, is the problem. It's like a bad tooth that needs to be pulled and replaced with a good tooth in order to provide a full, beautiful smile. It can also be comparable to having a flat tire. In order to get rolling again, the tire must be replaced. There must be some form of compensation. So, what I have devised is a method that illustrates how this unique equation works. It can be applied to any disorder or situation that plagues modern society. It empowers those individuals who so desperately want to rid themselves of the "vehicle" that is causing them major problems.

Since (B) the vehicle, is what needs to be replaced, we need to have a motive. In the toothache example, the motive to get rid of the tooth was not necessarily because the mouth was in pain, but to create a healthier looking smile. The motive to change the tire in the flat tire example was not because the car was damaged, but to get the car back on the road again. Therefore, that's what many ailing people would like to do with their lives — put a smile on their face, be happy and get rolling again on the good road to a prosperous life.

So, what is our motive in the Hedonic Equation? Three motives must be present in order to be successful in replacing the old vehicle (B) for a new one. After years of living with your present vehicle (B) it may be difficult prying you out of what you have become accustomed to. Old habits go out kicking and screaming, but they do go out. You must first understand that to be jettisoned out of your deep-seated vehicle (B) you are going to need some very strong motives. There are three very powerful motives that we have used throughout our lives to move from one pleasurable experience to the next. They are what I call the *ICI to change,* that is, *Inspiration, Compensation* and *Imagination.* These are the keys to powerful motivation and positive behavior change.

When we are inspired by "compensation" it captures our imagination!

The most important factor that governs motivation is "*inspiration*" (excitement). When someone is inspired, they need little in the form of a push. They don't need to be threatened, warned or bribed into taking action. They become truly excited about the benefits that are associated with any activity that will produce pleasure or happiness. Most of us know that even plants gravitate towards light, just as a person who uses drugs will do just about anything to get their hands on more. After a car salesman tells you about all the options on a new sports car or truck, you just may get excited enough to consider buying it. It is not so much the activity that moves us, but also the importance we place on that activity. The value system that governs our behaviors is always centered on the principle of importance. If something is important to us, chances are we are going to be inspired do it. If we are inspired by something, you better believe it is important to us. Therefore, if it is important for us to quit smoking, we will be inspired to give up our cigarettes.

Changing for the sake of change is not enough to change our behavior!

For anyone to tell you that you should stop smoking because it's not good for your health is following their agenda and not yours. Your agenda is to experience satisfaction. The ideal approach in overcoming harmful addictions such as smoking is to offer another activity that will provide both good health and personal satisfaction. Remember, it is not so much the addiction as it is the "*pleasure principle.*"

We humans are moved by inspirational people, places and things. Threat is not a good motivator. It may not even be an appropriate deterrent. Studies show that *threat* hasn't been very effective in preventing drug use, crime, alcohol abuse, violence or even war. As a result, many of these hideous events are still running rampant today, so why use the fear of threat? Telling someone they are going to die if they continue to smoke usually prompts a perfunctory response such as, “we’re all going to die someday” or, “if I get sick, I can always go to the doctor.” So, threats aren’t very effective motivators to get people to change. They just serve as scare tactics with minimum effect, if any at all, on getting people to change their behavior.

As with inspiration, *“compensation”* plays a very big part in motivation. It is the *biggest* motivating factor of all. We experience compensation in employment. Most of us would not work for any company if we didn’t expect to get compensated for our efforts. We would not spend our money if we did not expect to get something in return for our hard earned dollars. Even volunteers are compensated by receiving personal satisfaction for helping the needy. The rewards for volunteering their services generally have a more sentimental and emotional payoff than the monetary remuneration one gets from employment. Even though it is not in the form of currency, it is still compensation all the same. Everything we do is based on the principle of compensation.

Very few of us do anything just for the sake of doing it. Often, we expect to get some form of pleasure for our involvement. A leisure walk on the beach compensates us with a beautiful view of the ocean, a sunset and calming sounds of the ocean crashing along the shore. Television provides us with entertainment just as our friends share their companionship and love with us. Since we are hedonistic in nature, pleasure will always be that motivating factor.

If our goal is to be clean and sober, there must be some form of compensation that will direct our attention to developing healthier living habits. For sobriety is not a direct goal, it is the result of a process. That process is in following Qualitative Recreation Lifestyle Principles.

Although traditional treatment centers have helped many people overcome more serious addictions, we still find in almost every recovery program, new addictions such as excessive use of coffee, cigarettes and sugar. These soft addictions are acceptable, but they are just as deadly. A drug is a drug is a drug. Unfortunately, excessive use of coffee, cigarettes and sugar is no consolation to previous behaviors. In actuality, these behaviors are no better. Even though someone may have resorted to soft addictions, they are still displaying the behavior that can prompt them back into hard drug and alcohol use. Many who use these soft chemicals would beg to differ. Nevertheless, the use of coffee, cigarettes and excessive sugar are poor roads to dead ends and not a viable form of *compensation*. Is there any wonder why many people choose to wait until they are seriously ill from the death hold of their alcohol and drug addiction before getting treatment? That's called *hitting bottom.*

You can't expect people to go willingly into a situation where they know that their use of a perceived pleasure will be taken away without some form of compensation. There are many programs where the positive approach of compensation for old behaviors works wonders. People will beat a path to your door if they knew that they were going to be compensated in one form or another.

Take the Chicago Police Department "Goods for Guns" program. In the winter of 1994 they spear-headed a program to get guns off the street and out of the hands of criminals. They *managed* to get hundreds of people to turn in their guns for cash or gifts with no questions asked. People and guns came from everywhere. You see, these people knew that they were going to be compensated for their wares, plus people were assured that there would be no repercussion for having a gun. This is called win/win negotiating and it works!

This method worked so much better than the threat: "If you use a gun, you go to jail." Not one gun was turned in using this scare tactic, why? *No compensation*. More importantly, they were afraid of the consequences.

In most treatment centers, recovery homes and similar institutions, the *main* focus is that of the program, therapists, doctors or psychologists. They are the experts and you are to listen to what they feel is best for you and your well-being. Unfortunately, your interests in all this is to sit tight, abstain and follow instructions. In doing so, you just might get sober. What about your need to experience happiness, fun, pleasure, recreation, leisure and laughter. Well, what about it? The reason why these effective measures to recovery are not practiced is for one simple reason. Most insurance companies will not *"compensate"* medical agencies for this kind of therapy. I've worked in many institutions as a recreational therapist and was instructed by administration that I could not document that a patient's condition had improved due to their experience of fun, laughter and excitement during a recreational activity. The reason for these measures was because patients are not in the hospital to have fun. They are there because they are sick. Insurance companies are not paying for patients to have fun. The patients are to get better and then they should be discharged. More than most, it is recreation that brings about a state of ease as opposed to the pain of dis-ease that many patients suffer as a result of having to take a multitude of powerful mind-mood altering drugs.

Recreational activities help teach clients better coping skills which results in using their free time more effectively. It is my experience that recidivism decreases when patients learn better ways to utilize their free time. Therefore, I can only speculate that the reason why many clients are not getting the kinds of treatment necessary to keep them out of the hospital is because the medical profession profitability margin would seriously fall. Unfortunately, it is the patients that generally fall. That is, fall right back into the hospital after their drugs have run out. As a result, many patients feign illness just to get a few more weeks of three hots (meals) and a cot. Many of these patients get excellent coaching from the admission coordinators and nursing staff in order to increase hospital census and profitability. So, these poor mental patients are herded in and out of these holding pens like cattle in a slaughter house.

Hospitals have a responsibility to their patients. It just so happens that they also have a responsibility to their employees and their stockholders. When it comes right down to it, the upper echelon get their cut first. Employees get the leftovers. That leaves the patients scavenging for the crumbs. They are the last to be considered in the never ending pursuit for those extremely high medical profits. As a result, these patients suffer the most, and in most cases will have to rely on the medical profession for most of their lives. You see, hospitals want to keep things status quo.

It seems to me that compensation for these patients' recovery is not in the best interest of these institutions. If it were, many of their patients would develop the means to go "Beyond Recovery" and on to a whole new way of living healthier, happier and more productively. Therefore, *compensation* should be, of course, to provide *an equal or greater form of pleasure* that will motivate these patients to give up their old habits. When we human beings expect to receive something special for our troubles, we begin to *imagine* ourselves in a better situation and we develop a positive outlook on life.

The third motive that will help jettison you from the seat of destructive behaviors (B) is "*imagination!*" Although *inspiration* and *compensation* are strong motivators, *imagination* is the most powerful one of all. It is the only motive that directly originates from the power of the mind; and you own one free and clear. The power of the mind has the capacity to create unlimited images of success or failure. That's why it is very important that you understand this awesome power. Having this power and not being aware of its potential can be like driving a semi downhill without brakes. It's also like having a nuclear power plant. That is, it can be constructive as well as destructive. When creating images in your mind you must be careful not to create a negative image of yourself because the mind's eye will send instructions to your subconscious mind. Once your subconscious mind has accepted those instructions, it will carry out those orders by bringing into reality whatever it is you dwell upon.

For example, have you every imagined yourself living on a tropical island, being with the one you love or eating your favorite foods? Have these images been so strong that you actually set out and made them happen? Sure you have. We human beings do this all the time through the power of visualization. Visualization is a function of imagination and is the foundation of all our actions and behaviors. Before we move on anything, we must see it in our mind first. This is why our minds are a powerful force to have at our disposal. It is the mind's eye that first initiates the creation of reality. Therefore, what you visualize in your mind, is what you are going to get in reality. It doesn't take a mathematician to figure out this simple and unique law of visualization.

The Power of The Mind's Eye

The mind's eye is the creator, architect and projector of your corporation. At any time you can *re-create* your outer world with a single thought. The outer eye can only see what is, but the inner eye has the power to see what can be. Therefore, it is the power of the inner eye that can reshape our future, health and our outlook on life.

> ***The mind's eye creates an image and gives the body instructions to produce what the inner eye sees.***

The outer eye in turn sees what appears, confirms it and relates back to the mind that what it mentally created has been produced. This is called the checks and balances of your thought processes. For example, if you see yourself as a successful student, it's very likely you will become a successful student. If you see yourself as a failure, that image in your mind will manifest itself in reality.

Life is a self fulfilling prophecy. And what you see in your mind is basically what you're going to get. There are two kinds of people in the world, those who think they can and those who think they can't, and ironically, they are both right. So it's important to be careful what you think and how you see yourself with the mind's eye. Our inner visions and thoughts are the essence of who we are. The inner eye creates an image of our own fashion based on what we believe. These images of ourselves can be either negative or positive. It then sends instructions to the mind for its manifestation.

The human body can only react to those instructions it receives from the mind.

Therefore, we carry out those instructions by becoming the very thing we imagine in our mind's eye. If you see success, you'll get it. If you see failure you'll get that too. Although we would like to blame our misfortunes on environmental forces, we are totally responsible for our reactions to those forces. Understanding the process of how our inner vision governs what we become empowers us to see ourselves in a whole different light. We can reshape our entire lives by creating positive images of what we'd like to become and having faith that those images will in fact appear in reality. Those instructions we receive from our mind's eye are what makes things appear. That's why what we see is termed appearance. This process of seeing with the mind's eye and then becoming what you see, is living from the inside out. Looking at the world as it is and allowing that to influence your image of yourself is living from the outside in.

We become more in tune with nature when we live from the inside out. For everywhere in nature, the creation of beauty flows outward into infinity. Things that flow inward have a limited capacity to expand and are restricted by their inner boundaries. Take a flashlight and point it into a closed container. You'll notice that you're not going to get much of a "glow" going inward. Also, imagine if the sun shined from the outside in. It would have a dim and gloomy appearance. On the other hand, the sun shines from the inside out and lights up the entire universe. It can be seen for millions of miles, considering the sun is 93 million miles from Earth. The sun reaches every corner of the universe. The light reflects off every planet in its path increasing its capacity to shine its brilliance throughout time and space. Therefore, what the outer eye sees is limited because it only verifies what is. It is not a good representation of your true nature, or the power of your subconscious mind. Whereas the inner eye has unlimited capabilities to create an endless array of positive or negative images. This is why it is better to project positive images of yourself because everywhere around you are mirrors of people who will reflect the warmth or coldness that you emit. With this in mind, you can see why imagination is the most awesome force of all the motives behind your actions. It is the most reliable means towards ejecting you out of your old vehicles into ones that will provide healthier ways to live your life.

The Dynamics of The Pleasure Principle Illustrated

The Dynamics of the Pleasure Principle (DPP) that follows, will provide you with a better understanding toward making positive behavior changes in your life. This innovative approach can help anyone acquire healthier living habits and better ways to enjoy life.

Our quest for health and happiness should not stem from fighting a disease, but in promoting health. When we promote health, our diseases, negative addictions and compulsive behaviors will diminish.

Promoting health is similar to lighting a candle in a dark room. Curse the darkness and nothing happens. Light a candle and two things happen — the room brightens and the darkness disappears. Fighting a disease is similar to cursing the darkness. You can curse all you want but the darkness will remain. On the other hand, the darkness will automatically diminish when you light the candle of health. It's as simple as that. We human beings spend too much time, money and energy on fighting, when we should be making peace with our bodies by giving it what it needs in order to *compensate* (there's that word again) for the demand we place on it. For example, fight in our case can be linked to disease. When we put garbage in our bodies, it doesn't like it. So, our bodies rebel by making us sick. We in turn give it medication which it doesn't want either. We go back and forth until we are so out of touch with what our bodies need that we wind up falling victim to the disease and then have to rely on doctors, hospitals and the pharmaceutical industry. This is what I call the "Yo-Yo Syndrome of Disease." It's a war more than a fight, and we all lose in the long run. But there's a much more powerful way to create harmony in mind, body and soul without all the hassle. The magic of this positive transformation is in understanding the *Dynamics of the Pleasure Principle* and the *Hedonic Equation* (see Figure 8.1, page 254).

In reviewing the DPP, you will notice that self (A) and our need to experience pleasure (C) will always be constant. It is the vehicle (B) which is also the variable that will change throughout our lives. These variables can be positive or negative depending on the way in which we use them and

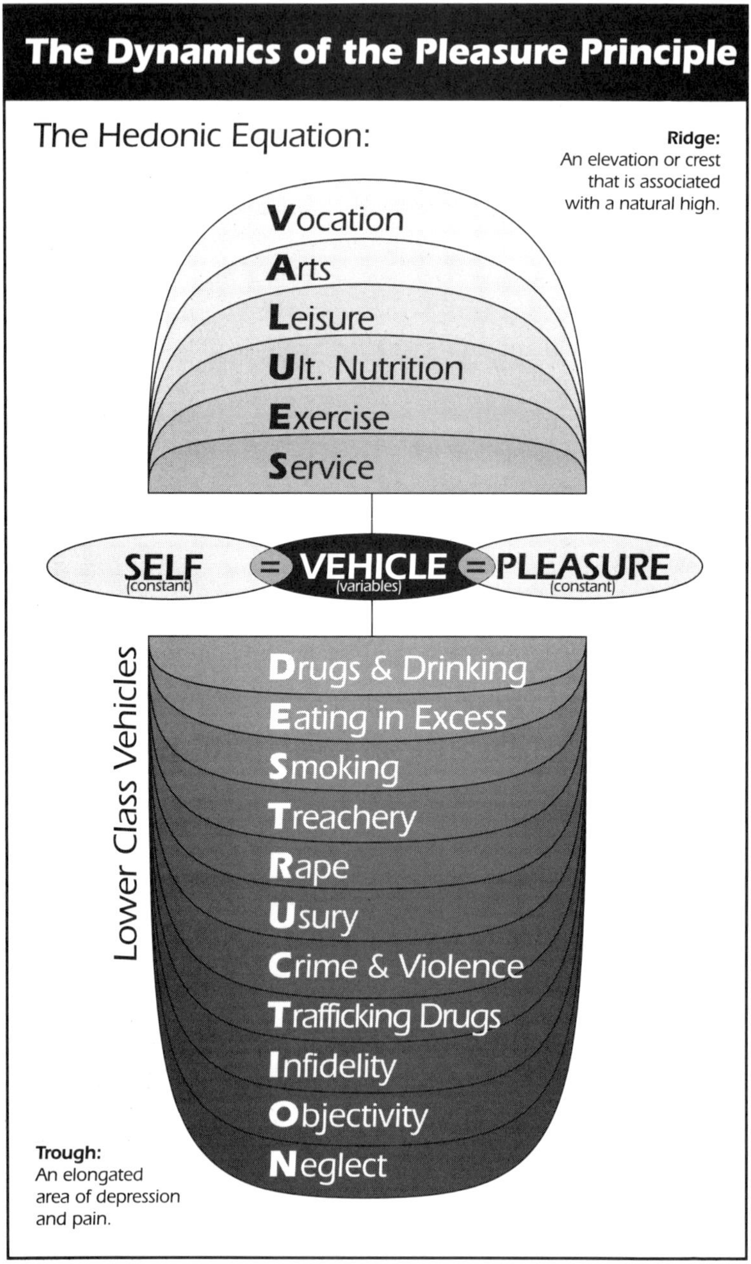
The Dynamics of the Pleasure Principle
The Hedonic Equation:
Ridge:
An elevation or crest that is associated with a natural high.
Vocation
Arts
Leisure
Ult. Nutrition
Exercise
Service
SELF (constant) = VEHICLE (variables) = PLEASURE (constant)
Lower Class Vehicles
Drugs & Drinking
Eating in Excess
Smoking
Treachery
Rape
Usury
Crime & Violence
Trafficking Drugs
Infidelity
Objectivity
Neglect
Trough:
An elongated area of depression and pain.

Figure 8.1

how often. Remember, too much of a good thing can be just as destructive as too much of a bad thing. Too much of any one thing can lead to a negative addiction and consequently dis-ease. Again, we do not deliberately set out to destroy our health. Poor health is a consequence of poor behavior trends. Our need to experience pleasure without balance can become a problem. This is why a balanced lifestyle leads to positive addictions and ultimately superior health. What this suggests is that it is not the addiction that causes our problems, it is the vehicles and the improper use of any one thing. Addiction is a natural human characteristic that's shared by all. Call it what you may. An addiction is no more than a need, passion, want, like, affinity, craving or hunger to experience pleasure. Any attempt to rid yourself of this natural characteristic would only lead to frustration and deprivation. Each and every one of us are a part of this Hedonic Equation where we apply a *means* to experience the *ends*. That ends just happens to be our pleasurable experiences.

Since it is not our addictions that create the problems in our lives, it would be best to focus on replacing those vehicles that create the problems with ones that create the solution— thus compensation! We've discussed the process of replacing our old vehicles with new and improved ones. Again, it requires the motives *ICI.* That is, *Inspiration, Compensation and Imagination.* To uproot those old behaviors demands equal or greater experiences of pleasure in the form of health promoting activities (HPAs). In *Discovery* 6 (Figure 6.3), I have listed a variety of activities that one can participate in toward developing desirable lifestyle values (DLVs). Values are the granddaddy of enhancing one's lifestyle and overall well-being. As indicated in *Discovery 1* (Figure 1.1) the word *values* is also an acronym that stands for: Vocation, Arts, Leisure, Ultimate Nutrition, Exercise and Service. These powerful components of life all lead towards developing total mind, body and spiritual health.

Why should our focus be on pleasure instead of improvement? For the simple reason that the ultimate goal in life is to be happy. Happiness comes from our involvement in pleasurable experiences. We are happy when we are involved in healthy and loving relationships. We are happy when we sit down to enjoy our favorite foods. We are happy when we are gainfully employed. It is no doubt that pleasurable experiences *contribute* to our happiness. Have you ever seen a person after winning the lottery who looked sad? Have you ever seen anyone upset after getting that job they've always wanted. How about the person who has just been reunited with a long-lost relative. The problem with some of the *vehicles* we use to produce happiness is that they produce *false feelings of euphoria* and are destructive in nature. We may perceive them as producing pleasure or happiness, but these substances only distort our perception of reality by altering our ability to think clearly. The substances that I am referring to are mind-mood altering chemicals such as: drugs, alcohol, cocaine, crank, heroin, crystal, crack, prescription drugs, food and a host of other debilitating substances.

A better example of how the hedonic equation can best be applied toward getting us out of the rut of destruction is similar to using our vehicles to get us to work. First, there is our place of origin, home (A). Then there is our need to get to where we earn a living, work (C). Our goal in this scenario is not to get from point (A) to point (B) but to use point (B) to get from point (A) to point (C) and vise versa. (B) is the means of transportation that will get us to our destination and back to our point of origin. The options that are available to get to work can be compared to the options we have to enhance our health. In order to get to our place of employment we can walk, drive, bus, taxi, cycle, run, fly or carpool. There are a number of ways to get to point (C). Our need to earn a living can be compared to our need to experience pleasure. If the vehicle that we are using to satisfy those needs are of a destructive nature, we can lose both our health and our job. So the problem does not exist in our needs, wants, affinities, passions or addictions, it exists in the vehicle.

For example, if the vehicle we use to get to work begins to break down, it could create a big problem at our place of employment. If we call in late on numerous occasions because of car problems, it could possibly put our jobs in jeopardy. As you can see, the problem does not exist with the job, or the *need* to get there. It exists with the vehicle that you are using. In this case, it would be appropriate to get it fixed, or get a new vehicle of *equal or greater value.*

Now that you have developed an awareness and a better understanding of how to develop healthier ways to live and enjoy your life, you are ready to live your life to its fullest. The most important thing to remember is to practice balance. Too much of any one thing can create just as many problems as using harmful substances. Keep in mind that whatever vehicles of pleasure you choose to use, make sure they are health oriented, varied and moderated. In other words, maintain your center.

Staying Centered: The Power of Balance

When you develop the understanding that addiction is only a link (vehicle) to a stimulant that we perceive as being pleasurable or that provides happiness, we must then find a happy medium within those pleasures of life. Some of the healthiest people in the world participate not in one or two health promoting activities (HPAs), but a variety of activities. Varied activities maintain the excitement and spark in life that produces desirable lifestyle values (DLVs). Since we renew ourselves through our projects, we are forever living in that creative force of life. That's why following Qualitative Recreation Lifestyle Principles are so effective in helping people change their lives for the better. As stated earlier, recreation is not an activity, but the result of the activities we engage in. Therefore, recreation is an attitude. It's not necessarily what you do or how you do it. It boils down to how you think. We can eat well, exercise, recreate, play, work and socialize with positive people, but if our attitudes are unhealthy we won't produce optimum health. For example, you can have your car serviced at the best automotive service center. They can give your car bumper to bumper service until it looks and runs like a new car. But the longevity and performance will not only be determined by the service it receives but by the attitude of the driver. If your attitude stinks, you could easily go out and trash that car in a matter of days. However, if your attitude is such that you have respect, pride and value for that car, it can maintain its performance and good looks indefinitely. Therefore, balance requires that you not only take good care of yourself through ultimate nutrition, pleasurable exercise, recreation, education, good relationships and public services, but also with a positive attitude and a healthy outlook on life.

Balance is staying centered when riding those vehicles of pleasure and satisfaction. Many people get caught up in overworking themselves, using too much sugar, eating excessive amounts of fat and getting too much sun. Although these vehicles can be pleasurable, over indulgence can cause dangerous consequences. That's why I state that poor health is not a quest or even a decree. We do not deliberately set out to destroy our health. Poor health is a consequence of behavioral trends due to gluttony and inactivity. A variety of activities keep our interests high and our disease rate low.

Recovery: It's not just a "Factor of Time," it's more a "State of Mind"

Many people who are accustomed to certain stimulants believe in their *minds* that it's close to impossible to break the chains of addiction without having to go through hell and high water. Well nothing could be further from the truth. All it requires is that you allow yourself to change your old ways of thinking by becoming a silent witness. You must allow yourself to establish new thought patterns that transmit positive affirmations of well-being. It's as simple as saying, I don't need these negative addictions anymore. I choose to live healthy and happy by changing the vehicles that are causing me problems. You can go further by stating, "I'm off the negative stimulants and have found more exciting things to do in my life now." Then make a list of those things and live by them.

These affirmations work, but you must say them with conviction, determination and believability or you'll go nowhere. Many people are finding happiness in life by utilizing this powerful thought-change process. Since our thoughts are the essence of who we are, there is no doubting that this method works. Whatever you think about, you become. What are you thinking about right now? Whatever it is, you're going to get it if you think about it long and hard enough.

Many people who are experiencing problems with addiction and compulsive behavior are usually aware that problems exist, but are lost about what actions to take in order to find solace or a positive and reliable solution. It is a fact that finding the cause of a problem assists in finding a solution, but in the human experience, finding solutions to problems are much more complex and subconsciously guarded. In some practices, too much emphasis is put on researching the causes instead of focusing on promoting health. Again, addiction is only the linking of a stimulant with a perceived pleasure or happiness. Replace the negative stimulant with one that is healthier and more positive and you are cured. It's a proven fact. Throughout our lives we have moved from one stimulant to the next. Those that provide extreme pleasures tend to overshadow our old stimulants. Why do you think a person will go from beer to pot, then pot to cocaine, then cocaine to a more powerful substance. They have just changed the link (vehicle) of their addiction to a more powerful one. We can do this to acquire healthier vehicles. We don't have to waste our time trying to get rid of a characteristic common to all human beings. What we need to focus on is making positive choices by selecting vehicles that will provide us with optimum health and a zest for life.

In order to acquire this innovative approach to optimum health, we must be willing to get rid of, not the addictive behavior, but some preconceived notions about what addiction is. Addiction is something that will remain with us for life. We are always going to have a need to experience pleasure so let's get off the addiction band wagon and get on with living our lives to the fullest. The negative addictions will cease once we focus on bringing new behaviors into our lives that give us that feeling of a natural high. That's why we used harmful substances in the first place. To get high.

The thought of not being able to get high again will only make us hold onto the negative behaviors that created our problems in the beginning.

It only makes sense to me that a person is motivated to change by *compensation* instead of *degradation.* Reviewing a person's past and having them talk about their shortcomings only lowers that person's esteem and plunges them into a sea of guilt. On the other hand, recognizing that we are all human beings who have made mistakes and that they are forgivable ones, empowers the individual towards forward movement and, ultimately, optimum recovery.

Many people who work the traditional recovery programs believe that solid sobriety is based on a factor of time. In other words, sobriety comes with time. These individuals spend much of their energy acquiring sober time as if they were trading stamps. Then they brag about how much time they have as if it were a badge or a certificate. But this "factor of time" means nothing if they haven't developed a new "state of mind." Unfortunately, if they should relapse, all the marbles they have saved come falling out of their time frame of sobriety. Those who have developed a whole new way of living healthy and successfully believe that it's not just a factor of time but a state of mind. States of minds can be changed in one day. These people develop healthy living habits *in no time.* Whereas people who live by factors of time will always be asking, "how long is it going to take to get my life back together?"

All one has to do is to believe in the power of the human mind. All it takes is one (1) day to develop a mind set that's going to give you a whole new lease on life and a zest for living. Although the body moves at a snail's pace, the mind can move as quick as a lighting bolt. But change must first occur in the mind before the body will follow, and that can happen in that one day. You see, you can change your mind anytime, but your body must wait until it receives orders from your brain. That's why what you see is not a good representation of who you are. Within your mind, you *must* maintain a clear picture (imagination) of your dreams if you expect to see the end result.

Since thought is the essence of who we are, we can change our entire life with just a single thought. What the human mind commands, the body will and must follow in kind and in time. If you are waiting for your body to change in order for your mind to change, then you are operating from the outside in. That kind of thinking is not in accordance with the flow of nature. Remember, all of life as we know it flows from the inside out. We human beings are brought into this world from the inside out. If you drop a pebble into a pond you will notice that the ripples flow from the inside out. The happiest people in the world are successful not because they have things. They have things because they are happy people. It is that inside happiness that produces their good fortune. Although they are excited about their wealth, they know that their true wealth is their good health. They see themselves as rich in mind, body and spirit as opposed to having ownership of possessions. If they should somehow lose their material possessions, they know that whatever they have produced in their past can be produced again. They are the goose that lays the golden eggs. As long as they keep that in mind and do not get hung-up on the eggs, they will continue to provide the nurturing necessary for the continued well-being of their body, mind and inner spirit.

Whatever the human mind can conceive it can definitely achieve. We've proven that premise repeatedly throughout our lives. We are the embodiment of the sum total of all our thoughts. For example, if you want to know what you were thinking five years ago, all you have to do is examine your current physical and mental conditions. If you want to know where you are going to be five years from now, all you have to do is examine your mind. Whatever you believe, think or imagine at this very moment will undoubtedly be your outcome in reality. "What a man thinketh, so shall he become." "I think, therefore, I am." With this in "mind," it is easy to realize that we are the creator of all our experiences. Change the way you think and you change your entire life. The next section will provide you with an innovative approach to re-newed thinking—The Dynamics of Development and Positive Behavioral Change.

The Dynamics of Development and Positive Behavioral Change

The dynamics of optimum health lies in our ability to *respond* to our *thoughts* and *actions* in a *positive manner.*

Also, positively responding to our internal cues as well as to what's happening in the environment is the key to overcoming our problems. We respond by making choices about our internal and external environment. Since our responses to life's situations are a function of our thoughts, we can change our response just by changing the way we think. It is only fitting then to say that it is not what happens to us that creates our problems, it's how we think and respond to the situation and circumstances that occur in our lives. Based on this same assumption, we can also significantly improve and enhance our health and overall well-being by generating positive and healthy thought patterns and acting them out accordingly. This is no theory but a proven fact. Everything that you have ever accomplished, gained, or achieved has, is now, and always will be, the dynamics of how we develop.

Understanding the dynamics of human development and *positive* behavior change empowers us to re-create ourselves and our lives just by allowing ourselves to be *exposed* to *fresh ideas* and *new sensory experiences.*

What gives this process credence and reliability is the fact that we have all experienced and witnessed these past actions over and over again. It may have been through our own personal development or the development of others we have come in contact with over the years. Nevertheless, this process works regardless of the current situation or condition we may be in at this time. It has worked for us in the past and can definitely work anytime we so desire to call on those powerful forces from deep within our subconscious minds. In essence, we are the creator of all our experiences. We are the metabolic end products of our sensory experiences and the interpretations of those experiences. Most of our experiences originate from the way we think. What this suggests is that our thoughts are the essence of *who we are? And since we are the thinker of our thoughts, we can, at anytime regenerate new thoughts and consequently recreate ourselves!* (see Figure 8.2)

The following flow chart, that I also call "Mind Design" was created based on ten years of actual human research and study. It *represents* and *defines* the dynamics of *human development* and our potential for *positive behavioral change*. From the day we are born to the present, we are constantly operating in the following mind design process. There are two approaches to development that we go through that's responsible for *who we become* and *how we change*.

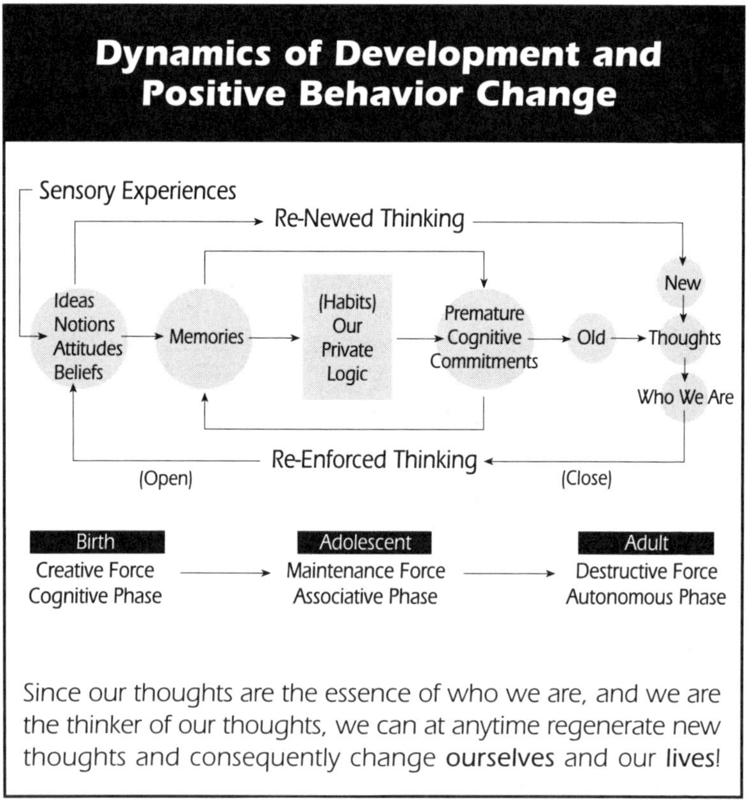

Figure 8.2

One is a positive approach to life that's demonstrated by a willingness to learn, prosper and grow. In this example, individuals are motivated, excited and have a passion to learn from the things that life has to offer. The second approach to human development is a "do or die" method to learning. People who follow the "do or die" method are generally threatened by severe consequences. In this example, many people feel that if they don't perform a certain way, they could probably wind up in dire straits.

When I was just a child, I remember my parents saying to me, "if you don't do your homework, you're not going to get good grades." Even some of my elementary school teachers stated at times, "if you don't do well in your school studies, you'll grow up to become a nobody." What a cruel and unjust thing to say to a child. This negative conditioning from our environment has a detrimental effect on impressionable children as well as older human beings. As a result I had a difficult time getting through school assignments and eventually flunked out of the ninth grade. Only after joining the military, did I finish my high school education and receive my diploma, which was ten years later. From there I enrolled at San Diego State University in California where I graduated with honors. Had I been given positive reinforcement instead of negative threats, I am sure I would have been inspired to be great during my earlier years in school.

As a result of my honorable achievements in college, I was recognized as the class nerd. At 45 year of age, it was somewhat of an honor, to have bestowed upon me, since at one time in my life I was considered the one least likely to succeed.

As children, our first attempts to walk were encouraged by our parents in a proactive approach to learning. We were motivated by the loving concerns of our family members to get on our feet and move. They would use encouraging statements such as, "Come on honey, show mommy you can walk, you can do it, that's a good boy (or girl)." Had our parents used a threatening approach to that particular learning such as, "If you don't get your butt off that floor and move, you'll never learn how to walk," chances are we'd still be on the floor today. Unfortunately, some parents do use this cruel and unusual approach to teaching. Some of us have been taught this way all of our lives. These approaches generally result in a defensive and resistive approach to learning. I've seen this negative approach to learning and development used between married couples, in families, with friends and throughout the work force.

A father insults his child because she is having difficulties learning how to drive. A wife scolds her husband because he's having a hard time finding a job. An employer threatens his employees with unemployment if they can't do their job right. This is only one way to get people to look at themselves, but it is not the best way. The key to maximizing one's potential is in positive reinforcement through positive encouragement, support and understanding. Those who are taught the proactive way to learning throughout their lives are the ones who become highly successful people. On the other hand, those who are threatened to learn generally fail to develop successfully.

If we give up on learning how to walk or anything else, it's probably because of a negative approach to teaching. In this approach, we would wind up living out the rest of our lives on the *ground floor* of development. Fortunately for us, our minds have not developed the idea of failure. So, we push ahead and learn how to maneuver gracefully on our feet within a year's time. During the early phase of our development we are generally open to learning, since we have yet to acquire the idea of fears, limitations and doubts.

The concept of the "Mind Design" is provided here to help you *understand* and realize that change is possible. If you understand how something works, you can better apply the knowledge you have gained. For success is an understanding, not just something that you do. Anyone can change and transform their life far *beyond recovery* if they are willing to believe that change is possible. In other words, we can live our lives to the fullest through the understanding and the applications of the "Mind Design."

Our potential for change can be miraculous just by following the mechanics of the "Mind Design." It is the essence of how we think, act and respond to the stimulus we receive from our environment and surroundings. In doing so, it is possible for us to change our entire life in just one (1) day, whereas with other methods it has taken years.

All we have to do is first *understand*, then apply ourselves as we did during our early years. Allow that kid inside you to come out and recapture the true art of learning and becoming again.

In observing this particular flow chart, it is obvious to see that we are the products of our environment as indicated by the Sensory Experiences label (Figure 8.2). Every *idea, notion, attitude and belief (INAB)* that we have acquired over the years have come from our continuous exposure to *outside experiences*. If we are told continuously at a tender young age that smoking is cool or certain groups of people are inferior, there's a good chance that those ideas, beliefs, attitudes and notions may become our own. Since we come into this world knowing absolutely nothing, our minds are primed to be formed by those we meet within our environment. And our chances of becoming just like those who have come before us, are extremely high. Similar to how computers are programmed, our minds are basically like an empty hard drive. We are actually ignorant until we are influenced by those who are our teachers, parents, mentors, friends and guardians. In most cases, their ideas, beliefs, customs, language, dress, diet, mannerisms and biases become our own.

For example, if you were born in California, USA, but raised in China until your teens, what language do you think you'd be speaking? You'd be speaking Chinese, of course. What do you think your diet would consist of? Let's try fish, rice, vegetable, grains, noodles, tea, etc.

Just because you were born an American in America doesn't mean you automatically inherit the American language and customs at birth. They have to be taught to you in America, exposed to the American customs and its people for many years. Although we are the product of our environment, we are also the result of our choices. Therefore, we also develop our own ideas and beliefs about our world from the people, places and things we come into contact with. As a result of our good or bad experiences, we develop good or bad memories of those experiences. We make every attempt to repeat the pleasurable ones while at the same time we try to avoid the painful ones (hedonism). The habits that we develop are the result of our urge to repeat the same pleasurable experiences — the innermost box (as illustrated in Figure 8.2).

In the process of developing these habits, we tend to make strong commitments to relive our pleasurable memories. We also tend to "deny" any harmful side effects that may result from that behavior.

The flow arrows in between the inner and outermost boxes illustrate the strong commitment we have with our memories. If our experiences are pleasurable ones, we tend to make a *habit* of repeating those experiences. We often see people who have problems with drugs, alcohol, gambling, shopping and eating, who demonstrate these kinds of behaviors. It is, without a doubt, that many of our problems stem from *over indulgence.* However, people with eating disorders generally don't think about the things that can help them recover from their dis-ease. They are plagued with thoughts that have been artificially inseminated into their minds. Many of them have been conditioned by the fashion industry that to be beautiful, they must possess a body that is thin, trim and shapely. Now, there's nothing wrong with wanting to be thin, except what this industry has created are *mind sets* that focus on outside packaging instead of the beauty that's within.

For example, many young women are concerned more about the glitter of the outside litter instead of the solid gold of their inner soul.

These *thoughts* that are passed on to us from the outside world represent the strength of our subconscious minds. Those learned thoughts refuse to allow any other thoughts to enter the mind that just may help that person understand the dynamics of their disorder. You see, people with eating disorders spend most of their time defending that they are fat instead of recognizing the beauty they have inside. These beautiful people are just as gifted as any spiritually oriented person. The problem with people who experience eating disorders is that they are more into the packaging than the contents of their total being.

The gift of beauty that one holds inside can never be revealed if they're making a fuss over the wrappings. They need to get a grip that, if the insides are beautiful, the outsides are going to be just as lovely.

Again, beauty and happiness are an inside job. All anyone has to do is to allow themselves to go beyond the surface of their human form and discover the depths of their inner spiritual being.

A Poem to Remember

Love From The Inside Out

Look within and see your heart,
Know the mind and understand your part,
Live and learn without the doubt,
And learn to love from the inside out.

People who are plagued with eating disorders are living from the outside in. Their attitudes are such that in order to feel good inside, they must look good on the outside. There's nothing wrong with wanting to look good on the outside, but the inside beauty must supersede the outside packaging before that beauty can become solid gold. Otherwise, a person's outside beauty becomes superficial. It's similar to having jewelry that is gold plated instead of solid 14k gold. Beauty that is just painted over rust will easily and eventually wear off if the surface isn't continuously reinforced with more outside glitter. But solid gold beauty is to the bone, and will always present its lustrous shine no matter what. People who are beautiful on the inside first, can never lose their magnificence.

The beauty one sees with the outer eye is a result of the beauty they see with their inner eye.

On the other hand, if a person who relies on their looks should somehow lose that outside beauty, they also lose themselves. People who live to create happiness based on these superficial means can only feel good about themselves if they can get the approval and favorable comments of those around them. That's the outside glitter. The reason for this is that they are not aware of their inner beauty that expresses itself from the inside out. Therefore, they rely on this outside glitter to feel good about themselves.

The glitter I am talking about are those comments from people who see and know us from the outside. When they truly get to know us from the inside, they just may find that we're mostly packaging, and then realize how shallow outside beauty can be. What really makes this backward loving so sad is that it has nowhere to go. It can't be shared. It is projected inward. The only person that receives this pseudo loving is the person themselves. This is one of the main reasons why people with all kinds of disorders very seldom receive love from others.

Love should radiate from within, project outwards, touch those in its path and reflect back to its origin.

The love we project may not always return when and where we want it. But as long as we maintain the *projection*, it will reflect off others who will eventually respond in kind.

Therefore, the way a mirror reflects our facial and physical features, so do the eyes of others reflect the warmth or coldness that we emit.

It's important to realize that giving love is mandatory but receiving it is, at best, random and optional. The bottom line is that if we are not emitting positive energy, there's a good chance we may not get any returns from outside sources.

Although our emotions play a monumental part in governing our behavior, we still maintain the *power* to make positive choices and healthier responses to the emotional setbacks that happen in our lives. A point to remember is that our emotions are not the cause of our problems; they are the result of our problems. In turn, our emotions add to our problems and eventually become the main focus.

This process is often characterized by people with weight problems. First comes the desire to experience pleasure through eating. Over a period of time, a person may become obese (primary problem). As a result, the person becomes *emotionally* distraught (secondary problem). In their attempt to deal with their weight problem, the *emotional factor* that was secondary to the weight problem, now becomes the primary factor involving the individual's situation. This person may attempt to find solace in eating more food to deal with the *emotional factor* of their problem. In doing so, they become more overweight and significantly more distraught. This is known as "double trouble" and is a hideous state for anyone to endure.

This situation has the characteristics of every disorder that plagues modern society. All we have to do to break this devastating "cycle of dis-ease" is to understand its process and know in our hearts that *we have the power to stop it!* Change the way you think and you change your entire life. But how do we change our thinking once our minds have been set to believe otherwise? Read on.

The process of repeating the same old pattern results in the same old conditions and the same old thoughts. These *old* thoughts become *who we are!* We retain these old thinking patterns by re-enforced thinking. For example, your encounter with a fabulous restaurant may produce memories of delectable dining. Every time you get the notion or thought to dine out, you may very well choose that particular site again. The scenario of *re-enforced thinking* may sound similar to this: "There's this really great seafood restaurant that serves the best broiled swordfish. The fish is so fresh that it melts right in your mouth, let's check it out!"

First, there is the exposure to the *sensory experience* of the restaurant. Due to the terrific experience you had there, you make a conscious effort to *remember* that restaurant the next time you want to dine out. As a result, you make a *commitment* to the *memory* of that experience and repeat the act of visiting that site sometime in the near future. After a number of repeated visits, it becomes a habitual — addictive — experience (see bottom half flow arrows in Figure 8.2).

It is interesting and important to note that of all the *flow arrows*, the bottom half is indicative of re-enforcing old thinking patterns and behaviors. This pattern is one that people seem to get stuck in most of the time.

To break the pull this pattern has over our inability to move out of that *accustom zone*, we need to understand and realize the trap we have inadvertently put ourselves in. We become stuck in this trap as a result of our *resistance* to fresh ideas and new sensory experiences in the developing stages. This process is illustrated by the flow arrow extending out from the *Sensory Experiences* label located above the upper left corner of the "Mind Design." This arrow demonstrates how information we receive from the environment gets directed to the intersection of the main receiving gate—INAB (Ideas, Notions, Attitudes and Beliefs). It is at this gate where the conscious mind carries out its task of programming the subconscious mind.

The sensory instructions we receive from our experiences with people, places, events and things all come to us in the form of either positive or negative stimuli. This demonstrates that much of what influences our behavior lies outside of us and has a tremendous effect on how we think, feel, act and respond (see "Mind Design," Figure 8.2). To create *re-newed thinking* that leads to positive behavior change within self, we must first understand the dynamics of this process and allow ourselves to be continuously exposed to fresh ideas and new sensory experiences when change is in order. Otherwise, we will continue to follow the same old living patterns that make it difficult for us to change our negative thinking and our old ways of living. This process of how our minds are *set* can be of a positive or negative nature.

The "Mind Design" represents how our mind sets and resets through the power of thought generated by our continuous exposure to our surroundings. Much of how we think and feel is strongly influenced by our contacts.

To the left of this imaginary *hard drive* is the opening (the main gate) where most of your new software is entered. This is the entrance to our subconscious mind that we call the INAB (Ideas, Notions, Attitudes and Beliefs). Whenever new information tries to get past that gate without your *conscious* mind's permission, it will be "NABBED" by your own ideas of how things are supposed to be. This is known as resistance.

Why is resistance to learning new behaviors so prevalent and difficult to overcome? The following theory (I like to think of it as fact) may explain why many people find it difficult to change. This new discovery of our inner mind and how it works can shed some new light on our resistance to change. You will be amazed to know that there is much more to the mind than just a conscious and subconscious.

We are all familiar with the fact that our conscious minds do the programming while our subconscious minds carry out those orders flawlessly. In other words, the conscious mind gives the orders and the subconscious obeys without question. That's why when someone commits a senseless act of crime or violence, the typical expression describing the perpetrator is that they acted with *no conscious.* Meaning that the subconscious acted on its own due to years of negative conditioning and programming. It is the conscious mind that determines right from wrong or good from bad. But once the subconscious mind has been programmed, the conscious mind becomes relaxed or lazy, allowing the subconscious to carry out its orders automatically.

Now, you ask yourself, "Why doesn't the conscious mind take over and reprogram the subconscious mind?" It's very simple. The subconscious is much bigger than the conscious mind. The entire mind is similar to a giant iceberg. Only a fraction of it is above the surface of the water while the bulk of the ice is submerged. The part above the water is comparable to the conscious mind while most of the submerged part is comparable to the subconscious mind. Another example of how the two can be compared would be like trying to fight off King Kong with a pea shooter. No disrespect intended, but your conscious mind takes the honors of being the pea shooter whereas your subconscious takes the part of being King Kong.

The subconscious is a very powerful force that took years in the making. But if you understand how this great source can be tapped, you can gain control of one of the world's most powerful forces known to man. Everything you have ever been *exposed* to resides in your subconscious mind and you are about to learn how to tap into that great source of yours. Similar to how King Kong was captured and forced to work for peanuts, you can do the same with your mind just by allowing yourself the time to understand how those two parts of the mind relate.

You see, success is not in doing; it's in understanding. If we understand the process of how something works, we can better apply ourselves and the principles that lead to total health, happiness and well-being. Now, let's tap into that inner world of your fascinating mind and learn how it works.

The "Mind Design"

What makes the subconscious so powerful other than the fact that it outweighs the conscious mind a hundred to one? The subconscious mind is more complex. It incorporates a powerful circuit of representatives that diligently strive to maintain consistency in your thinking. Once the *dynamics of development* has set its representatives in place, it would take an *act* of *congress* to change them all (this congress is your conscious mind). What are these representatives of your conscious mind?

If we probe deeper into our *total mind*, we will find that there exists five (5) subdivisions that many of us are not aware of. I call them your *Automatic Defense Systems (AutoDens)*. These (5) subdivisions are responsible for our refusal to accept and respond to fresh ideas and new sensory experiences. The *gatekeeper of our total mind* houses the INAB—our Ideas, Notions, Attitudes and Beliefs. This first line of defense determines what we allow past that gate into our subconscious mind. These defense systems act as bouncers guarding the door at an exclusive night club. Instead of one bouncer, we have five. If we don't produce proper identification, it's likely that we are not going to get in. And if we try to force our way in, there is a good chance that we will meet with strong confrontation and be bounced right out on our rear.

The conscious and subconscious minds work in much the same way. Anytime someone attempts to tell you something that does not coincide with what you now hold to be true, in most cases, you will not buy into it even if it is the truth. In other words, the information given — even if it is true—must agree with the perception of the beholder, otherwise, the mind will not accept it.

These AutoDens are the five subdivisions of our total mind that are located throughout the entire flow chart with the INAB representing the gate of the subconscious mind. See "Mind Design" in Figure 8.2 on page 264. These (5) defense systems are as follows:

1. *INAB (our Ideas, Notions, Attitudes and Beliefs)*
2. *Memories (everything that we have learned and experienced about ourselves and our environment)*
3. *PIC - (Protective Inner Core — our habits)*
4. *PCC - Premature Cognitive Commitments we make to our memories*
5. *Our Old Thoughts - Who we are*

When we are new to this world we have no ideas, notions, attitudes or beliefs until they are acquired through our contact with our environment. But once they are set, there is a chain reaction throughout our entire subconscious mind. During the many years that we are exposed to our surrounding environment, our mind is being conditioned by the people we meet, the things we see, the foods that we eat, the things that we do and the words that we hear. Our INAB begins the powerful chain reaction by setting our *standards of living*. By following the center arrow in Figure 8.2, you will notice that it is our *INAB* that is *set* first by our exposure to new *sensory experiences*.

The next reaction that occurs in this chain of events is that we acquire *new memories* from our ideas, notions, attitudes and beliefs about our experiences. Our *memories* are then reinforced by both our INAB, and the commitments we now make to the pleasurable things that we remember about those sensory experiences. Now, if these experiences are positive, or perceived by us to be good memories, chances are we are going to make every effort to repeat these experiences often. This ongoing process will then set up *premature cognitive commitments (PCC)* to our memories.

The commitments that we make to the memory of our experiences will eventually become our *habits.* Our habits become set and very difficult to change as they are reinforced every time we indulge in the same experiences of pleasure. Our habits, also known as our protective inner core (PIC) then become automatic and guarded. Our protective inner core (PIC) now becomes the governor of our *thoughts*, just as the governor of a community holds office for many terms. We become rigid in our ideas, notions, attitudes and beliefs which makes it difficult for us to change. In essence, we have become set in our ways. As you can see, there are five (5) barriers that *"new information"* must break through before we are ready to accept a change in our way of thinking.

If you can control your thoughts through understanding how your mind works, you can change your entire life in just one day. If you have difficulty with believing that statement, you are now experiencing how your (PIC) jumps right up to resist change, instead of considering that it just may be possible.

Allow yourself to *imagine*. Let's see how this powerful system operates when new information becomes available to you. Let's imagine that you are overweight and want to lose a few pounds of fat. You have decided to enroll in a local fat clinic that's going to cost you an arm and a leg. Although you'll be paying through the nose, you are desperate and will pay anything to get rid of the fat. Your idea, notion, attitude and belief (INAB) about your plan are set that it is the clinic that's going to do it for you. You begin to feel good about your decision and you share your aspirations with a friend. Unfortunately, your friend does not share your excitement of having to pay top dollar for something they feel you could do on your own. They begin to share their experience about a more economical process that has worked for them. But you are desperate and have already made your decision to attend this new program. The first thing that occurs within your mind is that your INAB refuses to go along with what your friend has proposed. Your *memory* of the program and how it works is then reinforced by your premature cognitive commitment (what you have learned about the program up to this point). Your commitment to those memories kicks in only to support your own private logic. The protective inner core (PIC) governs your old thoughts and you then reinforce your INAB by telling your friend that no matter what they say, you are going through with your plans.

The problem with this entire scenario is not in agreeing

with or disagreeing with the advice of the friend. It is not about defending your own private logic, and it is not about making the right decision. The problem is there but it's not an obvious one. Many people are unaware of the mechanics that create problems in situations similar to the one above. The problems that occur in most social, personal and professional verbal transactions are very subtle, and many people will miss what can be seen so easily. We spend tremendous amounts of time, money and effort, trying to change, alter, and improve our standards of living all based on the mechanics of the above scenario. If we took the time to understand the dynamics of development and positive behavior change, we could change in a few days, what has normally taken others years to change.

So, what is the problem in the above scenario? Before I share the secret with you, let's imagine another situation. You are a smoker who is considering quitting but you are not sure you can do it. Your INAB on smoking has left a very strong impression in your memory banks on the pleasure of smoking. It is our *memories* that have the biggest influence in maintaining constant behavior patterns. The reason for this is because our memories store all of our wants, likes, pleasures, fears, limitations, dislikes, prejudices, goals, skills and knowledge.

Of all the characteristics that make up our memory, knowledge is the predominant power that we try hard to harness. Since knowledge is power, our memories have a very strong influence on how we behave.

On the chart titled the "Mind Design," (Figure 8.2) notice the flow and direction of the two arrows leaving the memory phase. The first arrow leads directly to our protective inner core (PIC) that sets up the development for good or bad behavioral habits. The second arrow depicts how our minds create *a memory—commitment continuum* (flow arrows around innermost box). This is due to our need to repeat memorable experiences. In other words, we tend to repeat the things that give us pleasure.

For you, smoking may be a perceived pleasure, so chances are you are going to be pressed to smoke repeatedly. Your *commitment* to the pleasure of smoking stems from your memory of the experience. As a result of these continued behavioral patterns, you develop lasting behavioral habits that become very difficult to change. Deep within your subconscious, your habits become so ingrained in your mind that you continue to reinforce the protective inner core (PIC). It is this PIC that works in conjunction with the other four AutoDens in your total mind that prevents most people from making successful changes in their lives. Lastly, since your PIC governs your thoughts, it strongly affirms that smoking is a part of *"who you are"* (illustrated by the *"Old Thoughts" phase*).

These five AutoDens of our conscious and subconscious mind work so efficiently that many of us actually believe that our body needs and enjoys smoking. When in fact, nothing could be further from the truth. Instead of admitting that we have given in to the stronghold of the behavior, we *rationalize* our actions and defend our rights to destroy our inner spirit through the use of destructive substances such as cigarettes. I personally believe that if science discovered an easier and more effective way for people to give up cigarettes, many of them would douse the fires of their smoking habit. This "if you can't beat'em join'em" attitude is the result of a strong automatic defense system (AutoDens) of the subconscious mind. Therefore, people would rather *"fight than switch."*

Lastly, let's imagine someone who has just been diagnosed with cancer by their doctor. Our knowledge of this disease would lead us to believe that it is terminal. Where did this idea originate? Do our *attitudes* coincide with the commotion over the *notion* of this disease? If we believe that this dis-ease is terminal, then it will be. Again, our INAB set into motion a chain of events that signal our subconscious mind that we are going to die. Remember that the subconscious mind just carries out the orders that the conscious mind provides. What orders are you giving your subconscious mind about your ability to overcome cancer? If the mind can make you sick, then the mind can make you well. But you must be willing to get past your automatic defense systems (AutoDens).

When people tell themselves they can't do something, they are unleashing a power that has no limits. You are commanding a tremendous amount of power to carry out your orders about your abilities to succeed or fail. There are people on both sides of this argument that will tell you that what they believe and conceive they will achieve. Let's keep in mind that there are two kinds of people in the world — those who think they can and those who think they can't, and they are both right. So if you *think* cancer is terminal, it is—for you. If you think it isn't, it's not.

There are people who will argue that both are correct and they are. There have been many deaths due to this dreadful disease but there are those who have overcome the disease of cancer just by the way they think. If you want more proof, just check the many case studies at Harvard Medical School on the countless number of people who used their minds to heal their bodies. There is evidence for and there is evidence against. Your current health status all depends on which evidence you choose to believe.

If your idea of cancer is that it's terminal, you may want to tap into that powerful resource of your subconscious mind. It has the power to heal or destroy, but it can only do one or the other based on the orders it receives from your conscious mind. Your AutoDens can seriously and unconsciously affect your ability to overcome any obstacle if you do not allow your conscious to pay attention. If you refuse to believe that you possess this power, then you are allowing the protective inner core (PIC) of your subconscious mind to step in and defend your idea that this power does not exist.

To deny that you have this power is similar to carrying around highly explosive material and being unaware of the cargo you're carrying. In times of anger, rage, frustration, or excitement, your mind and body automatically produce powerful body chemicals to help you cope in times of stress. These powerful chemical substances are known as cortisol, noradrenaline, adrenaline, dopamine, acetalcholine, serotonin and other powerful hormones that help the body in times of trouble — "flight or fight."

To get to the heart of our problems, we must be willing to allow our subconscious to work for us. We first have to be aware of how our AutoDens prevents us from using the power of the subconscious mind. Understanding how it shorts out our power works like this. Our INAB triggers our memory that cancer is terminal. Our memory, in turn, is reinforced by our commitment to what we hold to be true; that is, the societal expectation that cancer is terminal. We affix in our minds such statements as: cancer can't be cured; or I can never quit smoking; or I've tried everything and nothing seems to work. These affirmations set off by our memories, reconditions our habits and reestablishes our own private logic. This is our protective inner core (PIC). Finally, our (PIC) that governs our old thoughts only reinforce our INAB all over again. This closed cycle (infinity loop) of becoming allows no opportunity for creative thinking.

If somehow new information does bypass your INAB entrance, there is another entrance that has a tendency to keep you from acquiring it. Notice on the "Mind Design" how the outer sensory experience arrow goes through your INAB, over the top and down on the right side until it intersects with new thoughts. Right there is the second entrance to your subconscious that once you accept an idea, it may not get in due to the strong opposition of your *old thoughts* that linger at that intersection.

For example, Fran would like to attend college and

receive her BA in Physical Education but is unsure of herself. Bob told her about this new program that's being offered at U-Study State University. He said that she could easily obtain a college degree in two years. Fran: "I think I can do it." The idea to attend college got past the INAB. Fran later discovers that maybe college will be too difficult for her. She begins to doubt herself and states such affirmation as: "It's going to be too much trouble or I'm not smart enough." Maybe it's just wishful thinking on her part. This is a classic example of what happens when fresh ideas enter our minds only to be turned down at the back door where our old thoughts reside.

Of the three scenarios that we covered, each represented a classic problem that prevents positive behavior change. Have you discovered it yet? How could the person wanting to lose weight accomplish her goal successfully? How could the smoker have been successful in giving up their cigarettes? And how could the patient diagnosed with cancer overcome the idea that their disease is terminal? The problems of overcoming their difficulties all stem from not allowing themselves to *look, learn* and *listen*.

Their AutoDens (INAB, Memories, Commitments, PIC and Old Thoughts) simply refuse to accept any information that does not agree with what they now hold to be true. So, before we even allow ourselves to listen, the AutoDens automatically and subconsciously responds with our Own Private Logic. Many people prevent themselves from receiving valuable information because they would like to be recognized for what they already know, and people don't like to be told that they are wrong.

An important factor to remember for those who would like to succeed in their endeavors is to forget about what you know up to this point. It is your known that prevents you from growing, prospering and changing. If what you know now has not helped you reach your ultimate goal, maybe you should allow yourself to listen to fresh ideas and participate in new sensory experiences. This is not to say that you are ill-informed and don't know a bag of beans about how to run your life. That's not what learning is all about. It's about getting rid of certain prejudices and old thinking patterns. For now, put your stuff on the back burner until such time you can integrate it with new learning. Allow your creativity and imagination to kick in to innovative ideas. Remember, you don't have to agree or disagree. You don't even have to do anything. All that it requires is for you to listen:

- *Intuitively*
- *Creatively*
- *Indiscriminately*

There are five other reasons why this process of listening is significantly effective and reliable. The art of listening has been tested, proven and is used often by highly successful people throughout the world.

- *With listening comes understanding*
- *With understanding comes knowledge*
- *With knowledge comes power*
- *With power comes control*
- *With control comes success*

You are now in control of the most awesome force known to science: The power of the human mind. As the Owner and Chief Executive Officer of your Corporation, you now have the power to heal, grow, prosper and change. With this new understanding, you can now take control of your life and overcome any problems, disorders, or dis-eases that have held you back or have caused you pain in the past. There is no way this process can fail if you become a silent witness. That is, listening without:

- *Rationalizing*
- *Defending*
- *Judging*
- *Protecting*
- *Justifying*
- *Arguing*

These are very strong defense responses that support and maintain your own private logic, habits and old ideas of how things are supposed to be. The first time you attempt the art of listening, your Automatic Defense System (AutoDens) within your subconscious mind is going to try diligently to keep you right where you have always been, stuck. No matter how hard you try to suppress or deny those old ideas, they are going to be there until you allow your new ideas to settle in and take the place of those old ones. Those old memories must be replaced by new memories in order to acquire healthier habits and new ways of thinking. It only takes twenty-one to thirty days for anyone to develop new habits and skills. And if you can breathe, you too can create an entirely new you, but you must be willing to *practice* new ways of living your life until those new habits take form.

Acquiring the new memories should be obtained in the same manner in which we obtained the old ones: By exposing ourselves to fresh ideas and new sensory experiences. A more drastic way a person can easily learn new ideas is by falling on their head and causing amnesia. Is it any wonder why an amnesiac would be a great candidate for learning new skills? They have no memory that's going to defend old ideas or prevent new information from getting into their brain.

Since the mind of a child and an amnesiac are basically open to new information, they are capable of developing, learning and growing much faster than those who have already been living under the hypnosis of societal conditioning. Just below the "Mind Design" you will notice the three main forces that structure all of life that we talked about in *Discovery 6.* They are the creative force, the maintenance force and the destructive force. As you can see, the creative force corresponds to new birth and learning (cognitive phase). We are very much open to learning during this phase of our lives. The maintenance force corresponds with puberty and associates everything we have learned up until now with who we are. This maintenance force is where most people experience a stalemate in learning. They are very much set in their ways and are somewhat skeptical about who to believe or who to trust. Many teenagers have difficulties establishing their identity during this stage of their lives and are reluctant to change what they now believe. They are reaching that closed end in their lives where if what's being said does not agree with what they hold to be true, it won't get in. Most parents — all too often — know the difficulties that they have with their teens during this stage of development.

Lastly, there is the destructive force. This force is where most adult's habits, ideas and behaviors are set in stone where they have almost given up on learning innovative ways to live better lives. They are cruising on momentum. Their booster rockets have long been jettisoned. They are operating on old thoughts, ideas and concepts that they have learned years ago. To introduce them to new ideas would be like sticking their heads into the mouth of a lion. Most adults become cranky as they age. This is not normal. Crankiness is a learned response. Aging is not a decree, it's a decision that we make based on the decisions that people have made for us. When we see others get old and cranky, there's a good chance we are going to do likewise. We are a race of followers. Only a few become leaders. Leaders are always open to innovative ideas and new ways to enjoy and live their lives. Followers become whatever those people were before them without question or doubt.

While operating in the destructive force, most people

begin to decay, grow old and become plagued with numerous degenerative diseases. They sit at home, eat more food and don't move their bodies the way they were designed. They spend a lot of their time in and out of the hospital and consume pounds of medication each year in the form of pills, potions and elixirs. And they wonder why they contract all kinds of dis-eases. Is there any wonder why this is called the destructive force? Since most of our behaviors during this phase are automatic, we really have to get a grip that understanding is the key towards turning our lives around. We must realize that becoming a silent witness to our inner spirit and environment can make a tremendous difference in living a healthy and successful lifestyle. Remember, in order to recreate ourselves, we must be willing to understand thoroughly the *Dynamics of Development and Positive Behavior Change*.

Discovery 9

Soar With The Eagles– Developing Healthy Support Systems

Associations are relationships that mold and shape our character. Our ideas, notions, attitudes and beliefs (INAB) are birth by our surroundings. Seek healthy relationships, for associations bring about simulations.

Oliver Rhodes

Many people are out there scratching with turkeys instead of soaring with eagles. Developing a healthy support system of eagles is crucial to acquiring optimum health and overall well-being. It's as essential as water is to fish and light is to plants. But how do you find eagles? *Become One!* How do you find a healthy association of people? Same way, *Form One!*

In doing so, you'll attract other people who are following the biological laws of nature. The adages, "birds of a feather flock together," "monkey see, monkey do" and "it takes one to know one," are all truisms. For example, during the time that I was drinking and using, I sought out those who were using as well. You see, misery loves company. I wanted to be around people who wanted to get *high* with me. Similarly, people who are living in accordance with nature also enjoy interacting with those who relish that same lifestyle. *Healthy associations make it easier for people to develop healthy lifestyle habits.*

If you aspire to lose weight, but others around you are not encouraged to do likewise, it may be difficult for you to obtain your goal. It is the same way with trying to quit smoking. It's almost impossible to give up cigarettes when others around you are lighting up every time you look around. The environment can make us or break us.

There are many people I've worked with who decided to give up their drinking and using, but did not want to give up their old using buddies. People who soar with eagles live high on life. Developing healthy habits are more than just learning new behaviors. You also have to develop a new *circle of associates* that have the same aspirations as you. You want to move with the flow of traffic. Hanging around with opposing forces are similar to driving through a "do not enter" sign on the freeway. You undoubtedly would have to turn in their direction or face them head on. Most of us would like to avoid head on collisions, so we generally conform to the standards of our surroundings. Change is difficult enough without having to convince friends, family, colleagues and current associates of our new lifestyles.

We need support when making strides to change from worst to better and from better to best. Social support systems are paramount to the change itself. In contrast, a lack of support can stop us dead in our tracks. How often have enthusiastic people been discouraged from attending school, selecting a new career or learning a new sport all because someone laughed them out of it? Why do some people have a difficult time seeing others take to the sky? Obviously, they don't want to be left on the ground. It can be miserable watching others fly.

Remember the fairy tale "The Ugly Duckling?" It was the story about a baby swan that somehow got lost from its own and winded up with baby chicks. The chicklings thought that the duckling was terribly ugly. The chicklings were cruel and mean to the duckling calling it horrible names. Reluctantly the duckling was forced to fend for itself and go it alone. The little duckling was crushed and broken hearted. It never wanted to peer down into the pond to see its ugly face again. He stayed away from all others so that he wouldn't be reminded of his horrible looks. After months of surviving on his own, he begin to mature. One day as he peered into the sky, he noticed a flock of the most beautiful birds he had ever seen. These great birds flew with grace and poise. They were absolutely fabulous and danced with the wind displaying poetry in motion.

The ugly duckling sighed, "Oh how I wish I could be one of them, but no one wants to associate with an old ugly duckling." All of a sudden the great white birds peered down from the sky as if they were drawn towards a magical force from below. "It appears as if they are gazing directly at me," the ugly duckling cried. "I must hide before they come down to harass and make fun of me, too." But there was nowhere to hide. There was only the pond that the ugly duckling had sworn never to look into again. But this time was different. The pond was his only hope to hide, even if it meant seeing his own horrible face again.

The ugly duckling *spread his wings* and dashed for the pond to submerge himself beneath the waters. But before he entered the pond he was struck with amazement of the image that peered back at him. Instead of seeing the horror of an ugly face, he was now seeing the majestic beauty of a new style and grace. It was not the ugliness that excited and lured those swans to his side, it was his incredible beauty and most magnificent grace that brought those swans to his embrace.

A Poem to Remember

The Swan

The duckling was a swan, a beauty of his kind.
But those chicks with no shame, gave him one
heck of a time.
Filled with overwhelming grief and
mounting pain,
He fled the scene, holding his head in shame.
Over the months he developed, and fully
matured,
And an awesome symbol he became, through
the pain he endured.

He aspired to be great, with a new change in luck,
And much to his surprise, he became a swan and not that duck.
For weeks he ran, because his face he could not stand,
Until he gazed into the pond, and realized all along he was a swan.
A thing of beauty, a heart of gold, a majestic swan he now behold.
Beauty so striking, he just could not hide,
It was the lure of his greatness, that brought those swans to his side.
Months of hiding, had come to an end,
The duckling had found, a new set of friends.
He became more than their friend, he was picked as their leader,
And nothing could be better, or ever much sweeter.
They all took to flight, it was an incredible sight,
Not once gazing back, as he led his new pack,
And as he climbed to the top, he waved goodbye to that spot,
Where he once hid his face, in shame and disgrace.
But it's all different now, because he's far above the ground,
He went from ugly to beauty, and now he wears the crown.
There was never an ugly duckling, it was just a bad label,
That was given to him, by those chicks that weren't able.
They couldn't fly to the sky, so they played silly games,
Finding fault and shame, by calling him bad names.
These birds were nerds, that spoke ghastly words,

But the duckling turned swan, found a much healthier herd.
If you aspire to be better than you currently are,
Find yourself a supporting cast, and become that shinning star.
Be aware of certain groups, that try to play with your mind,
Take off like the swan and leave the turkeys behind.

Choosing Eagles Through QRLP

Although the story of the ugly duckling is a fairy tale of sorts, it is also a fable that reveals a truth. There are many true tales that are similar to this one. As aspiring individuals, we must be aware of those who yearn to have us fill their agendas. Those agendas may mean substance abuse, crime, violence, gluttony, dishonesty or infidelity. It can be poor conduct in school, to cruel and unusual punishment. Even in intimate relationships, one spouse may become intimidated if the other decides to pursue a more profitable career. Healthy relationships would support this move by encouraging their mate to give it their best.

As people, we need each other. Sharing ideas and experiences are essential to human life. We are social beings and must learn to get along with each other through supportive relationships. But how do we distinguish the eagles from the turkeys? Naturally we want to soar with the eagles. But too often we wind up with those who would have it no other way than for us to be stuck in a rut as they are.

In many relationships where one mate is more motivated and energetic than the other, conflict tends to be an issue. Eagles breeding with turkeys can become confused, disoriented and bogged down. Eventually, they may become disappointed with the others and may decide to pick up stakes. Finding healthy relationships, associates and colleagues can be as easy as understanding the dynamics of Qualitative Recreation Lifestyle Principles *(QRLP)*.

You may recall in *Discovery 6, QRLP Defined & Applied*, that choosing our associates should come under these standards. Also, since birds of a feather flock together, we cannot expect to develop relationships with people of high caliber if we don't live by those same standards:

Quality .... *A Standard for Excellence*
Recreation .... *A Restoration to Health*
Lifestyle .... *A Process of Balance*
Principles .... *A Code of Conduct*

- *Integrity*
- *Harmony*
- *Conformity*

If you're following *QRLP*, naturally you would want your associates to do likewise. On the other hand, if you're not practicing these principles you may be comfortable with those of your own fashioning. It is only when we decide to break away from the crowd that it becomes our most challenging task. Many people that we have associated with over the years may become bitter if they see us sowing a new road. Here are some behaviors that will help you develop healthy and loving relationships:

Become an Eagle. Live your life according to the biological laws of nature *(QRLP)*. Be honest with yourself and those you associate with. Learn to respect and appreciate who you are and others will do likewise. People tend to treat us the way we treat ourselves. The *choice* is yours. Eagles are leaders that attract other eagles. Be a follower and others will lead you. Be a leader and others will follow you. Make a difference in your life and the lives of your loved ones by following the *Eagle's Creed (Discovery 1, page 75).*

Develop Healthy Associations. If you are a follower, chances are you are being influenced by your associates. If you are a leader of good habits, then your association will carry with it opportunity to grow, prosper and develop. Select associates that are: *(Q)* Striving for excellence; *(R)* Actively involved in Health Promoting Activities; *(L)* Leading a balanced lifestyle; and *(P)* Conducting themselves with Integrity, Harmony and Conformity based on the laws of nature and laws of your community.

Stay Focused. There will be times others will want you to veer off course into turbulent waters. Taking risks are a part of living with challenge, but be aware of *unnecessary* risks that do more harm than good. Keep reflecting good will. And remember, the way a mirror reflects our facial and physical features, so do the eyes of other's reflect the warmth or coldness that we emit. In spite of the negative energy that you receive from the environment or other people, keep shining. Don't become their mirror; allow them to become yours. In this way, you can maintain your dignity and perhaps influence others.

Believe in Yourself. In line with staying focused, believe in yourself. You are the creator of all your experiences. Your thoughts are the essence of who you are as well. You are more than what you think you are. Therefore, you can change your life just by the way you think, because you are the thinker of your thoughts. *All things are possible if you believe*. Believing is more than seeing. We may not always see what it is we aspire to achieve, but believing can bring you everything you see.

We are social beings and can't get along without each other. Everything we do will somehow influence others and they in turn will influence us. Let's be assured these influences coincide with those laws set by nature. Active participation in Qualitative Recreation Lifestyle Principles *(QRLP)* will help you weed out those who are not creating healthy lifestyle habits.

Throughout your life you are going to be challenged

by your environment and those you associate with. As long as you're involved in Health Promoting Activities (HPA) you will continue to yield Desirable Lifestyle Values (DLV). There is no program, pill, medication, therapist or doctor that can surpass a strong values system when it comes to staying truly healthy. As a result, there can be no drug, alcohol, obsession, disease, criminal or violent act that can come between you and the value you place on yourself. Values cannot be found outside of your person. They can only manifest within self.

Once we understand that self-worth and appreciation originates from within self, there can be no dysfunctional aftermath. Everything outside of you is of a material nature, and can be taken away or lost at any time. If your identity is tied to those substances, your very soul can possibly be lost with them. There's nothing wrong with being attached to objects in the environment, but understand that *attachment* is the source of all human suffering. Some people get so wrapped up in objects, that *detachment* becomes a painful and stressful experience. We come into this world with nothing and will leave with nothing. This goes for relationships as well as material possessions.

If you find yourself down and out because you've been scratching with unhealthy chickens, not to worry, there's always going to be that swan or eagle soaring overhead. Hold on with all your might until you're *discovered*. Then you too will find that swan or eagle in you. Don't settle for less because you do have a *choice*. Believe in yourself and you'll always soar with eagles.

So, Spread Your Wings!

Discovery 10

Happiness: The Ultimate Goal Is Not In Recovery; It's In Discovery

We human beings are forever searching to find ourselves; therefore, the goal of happiness is to go Beyond Recovery into Discovery.

Oliver Rhodes

Pleasure and excitement are the keys to motivation and happiness. Wherever our desires lead us, you can be assured that the means are in some form of pleasurable experience. Unfortunately, many of our pleasures yield destructive lifestyle values. Although many of us fall victim to such painful consequences, it is not our intentions to become negatively addicted. Every situation that has befallen us has resulted from our need to experience pleasure. We set out on a journey from the time we are born to find that which pleases. Before we are ever conscious of our existence, we are reaching out for external stimulants of pleasure.

As a result of our need to explore new frontiers of pleasure, it is obvious that there is a Christopher Columbus in all of us. Recovery is similar to being shipwrecked on a deserted island that has no redeeming treasures. So, instead of getting back into our ships to further explore more promising worlds, we stay marooned on our little *island of recovery* hoping that *our ship will come in* to rescue us from our distress and unhappiness.

The above scenario actually happens in today's world. Many people are stuck in recovery with no place to go. They are there for the rest of their lives. It's similar to being handed down a prison sentence. However, there are many people who have broken the chains of recovery and have gone on to discover a new happiness.

People in traditional recovery programs are not taught to be happy. They are taught to be clean and sober. Sobriety does not necessarily lead to happiness. On the contrary, a great percentage of people in recovery programs are content to be clean and dry. Unfortunately, being sober just may not be enough motivation to encourage humans to live productive lifestyles. We are hedonistic in nature, meaning we are pleasure seeking beings (discovering what makes us happy) and are not happy with ourselves if we are not living a life of bliss. Therefore, the ultimate goal in life is HAPPINESS.

I have found in the recovery community that people go to these "programs" thinking that their outcome is going to be happiness. Most are disillusioned and find out that happiness is very much out of their reach. Many people think that they can become happy if they are sober. But to the contrary, it's the other way around. People who are the most successful in their recovery are not happy because they are sober. They are sober because they are happy first, for happiness is an inside job brought on by their involvement in personal reeducation, rejuvenation and recreation.

People need to be happy first before they can reap the rewards of a clean and sober lifestyle! Being miserable most of the time can only make you pick up that drug again. The confusion as to whether sobriety can make you happy or being happy first is similar to the question "What came first, the chicken or the egg?" What do you think? Well, in the case of sobriety versus happiness, it is clearly happiness.

Happiness is a function of following Qualitative Recreation Lifestyle Principles, and sobriety is the result, not the cause.

Happiness must come first before anyone can establish and maintain continuous sobriety. For example, if sobriety is cause for one's happiness, what happens when that person experiences a crisis? More than likely they will lose their happiness and everything that goes with it; including themselves. This relapse behavior is condoned and happens on many occasions to people who are in recovery for substance abuse. Many people who excuse themselves for relapsing often state that some other factor or factors *caused* them to fall off the wagon. Well if that's true, they are going to have a lifetime of falling.

People who sit around doing much of nothing during their sober days will need more than a few meetings to stay sober. If their life isn't filled with a variety of fun-loving activities, chances are they going to fall again. In that state of mind, all it would take is a minor crisis to nudge them into seeking their old drug of choice. And there are a lot of circumstances that can push a person off the wagon. Especially, if they didn't want to ride the darn thing in the first place. To some, a sober lifestyle just doesn't cut the mustard when it comes to having fun!

With so many alternatives to using, how in the world can a person choose to use? The individual who does not find alternate ways to enjoy their free time is just not owning up or facing up. Owning up means taking responsibility. Many of the excuses for relapsing are very common and widely used. Some of the excuses that I often hear are, "My wife left me; there was a death in the family; I lost my job; I could not cope; or, it's the disease that forced me to relapse." I very seldom hear: "I choose to use;" or, I just wanted to get high. Giving excuses takes responsibility off of the user. On the other hand, people who value their new found happiness will not allow anything to interfere with the value that they now place on themselves, even in the event of a crisis situation.

Qualitative Recreation Lifestyle Principles is to the chicken as happiness and sobriety are to its eggs. If you refer back to *Discovery 6, QRLP Flow Chart*, page 177, you will notice that sobriety is *part* of the *whole (Desirable Lifestyle Values)*. Sobriety is one of the outcomes (an egg) that results from our participation (Labor of Love) in Health Promoting Activities. Unfortunately, some of us get involved in activities that produce "Rotten Eggs." These "bad eggs" result from "labors of love" that are destructive. So naturally, what results is pain, suffering and dis-ease. As long as we participate in destructive "labors of love" we're going to produce dozens of "rotten eggs." There's nothing wrong with wanting to labor for love, but it must produce "golden eggs." You can't produce gold from lead, just as you can't produce happiness and sobriety from negative "labors of love." There are just too many people in recovery programs that are working on their sobriety, but are not involved in positive "labors of love." Therefore, it will be difficult for them to produce golden eggs of happiness.

Qualitative Recreation Lifestyle Principles is the chicken that produces the eggs (DLVs). Your participation in these health promoting activities is the labor of love. As a result of your labor in these activities, you give birth to sobriety. It then joins the rest of the eggs in your nest of desirable lifestyle values. The nest is your *personal value's system*. The more eggs you have in your nest, the more protective you become of the values you now possess. It's similar to the chicken and its baby chicks. They are proud and protective of what their labor of love has produced. Chickens that have no eggs have nothing to feel good about.

These eggs are to the chicken what *values* are to *Qualitative Recreation Lifestyle Principles.* Just like a certain number of eggs make up a *dozen*, a certain number of values make up a high sense of *self worth and appreciation.* Production begins within and results in positive or negative "outcomes" depending on your efforts or lack of responsibility. Eggs are also considered to be rewards or consequences. Like the eggs, they come as a result of your labor of love. What is your labor of love? The end result — where you are today — is an indication of your efforts or lack of responsibility within your chicken.

The things that are worthwhile in life must come from within and work their way out from our center. Looking for things outside of ourselves for happiness is like trying to produce fruit without nourishing the tree's roots.

As long as we can receive these things we are generally happy. If we don't get them, we're down in the dumps. Living from the outside in predisposes us to become dependent on outside stimulants. This predisposition can set one up for developing negative addictive behaviors. Positive eggs of happiness are based on an inside job by understanding that all things in nature breed from within and expresses its beauty outward. Baby chicks are born in the nest and when they are able to move on their own, they venture outward. It would be very difficult as well as impossible for this process to work in reverse. But many people are living their lives this way. They believe in order to be happy, something outside of themselves must come into their lives. Many are unaware of the power they hold "within." The power to act, produce, create, think and respond are all "within" their circle of influence.

Instead of realizing the power to produce golden eggs of happiness, too many are "concerned" about the "fox" of pain and despair. The only time chickens worry about the fox is when the danger is *clear* and *present*. They don't sit on their duff wondering if the fox is going to raid the hen house. That just doesn't happen. But, you'd be amazed by the millions who worry themselves sick over concerns that have already happened, have not happened or probably never will happen. It may even be something that they can't do anything about anyway.

The Serenity Prayer is a prime example of the above scenario. How often have we, as a society, recited these divine words only to misunderstand and follow just the opposite? In reciting the Serenity Prayer we ask God to grant us the serenity to accept the things that we can not change, the courage to change the things that we can, and the wisdom to know the difference. It is the last part, "the wisdom to know the difference," that get some people confused. They are trying to change things that they cannot, which is outside their circle of influence. And they are not changing the things that they can, which are themselves.

Take Harold P. for example, a 34 year-old who was married to Carol for ten years. They had two young children and the bills were mounting. Carol wanted to work in order to help with the finances. Harold, being the bread winner during the course of their marriage, felt that her decision to work was an attack on his manhood. He flat out refused and was strongly against Carol working. Carol, persistent and determined, stated she was going to work and that Harold was just going to have to live with her decision. Harold became upset and angry. He wanted to control Carol and not himself. Carol eventually divorced Harold. Harold just did not want to accept Carol's decision to work, and it cost him his marriage. He could not accept the things he could not change—Carol. And he did not have the courage to change the things that he could—himself. Harold could have produced golden eggs by allowing and accepting his wife's decision to work.

Fear is a learned emotion that occurs over years of experiencing pain, failure and frustration. I call this process, "Chicken in the hen house." Again, we produce golden eggs as a result of our "labor of love." As long as we have eggs to sit on, we're okay. But there's another factor of life that tends to disrupt our day—the fox! Those are the "things that we cannot change" in the Serenity Prayer. I call this the "fox fear factor."

During the course of our lives, the fox breaks into the hen house and steals some of our eggs, if not all of them. Now, we can sit and pout, or we can produce more eggs. Remember, production is an inside job. Unfortunately, many people choose to sit without trying to reproduce (re-create) for fear that the fox will return. They are afraid that the fox will not only steal their eggs, but eat them as well. So, they sit and do nothing. They are afraid to try again. The "fox fear factor" paralyzes and prevents many people from continuing to produce happiness.

Why do we stop producing and then blame life (the fox)? When man takes from the fruit trees, do they not till the soil to produce the next harvest? We humans don't have to produce just to have our eggs taken away. There is something we can do, and that is "chickens in the hen house shoo *fly* shoo." Who are the *flies* in this analogy? The fox and the people who bother us. How do we deal with them? Screen them out. That is, put screens up in your hen house.

As long as we stay a "chicken" in the hen house we'll find ourselves too afraid to come out to explore the beauty that life has to offer. We'll stop producing eggs and find life boring. The "fox fear factor" tends to cause a shutdown of our creativeness. In our youth, we are open to explore the wonders of life. As adults, we tend to lose that unique quality that only children seem to possess. What happens to us as we become adults? We become rigid. We learn how to become an adult—social reproduction. The most healthy and happy people in the world are producing golden eggs. Our ability to produce this happiness never ends. *We are taught to end it (e.g., "stop acting like a child").*

QRLP is the chicken, and the values are the eggs you produce as a result of your involvement (labor of love) in HPAs. If you don't take care of your chicken it could possibly get sick and die. The results could be devastating. *No more chickens, no more eggs, no more positive outcomes.* You have got to take care of your chicken if you want the chicken— your chicken—to take care of you.

All this struggling to stay clean and sober when all you have to do is be happy. Does this sound too easy? Well, it really is. You are happy when you are satisfied by what you enjoy doing. If what you do (your labor of love) promotes health, you're going to be happy for life. If what you do is of a destructive nature, that happiness is pseudo and will soon cause false feelings of euphoria that will eventually diminish.

In your attempt to regain that fake high, you'll try even harder to acquire what was first thought to be something of value. Over a period of time, you'll lose sight of everything else and become consumed by the mystery of the illusion that leaves no trail. Eventually, you'll come to the end of your search with nothing to show for your involvement but a ghost.

> ***The pursuit of false happiness leaves your inner spirit drained, strained and deranged. In spite of what many may believe, true happiness burns within the soul of our bodies, and not at the end of a joint.***

It is our love for labor that will give us what we seek. It comes to us, we don't go to it. Chasing that pot of gold at the end of the rainbow will end in failure and frustration. The more you pursue it, the more it eludes you. Pursuing happiness in this fashion is a perfect example of getting wasted on mind-mood altering chemicals. I know because I've been there.

> ***Pursuing happiness through the use of drugs never gets you what you want. You only get what you deserve.***

Sobriety is the same way. I tried for years to live a sober lifestyle but was not experiencing happiness. I was clean and free of chemicals but did not feel excited about where I was. Being sober without a labor of love is similar to having a new car with no engine. It looks good, but can't go anywhere.

> ***Sobriety is not an action word, labor is. A labor of love means to exert one's power of mind and body, especially with enthusiasm, determination and inspiration.***

Pursuing happiness is not something you look for, it's something that happens due to your participation in healthy activities of pleasure. For many people, it doesn't matter if what they choose to do is of a destructive nature, as long as they receive some form of *compensation* for their efforts.

For example, many people seem to enjoy stealing from others. But that's like cancer. These people become just like the free radicals (toxins) that infiltrate the body. These free radicals do not have enough eggs (electrons) to maintain their stability in the body, because they have no labor. They have no function whatsoever, but to destroy healthy cells. If you do not have a labor of love that produces golden eggs, chances are you are going to take from others. And you're going to keep taking until you destroy yourself in the process of trying to destroy the victim.

Sobriety is not difficult to obtain. But it must be an ends (egg) to a means (labor of love) instead of a means (labor) to an end (sobriety) (see Figure 6.2). In other words, you should not have to work hard to become sober. You should be happy participating in worthwhile activities, then watch your sobriety (eggs) appear. As long as you are happy in what you do, you'll remain sober for the rest of your life and without much effort.

By following *QRLP*, (health promoting activities) you establish and maintain a healthy value system that produces dozens of golden eggs. The more eggs you have, the more secure you become in your life. You see, you can afford to lose a few eggs and still have some to fall back on (or sit on). People who are not producing eggs generally fall apart in the midst of a crisis.

Happiness is a Process of Living

Living a productive lifestyle is a process, an enjoyable one that lasts. Everything in nature works on this idea of self = health = wealth. Just like with the chicken analogy, a fruit tree follows this same process of nature. Since we human beings are a part of nature, we also have the ability to produce the fruit of happiness. If you think of how a tree produces fruit, you'll get an even better understanding of how we can produce that happiness from the inside out.

A tree must be nourished from deep inside its roots. If those roots are neglected, that tree will eventually die. But before it does, it first becomes sickly, producing a sick looking harvest that's not even "fit" to eat. The tree may become infested with pests, causing further deterioration. Although it may be appropriate to protect your tree from these pests, this is only glitter that eventually becomes the outside litter. The tree needs to be nourished at its roots.

There are some people who don't mind decorating themselves up to look happy. But this method usually doesn't last long. The only other tree I know that you embellish on the outside is a Christmas Tree. Although it may look very pretty on the outside, it is dead and shallow on the inside. It is unnatural and won't endure a long and prosperous life, especially since it has been cut off by its "roots." There are many people who are living their lives in this manner.

As long as you nourish your roots within, you'll have continuous happiness. Even in the midst of a crisis, you'll be able to withstand the most difficult of circumstances because you value yourself more than your material possessions (fruit). If the fruits you "produce" fall from your tree, not to worry, because all you have to do is continue to nourish those roots of yours and more fruit will appear. Just like all plants in nature, they wither and die when their roots receive no nourishment.

Plants gravitate toward the light on their own. No one pulls them into the direction of the sun. It's a natural act of nature. All living things are a natural act of nature and must respond in kind. When we violate those laws of nature, we humans wither (get sick) and eventually die. It's the withering that causes the suffering. Dead people don't suffer.

Happy people know and enjoy what nourishes their soul. They set goals and then work on the *process* knowing that as long as they continue to live for today, the goals that they aspire to obtain will appear serendipitously. They don't directly seek their goal. They work on self, and the wealth follows — cause and effect. You take care of your cause (self) and the effect (wealth) will definitely come. This is your formula for true happiness. That is "Self = Health = Wealth." It is the same formula (some variable differences) illustrated in Figure 4.3.

This is also in accordance with Roots = Tree = Fruit. This formula can be used to demonstrate other analogies of nature. In studying how everything in nature progresses, you will notice that they are all an inside out process. It is what I call the Universal Formula of Happiness:

Self	=	*Health*	=	*Wealth*
Chicken	=	*Labor*	=	*Egg*
Roots	=	*Tree*	=	*Fruit*
Cause	=	*Response*	=	*Effect*

In nature, everything moves from the inside out. Global weather patterns move from left to right (from west to east). Any attempt to move contrary to those laws, and the opposing forces will most likely cause serious consequences. Most of us want what's on the right, but many people don't understand that if they want the finer things in life, they must work from the left side of this equation. Now there's nothing wrong with wanting to possess what's on the right of this equation, but our focus should be on the "root" of the problem. We can also come up with a similar formula on how unique and simple this law works.

Wood = *Fire* = *Heat*

I'm sure many of us are all too familiar with the warmth of a fire on a cold winter day. We know that if we want to experience the heat of the fire, we must pile in the wood first. Also, it takes effort to get that fire going. Then, and only then are we going to experience true warmth. There are literally millions of people in the world who expect to get more heat from too little wood. Some are getting no heat at all because they refuse to chop, carry and ignite the fire of wood in their lives.

We have to be motivated by the dynamics of sowing before we can reap. We are pure potentiality and have the power and the means to do "something" about our conditions. If you can breath, you have potential to be truly happy. If you can breath, then you are alive and being alive means you have the ability to think, feel, act and respond positively to the things that happen to you in this world. As a result of being able to do these four simple human tasks, you can change your life beyond your wildest dreams.

Now if you're thinking that you can't teach an old dog new tricks, you're in trouble because the only dog that's not teachable is a dead dog. You are alive and must realize that there is no such thing as the living dead unless it is in your head.

As long as you are working your fields, you will reap rewards. The process of growing food, promoting health, love, self-esteem, carrots or anything in nature all fall under the concept that what we reap (end results) is directly related to what we sow (taking action in our lives)

Successful people know that all they have to do is plant the seed of happiness within their minds and watch it grow. Unsuccessful people plant the seed of bitterness and it too grows. You see, we all have a plot of ground and whatever we plant there will sprout. Thinking is likened to seeding. It is a form of mental goal setting. Just like a farmer plants a seed. He doesn't doubt that it will sprout. He has *complete* confidence in himself and the miracles of nature. He knows that the seed contains all the mechanics for its growth. What are you growing, weeds or good deeds? If our plot of ground is producing a harvest of happiness, it's because we are seeding positively and attending the fields of our minds.

Happiness is directly related to optimum health and overall well-being. When was the last time you visited a hospital, recovery home or skilled nursing facility. Take a look around at the faces of the individuals who are there. Do you see happy faces or faces of pain and despair? I've worked in six hospitals over a course of twelve years. I have worked in residential treatment centers, recovery homes and nursing homes and have witnessed the bovine faces of pain and suffering that these people display. It doesn't have to be that way. We all have a choice and that choice is to be happy or we can choose to be sad.

Health and happiness are the result of self-love, self-respect and self-appreciation. Illness is a result of losing all of the above.

Remember, the formula for a lifetime of happiness is:

Self = *Health* = *Wealth*

You must take care of "*self*" by nourishing your inner body, soul and mind.

Most people in recovery are "trying" to abstain from *using* instead of "succeeding" in doing something more *amusing*. If it were our need to experience pleasure that got us there, why not allow that need to experience *wholesome* pleasure to take us out. Our quest to be happy was founded on false feelings of euphoria. It is only practical to find our way out of the darkness by seeking a program that puts us in line with pleasures that cultivate and nourish the mind, body and soul. I have personally researched programs that provide *COMPENSATION* and *REPARATION* instead of *RESIGNATION* and *DEGRADATION*.

Far too many recovery programs practice taking away someone's "perceived" happiness or pleasure and replacing it with solitary confinement. This approach has not been very effective. And, I don't have to quote any statistics. All one has to do is just watch the evening news or read the daily newspaper to see that we are not even making a dent in substance abuse prevention or rehabilitation. The reason why people "use" is not to become sick, but to experience pleasure. I say don't take away their happiness. Teach them how to become happy and high on life.

The most difficult thing in the world to do is to rob someone of their livelihood. No one likes to be mugged, raped, cheated or physically assaulted. Pain is something that we try to avoid while trying to experience pleasure. Why do so many people seek to fulfill their desire to be happy through drug use? I'll tell you why. We rob our young people of recreation, play, crafts and games by taking away programs that are conducive to helping these young people become upstanding citizens. We shut down recreation centers where teens can hang out. Worse than that, we provide very little, if any, leadership from true caring adults and the media. While our young people continue to suffer, the movie industry in Hollywood becomes waxed rich on the drug and violence oriented programs. These programs permeate the TV screens in our homes where children, barely old enough to talk, can get first hand lessons on violence right in the comfort of their homes.

Violence, drugs use and crime will always be set in the fabric of our society, but there aren't many ways to counter the devastating effects and strong influence these teachings have on society as a whole. What makes matters worse is that it doesn't seem to be getting any better.

The out dated "programs" for treating substance abuse, crime, violence and other disorders must be revamped. The old must give way to innovative and more creative means to uplift people's spirits and heal their pain. If something is not working, we can't blame the victims. We also have to take a close look at these so called "programs."

Those who are in business know that if their company is failing to produce, it is not because of the clients. The onus of responsibility rests with the business and its staff to provide a quality product. Many companies would go bankrupt sticking to one game plan. They must at least seek to augment their existing program by allowing other options for their clients.

As a caring person who does not like to see people suffer, I honestly do not believe we, as a society, are doing everything we can to help people recover from their diseases. Many programs are *supported and promoted* because of the massive revenue to be made from treating and fighting:

- *Illness*
- *Crime*
- *Substance Abuse*
- *Violence*
- *Dis-ease*
- *Obesity*
- *Drug Trafficking*

These are just the symptoms of a diseased society. What we are doing now is not even a drop in the bucket on healing our world. We need to stop fighting and treating these symptoms and focus more on promoting health. When we promote ease, dis-ease diminishes.

As you read this book, realize that you are the key to your happiness and overall well-being. Depending on others to look out for our welfare keeps us below the threshold of recovery. You are a magnificent human-being with the power and the means to go beyond those outside extremes. If you'd like to help our world heal itself, then it must come from you.

What has happened in the world is that we have turned our lives over to those who are not fully committed to providing for our needs.

The needs of the all powerful rich are the ones that stand to gain, while the client stands to become further dependent on the massive amounts of services that keep them locked into strict servitude. If you really want to help, pass this book on to others who may be seeking or have a desire to go beyond recovery. Beyond recovery is to help people go on to brighter and healthier ways of living and not become stuck in one-way thinking. It is my sincere hope that the words in this book will help you realize that you are that spiritual power that can provide for your every need if you believe.

The profit-making industry wishes to keep you ignorant ("Ignore"-rant) to the marvelous wonders that your mind, body and soul possess. We must wake up and live according to the biological laws of nature so our lives can be free of sickness, despair and pain. People need new and healthier ways to live so that they can fly on their own. So Spread Your Wings.

Qualitative Recreation Lifestyle Principles *(QRLP)* is your *nest to set.* Set on it and make yourself some golden eggs through a labor of love (see page 178). Everyone has something that they enjoy doing. Whatever your desires may be is your *Pleasure Principle*. Are your *P.P.s* producing golden eggs or rotten eggs? If you are not following *QRLP,* it's unlikely that they are golden.

Re-examine your goals (eggs) and participate in those labors that produce the *outcome* that you seek. You may enjoy getting high on pot, but that's not a true labor of love. It's a destructive form of labor that will eventually rip at your very soul. To deny your chicken of healthy labors will inevitably destroy it. It will become a "sick chicken" first, then it will die.

Happiness is a child. Most children have not been exposed to harmful and dangerous influences, yet! Regain your inner spirit and allow it to become that child again. Allow the words of the following poem to inspire you towards living from within. It is hoped that this poem helps you learn the real beauty of true happiness.

A Poem to Remember

A Father and His Child on Happiness

Dad, what is happiness, is it something that
you seek?
Happiness comes to us, when we're living at
our peak.
Can happiness be found in a bottle or a drug?
No, it comes to us, son, through a labor of love.
Dad, I hear people say, that they love to get high.
They are just using those drugs, as a sick way
to get by.
Isn't using those drugs, a labor of love?
It may be labor, but a destructive way to love.
Dad I'm confused, as to why people use,
Is it some playful way, to bring happiness to
their day?
There's no play about it, and I'll be the first to
shout it,
Harmful drugs can kill, and that's the real deal.
A lot of people use, those drugs, huh, Dad?
They really do son, and yeah, it's bad.
How can people be happy, living bad like that?
I thought people wanted to be happy, not live
on crack.
Son, people do want to be happy, there's nothing
wrong with that,
It's just the vehicle that they are using, that puts
the monkey on their back.
Do you think that our society will ever become
drug-free?
Not if they keep promoting it, in our music and
on T.V.
If drugs are so bad, why don't they just stop it?

It's just not that simple, when it's sold for
a big profit.
Well, they tell us at school, to just say no!
I know my dear son, but that's just not how
it goes.
So, tell me what's to it, to get people not to do it?
You have to learn to be happy, through some
other conduit.
Dad, what is conduit, I don't know that word?
It is important that you ask, about that word
you just heard.
Conduit is that vehicle, that I mentioned
to you before.
It takes you to your goal, just like the opening
of a door.
It's a means to an end, or a channel from above,
It's our transport to happiness, it's that labor
of love.
I don't think labor, can be one of hope,
When millions of lives, are being destroyed
on dope.
I don't understand, that kind of thinking, dad,
How could our world, let it get so bad?
They take away recreation, and places to play,
Put children in day care, where they tend to
waste away.
Children are special, and have special needs,
They need more than just love,
they need someone who leads.
Dad, I often hear, that we're the greatest resource,
But why does it have to come to this horrible
discourse?
Children having children, and hooked on drugs,
I think the biggest problem with children is that,
they're not getting enough hugs.
You're right, my son, but many adults are in
denial,

And it takes more than just hugs, it takes time
too, my child.
Well, if time is a factor, why don't parents try
and give it?
Time means careers, and there's no other way
to live it?
If parents' priorities, are to seek their careers,
Children sometimes become controlled by
their peers.
And when parents try to tell them what to do,
They get rebellious and say, "the heck with you."
Son, this kind of rebellion, has been going on
for years,
It has caused many children anger, and many
parents tears.
If we adults, don't soon wake up,
The youth in our world, will be dead out of luck.
We have already deprived this younger generation,
And that's no figment of this grim realization.
To have good kids, you got to be good folks,
Letting them to fall through the cracks, leaves
many with little hope.
Dad I'm concerned, and think I'm
experiencing fear,
Don't worry my son, for I will always be here.
With all that's going on, I may not stand
a chance.
I'm going to love you and hug you, under any
circumstance.
Dad, if I had millions, I would make everybody
happy,
By sharing it with the world, so things won't be
so crappy.
Where did you learn that word, it's not one of
mine?
I heard it from the kids next door, they say it all
the time.

Well, my son let me give you some advice,
That word you learned, "crappy" is not very nice.
Am I in trouble? I really didn't know,
It's all apart of learning, my son, and a part of how you grow.
We live and learn and you're my concern,
I was taught by my dad, and now it's your turn.
I'll teach you the best, in every possible way,
For, son, "I love you now," as I will everyday.
I love you too, Dad and I'm glad you're my friend,
For you are more than a parent, you're my shining light within.
I wish other kids, were as lucky as me,
To have good parents, that teaches the proper way to be.
Dad, if I had that money, I wouldn't give it away,
I'd spend it on recreation, so we could have a place to play.
Kids need attention, and parents that really care,
Not just providing room and board, but actually being there.
It's more than just physical, or being in plain sight,
Provide us with hugs, for our emotional appetite.
Give of your time, and do more than what you do,
Hug us with kindness, and say, "honey, I love you."
Son, you learn fast, and you're really on the ball.
Of course dear dad, it's you that taught it all.
Son, you're learning from me, but I'm also learning from you.
How's that dad, because I do what you do?
No! I provide the lessons, but you also have a choice,
To express your true feeling, in a positive and

clear voice.
Your desire to help others, in their time of need,
Showing a loving heart, to do a good deed.
Well, isn't that the reason, we're all here on this earth?
To live in good faith, after our initial birth?
You're so right, my son, and we should never lose sight,
That the difference in our world, shouldn't result in fight.
Dad, we always fight, I see it on T.V.,
Almost in every program, as if it were meant to be.
Is that how we should live, beating up on our neighbor,
Just because they exhibit, some different kind of behavior?
Do we slap them in the face, or call them a dirty name,
This kind of behavior, doesn't seem very tame.
I don't like to fight, I want us to all get along.
Fighting, and thieving, all seem so wrong.
Although this behavior is on our T.V.,
Does not really mean, this is the way it should be.
The way we should live, is to make love what you give,
The violence and the crime, is just a sign of the times.
It's nothing but a pest, and you're better than that mess,
So, get out there and perform, and give nothing but your best.
Dad, I think I'm learning values, and it more than owning wealth,
It's establishing and maintaining, an excellent state of health.
But does money make you happy, I see it on T.V.?
Some people think it does, but not completely.

There's more to happiness, than having
nice things,
It's an inside job, that nothing else can bring.
It's knowing who you are, and what you love to do,
It's that labor of love, that's deep inside of you.
You truly have been blessed, with a mind to use
and think with,
Don't waste your valuable gift, as a tool to go
and sink with.
Many people don't know, how fortunate they are,
To own such a marvelous brain, that can take
them high and far.
Dad, I'm all excited, and not afraid anymore,
I feel like I can tackle the world, when I go out
that front door.
When people rub me wrong, I will rub them right,
I'll keep a positive attitude, and won't give
way to fight.
Dad, you're my leader, and I'm glad that
you're here,
For it's your loving ways, that show me that
you care.
If all other parents, spent time with their kids as
you spend with me,
Imagine how wonderful, this great big world
could be.
I love you, Dad. I love you too, Tom,
Now may I go, and spend some quality time
with Mom?

There are two kinds of people in the world, those who think they can, and those who think they can't. Ironically, they are both right!

It's All About Attitude!

The above quote epitomizes the sole truth as it relates to each individual and how each person views their own individual experiences in life. How many times have you heard someone say with unmitigated realism, hopeless statements such as "I have tried everything and nothing seems to work," or "It's just too hard." Some have even convinced themselves that "Life Sucks," but we all know that this statement just isn't true, at least not for all of us. This statement only applies to those individuals whose beliefs are based on their own personal experiences with life. To say that life sucks implies that it sucks for us all. Realistically, life plays no favors. It just happens. This disgruntled individual is only expressing their own attitude (belief within their reality) on how they respond to that which happens in their life.

We often hear many people say, "I could never do that," or "all men are dogs," or "once a loser always a loser." These are figments of that person's imagination and are not within the realms of reality. These defeatist attitudes all represent a truism of that person's specific beliefs about their perceived potentiality. Our attitudes are the governing factors to much of our success or failures in life.

Our attitudes are what influence our thinking, feelings, actions and reactions towards our environment. Conversely, our attitudes are often, if not always, structured by what occurs in the environment and could possibly hinder our ability to grow. Consequently, it is our reasoning ability that determines whether we develop a positive or a negative attitude. If our attitudes are such that they create unhealthy behavior, it may be that we have allowed our environment to effect our good intentions. For example, people who view life as unfair or difficult may have been exposed to others who have responded in this negative fashion. Everything we learn in life tends to come from those before us. If a person sees another respond to others with violence, it's possible that this observer may *choose* to adopt that same attitude. It's the same way we develop *our attitudes* on smoking, racism, recovery, drugs, marriage, children and relationships.

Our attitudes don't have to be good or bad, negative or positive. They just may represent our likes or dislikes about a person, place or thing. What we may want to look at is whether our attitudes are contributing to our welfare, development and personal success. Are we making strides to improve our lives as we go through life, or are we allowing that which happens to us destroy that which we are trying to build? Are we able to overcome the negative influences in life, or are we giving in to those *outside forces* that could steer us too far to the right or left? How do we determine right from wrong, or good from bad? Who do we follow or who do we ask when faced with difficult decisions about our lives?

The main reason that we are here on this earth is to create *happiness* within ourselves by contributing to life. In spite of the negative influences that occur in our lives, we are all left with a *choice* from day one (this very day) to make things better. There may have been many unjust events that have happened to us in life, but does that give someone the right to live their current lives destructive, scornful or forever in contempt? Too many of us have developed the attitude that others are *responsible* for who we are and what we have become. That may be true, but we don't have to allow it to go on? We can stop it right this minute if we only allow ourselves to move on with our lives and stop living in the past.

Granted, such things as child abuse, dysfunctional families, fatherless homes and crime infested communities have contributed to our poor attitudes towards ourselves and to the world around us, but we cannot let these things continue to prevent us from taking responsibility for our actions. We must learn to *discover* healthier and happier ways towards overcoming these unfortunate past situations by living for today and looking to the future.

Remember, the past is just a review, not a major study. We are still spending too much of our valuable time in recovery. Happiness is not in recovery, it's in discovery.

We need to go beyond recovery and find our place in life. Recovery deals with the past, while *discovery* focuses on the future and our true headings in life. Our focus should be on where we are going, not where we have just come from.

It's similar to driving our cars. It's only natural to occasionally look in the rearview mirror, but most of the time we should keep our eyes on the road up ahead.

Characteristics of a Positive Attitude

The characteristics of a positive attitude are in our understanding that things will occasionally fall apart, but as they do, we should not allow ourselves to fall apart with them. People with positive attitudes believe and have faith that more good will happen in their lives than bad. Based on their assumption, they generally make better choices towards creating happiness in their lives. Knowing that we have choices empowers us to make positive decisions in a forever changing world.

Attitude is everything as Zig Ziglar says. "It is attitude, not aptitude that determines our altitude." Attitudes can be contagious. Therefore, we must be vigilant about the attitudes of others, and the influence our environment may have on our attitudes. Also, whatever attitude you project will be reflected by those who will act as your mirror. Your attitude, whether positive or negative is a creation of your own fashion. In spite of what attitudes have influenced yours, you're still going to be the bearer of your own bad or good tidings.

The truth of the matter is that whatever your attitude *projects* — others will reflect in kind. Therefore, if you are good to others, others will be good to you. If you treat yourself with respect, your body will respond in kind by providing you with excellent health.

When we follow the biological laws of nature, we will surely create *ease* in our lives, but when we are in violation of those laws, we will suffer the consequences. All attempts to side step those laws will end in failure. It doesn't matter what outside forces we may call upon to put us back together again (medical establishment, psychologist, treatment centers or recovery programs). As long as we take the attitude that something outside of us is responsible for our ills we're *doomed!*

It is the same way in which we take care of our bodies. Many of us strive diligently to maintain our health through fitness, diet and corrective surgery. But a large majority of society are unaware that it is our *attitude* that will determine the quality and longevity of our lives, not what we do on the outside.

In sickness and in health, your attitude can play a major role in the healing process. For example, there are many case studies at Harvard Medical School where patients have defied the laws of medical science. There are many case studies of people who have overcome some of the worst life threatening illnesses because they took the attitude that their disease was not only treatable but also curable. Similarly, there are those who are in chronic pain because they believe that there's nothing they or anyone can do to cure their illness. What we have here are two different attitudes with two opposing results. A healthy attitude can be the result of your outcomes, or your outcomes can be the result of a healthy attitude (Figure 10.1).

Attitude Check

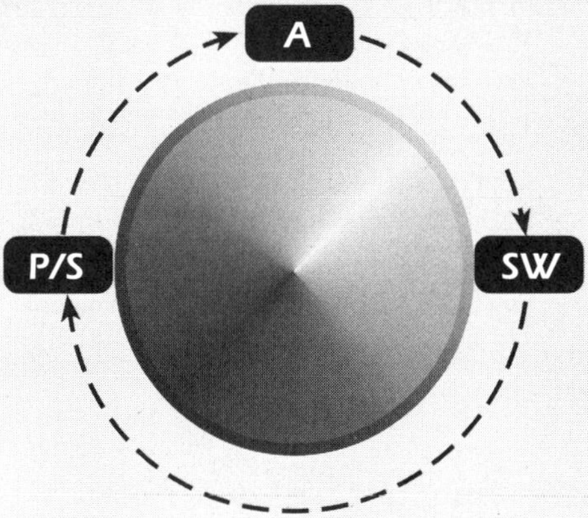

Spiritually Connected

Positive attitude **A** determines Self-Worth **SW**, that results in **P/S** (Position and Status in life) which in turn re-enforces **A.**

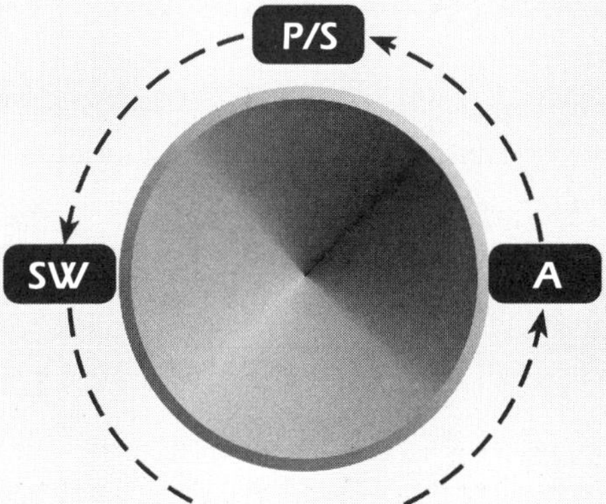

Materially Connected

Position and Status **P/S** determines Self-Worth **SW** that results in **A** (a good attitude). So, **A** is dependent on **P/S** & **SW**.

Figure 10.1

We have been conditioned by our society that when we look good we can also feel good. This is a backwards statement that's predicated on profitability. It's generally said to get you, the consumer, to purchase goods that *undermine* your better judgment and your good intelligence. Marketers claim that in order for you to be good, feel good and look sharp, you must buy their products.

You are a walking miracle and should be aware of that fact. It is your attitude about yourself that should determine how you look, feel and behave. Everything in nature moves from the inside out, not from the outside in. People with positive attitudes know that they possess the power to make their life and inner spirit whole.

Take our most prestigious possession, our car, for example. Everything that we do to it enhances its beauty. Why there are those who religiously clean, wax, oil and repair their cars better than they take care of themselves. But again, of all the things you have done to your car, it is still the attitude of the driver that's going to determine the quality, longevity, and its performance.

Understand that no one is responsible for your attitude, so steer clear of the *blame game*. There may be those who have behaved unfavorably towards you, but no one is at fault for your behavior after the fact. No one makes you do anything. Your *attitude* about that which happens to you determines your actions. And since you are the creator of your actions, you are also responsible for those actions.

Ten Steps to a Winning Attitude

If you want to develop a winning attitude, it is imperative that you follow Qualitative Recreation Lifestyle principles *(QRLP)*. These unique and reliable standards are what some of the most successful and happiest people in the world live by.

The Winning Ten

1. *See yourself as the creator of your own attitude, whether it be positive or negative.*
2. *Allow all those you meet to become the bearer of your good tidings.*
3. *Realize that no one can make you feel inferior without your permission.*
4. *Understand that people who hate can't hate if you don't reflect back what it is they are projecting. By maintaining your dignity, you just may influence theirs.*
5. *Be the first to offer smiles, hellos and apologies!*
6. *Live by the rule that the strength of a person is not the power to be aggressive but the power to restrain!*
7. *Make everyone you meet feel special. Remember, we are all connected, and if you see others as an extension of who you are, there can be no conflict and your relationships will become magical.*
8. *Give of your services with a smile! Don't wait for a tragedy to happen before rendering a helping hand.*
9. *In times of difficulty, offer a shoulder to lean on.*
10. *Take full responsibility in all that happens to you and refrain from blame. Recover and then discover and you'll create magic in all of your relationships.*

Healthy relationships, prosperity and happiness will always be your rewards when following these biological laws of nature. As a result of your change in *Attitude*, your *Gratitude* (appreciation) for doing so will have profound effects on your *Expectations* in life. With a positive attitude, you can "expect the best" and you will get the best! Be the creator of your "New Attitude," new life and new you! Recover and then discover your true nature and potentiality starting today!

What's Beyond Recovery?

Discovery!

And That *Discovery* Is *You*!

Reminiscence of Discovery

Overcoming Addiction Without A Twelve Step Conviction was written from the hearts of many caring, loving and spiritual human beings. The stories, claims, successes and miracles outlined throughout these pages were derived from over 30 years of personal and professional experience on the dynamics of spiritual health and healing.

Of all the factors governing spiritual health, success and happiness, there is only one factor that surpasses them all. It does not rest with traditional medical or psychological means. It is not about breakthroughs in pharmaceuticals or corrective surgeries. And, it is not about following a *program* of strict servitude. It is knowing and understanding that all human beings have been blessed at birth with the single most important factor of them all—Common Sense Intelligence (CSI).

This, my friends, is the greatest gift that God has bestowed on all human kind. Before there were books, art, music, dance or culture, intelligence was the catalyst for every living and non-living thing. It precedes every idea, discovery, philosophy, invention, theory or doctrine, and you my friend are in possession of the most powerful force in the universe. It is today the key to invincibility and immortality.

Therefore, the basis for succeeding in everything that you do is contained within the depths of your marvelous mind. When thought is allowed to flow in accordance with the biological laws of nature, there can be no disease, war, hate or personal conflict. Your mind is a link to all that exists because we cannot do it alone. Use your gift wisely, and you too will discover that all things in life are possible if you believe! Conceive it, archieve it and you *will* Overcome it!

From the heart of the author,

Best Wishes in Your New Discoveries